What People Are Saying About *Chicken Soup for the Single's Soul* . . .

"This book chronicles the meaningful, challenging and ultimately amazing realities of being a single person today. Anyone who was, is or may be single should keep a copy close at hand."

Trish McDermott
single's coach and
advice columnist, *Match.com*

"Thank you for recognizing singles! These stories help us to 'make being single, the single best time of our lives.' I suggest that all singles read the entire book, as it will help us all remember to 'Make every Single moment count.'"

Ric Mandelbaum
founder and president
Singles Source organization

"*Chicken Soup for the Single's Soul* is the perfect companion if you're seeking love, laughter and loyalty. These inspiring tales will never let you down no matter how often you turn to them."

Andrea Engber
editor, *SingleMOTHER*
coauthor, *The Complete Single Mother: Reassuring Answers to Your Most Challenging Concerns*

"The secret to being happily single is recognizing one's self as a true friend. *Chicken Soup for the Single's Soul* expresses this perfectly."

Janet Sussman
spiritual counselor, writer and musician

"All of us have days when we just need warm bowls of fresh encouragement from others. That's what *Chicken Soup for the Single's Soul* does. It presents the stories of men and women like you and me, who, amid the busyness of everyday hassles, stopped to hear the greater lessons life was teaching them. As you and I read about *their* journeys, may we find fresh strength to continue *our* journeys—every 'single' one of us."

Dr. Lynda Hunter
editor, *Single-Parent Family*

"Tempted to have a "poor ol' single me" party? Forget it! Pick up *Chicken Soup for the Single's Soul.* These stories have something to say to *every* single adult—including you! Some of the stories sneak up on you and catch you off guard. While you're at it, buy a couple of copies. Because some single adult you know needs this book. Now!"

Harold Ivan Smith
author, *Singles Ask*

"This book provides a spiritual, inspirational lift for every single."

Janet L. Jacobsen
editor, *Arizona Single Scene*

"*Chicken Soup for the Single's Soul* is like a best friend, giving you the support, inspiration and laughter you need on the journey through 'singledom'."

Anthony Lawlor
author, *A Home for the Soul*

"*Chicken Soup for the Single's Soul* is a heartwarming book, filled with love and laughter to lift and renew the soul!"

Gary Gray
publisher and editor, *Living Solo Magazine*

CHICKEN SOUP FOR THE SINGLE'S SOUL

Stories of Love and Inspiration for the Single, Divorced and Widowed

Jack Canfield
Mark Victor Hansen
Jennifer Read Hawthorne
Marci Shimoff

Health Communications, Inc.
Deerfield Beach, Florida

www.bcibooks.com
www.chickensoup.com

We would like to acknowledge the following publishers and individuals for permission to reprint the following material. (Note: The stories that were penned anonymously, that are in the public domain or that were written by Jack Canfield, Mark Victor Hansen, Jennifer Read Hawthorne or Marci Shimoff are not included in this listing.)

Room at the Table. Reprinted by permission of Vivian Eisenecher. ©1999 Vivian Eisenecher.

The Professor and the Soulmate. Reprinted by permission of Bryan Aubrey. ©1999 Bryan Aubrey.

Is Fire Goddess Spelled with Two Ds? Reprinted by permission of Linda Stafford. ©1999 Linda Stafford.

Lessons from Aunt Grace. Reprinted by permission of Nardi Reeder Campion. ©1984 Nardi Reeder Campion.

Seeing 20/20. Reprinted by permission of Bill Asenjo. ©1998 Bill Asenjo.

(Continued on page 388)

Library of Congress Cataloging-in-Publication Data

Chicken soup for the single's soul: stories of love and inspiration for the single, divorced and widowed / Jack Canfield . . . [et al.].

p. cm.

ISBN 1-55874-706-0

1. Single people Anecdotes. 2. Single people—Conduct of life. 3. Divorced people Anecdotes. 4. Divorced people—Conduct of life. 5. Widows Anecdotes. 6. Widows—Conduct of life. 7. Widowers Anecdotes. 8. Widowers—Conduct of life. I. Canfield, Jack

HQ800.C43 1999

305.9'0652—dc21

99-35448

CIP

ISBN 1-55874-706-0 (trade paper) — ISBN 1-55874-707-9 (hardcover)

Publisher: Health Communications, Inc.
3201 S.W. 15th Street
Deerfield Beach, FL 33442-8190

Cover redesign by Larissa C. Hise
Typesetting by Lawna Patterson Oldfield

With love, we dedicate this book
to all single people
on the journey of life.

Contents

5. SINGLE PARENTING

6. SINGLE AGAIN

7. LOSING A PARTNER

8. WE ARE NOT ALONE

9. FRIENDS AND FAMILY

Acknowledgments

Chicken Soup for the Single's Soul has been a true labor of love for all of us. One of the greatest joys of creating this book was working with people who gave this project not just their time and attention, but their hearts and souls as well. We would like to thank the following people for their dedication and contributions, without which this book could not have been created:

Our families, who have given us love and support throughout this project, and who have been chicken soup for our souls!

Inga, Travis, Riley, Christopher, Oran and Kyle for all their love and support.

Patty Hansen, and Elizabeth and Melanie Hansen, for once again sharing and lovingly supporting us in creating yet another book.

Dan Hawthorne, and Amy and William, for their constant love and affection.

Maureen H. Read, for always being there.

Louise and Marcus Shimoff, for their eternal support and love—and for being two of the best parents on Earth.

Beverly Merson, for once again putting her heart and soul into another *Chicken Soup for the Soul* book. We deeply appreciate the extraordinary work you did in connecting with writers nationwide, researching stories, handling millions of details and fostering relationships with many people and organizations in the singles world. We couldn't have done it without you.

Bryan Aubrey, Natalie Cleeson, Wendy Miles, Linda Neukrug, Daniel Schantz and Teresa Williams for their brilliant editing of numerous stories. You beautifully captured the flavor of *Chicken Soup for the Soul.*

Suzanne Thomas Lawlor, for her dedication and perseverance in reading thousands of stories and helping us select the gems.

Craig Herndon, our manuscript and information management hero, for his devotion, patience and commitment to perfection.

Cindy Knowlton and Sue Penberthy, for their devoted care and support of Jennifer's and Marci's respective lives. Your loyalty, heart and attitude of service touch us deeply and help our lives flow more smoothly.

Patty Aubery, for being a great friend and colleague—and the real soul that holds the central *Chicken Soup for the Soul* office together.

Jeanette Lisefski, for continuing to keep parts of our office impeccably on track.

Carol Kline, for her ongoing support, feedback, input and help wherever it was needed. You are a wonderful friend, and we're so lucky to have you in our lives.

Joanne Cox, for her excellent contribution to helping prepare our initial manuscript.

Peter Vegso at Health Communications, Inc., our publisher extraordinaire, for his vision and commitment to bringing *Chicken Soup for the Soul* to the world.

Heather McNamara, senior editor for the *Chicken Soup for the Soul* series, for her wisdom, experience and heartfelt dedication in completing our final manuscript.

Nancy Autio, for overseeing the permissions process for

the stories used in this book and for her ongoing support.

Teresa Esparza, Leslie Forbes, Rosalie Miller, Veronica Romero and Robin Yerian for the great job they do in running Jack Canfield's office. It's a joy to work with you.

Laurie Hartman, Laura Rush and Lisa Williams at Mark Victor Hansen's office, for helping in the marketing and promotion of our books.

Kimberly Kirberger, for her ongoing support in all areas.

Mark and Chrissy Donnelly, for their friendship, support and marketing efforts on our behalf.

Christine Belleris, Matthew Diener and Lisa Drucker, our editors at Health Communications, Inc., and especially Allison Janse, our managing editor, for their expertise and willingness to work with us on every aspect of this book.

Terry Burke, Randee Feldman, Larry Getlen, Kelly Maragni, Tom Sand, Kim Weiss and the marketing department at Health Communications, Inc., for bringing their talents to the support and promotion of this book.

Larissa Hise, Bren Frisch, Shepley Hansen and Robbin O'Neill for working with us so patiently and cooperatively on the cover design of this book.

The following people, who completed the monumental task of reading the preliminary manuscript of this book, helped us make the final selections and made invaluable comments on how to improve the book: Fred C. Angelis, Barbara Astrowsky, Bryan Aubrey, Carolyn Burch, Tom Davenport, Linda DeGraaff, Trina Enriquez, Corina Garona, Larry Getlen, Pam Gordon, Elinor Hall, Amy Hawthorne, Dan Hawthorne, Paul Hindman, Carol Jackson, Carol Kline, Cindy Knowlton, Robin Kotok, Barbara LeMonaco, Suzanne Lawlor, Jeanette Lisefski, Donna Loesch, Barbara McLoughlin, Karen McLoughlin, Heather McNamara, Barbara McQuaide, Beverly Merson, Linda Mitchell, Monica Navarrette, Sue Penberthy, Dick

Purnell, Maureen Read, Wendy Read, Carol Richter, Heather Sanders and Marcus and Louise Shimoff.

Dan Hurley and Bill and Patricia Rayl for administering our America Online contest for stories.

Jim Rubis and the Fairfield Public Library (Iowa), for their outstanding research assistance.

Fairfield Printing (Iowa), especially Cindy Sharp, for their enthusiastic support of our work.

Jerry Teplitz, for his inventive approach for testing manuscript and cover design.

M., for the gifts of wisdom and knowledge.

Ron and Elinor Hall, for their constant support, encouragement and love.

We also thank the following people who took the time to spread the word about this book, helped us network with other writers and researched stories: Doris Booth, Dan Davidson, Reg A. Forder, Gary Gray, David Hargrove, Lynda Hunter, Janet L. Jacobsen, Eileen Lawrence, Patricia Lorenz, Trish McDermott, Ray Newton, Penny Porter, Dick Purnell, Barbara Schiller, Jeff Shepherd, H. Norman Wright and Steve Zikman.

We deeply appreciate all the *Chicken Soup for the Soul* coauthors, who make it a joy to be part of this Chicken Soup family: Patty Aubery, Jeff Aubery, Marty Becker, Ron Camacho, Tim Clauss, Barbara De Angelis, Mark and Chrissy Donnelly, Irene Dunlap, Patty Hansen, Kimberly Kirberger, Carol Kline, Hanoch and Meladee McCarty, Heather McNamara, Nancy Autio, Maida Rogerson, Martin Rutte, Barry Spilchuk and Diana von Welanetz Wentworth.

We also wish to acknowledge the hundreds of people who sent us stories, poems and quotes (especially Rochelle Pennington!) for possible inclusion in *Chicken Soup for the Single's Soul.* While we were not able to use everything you sent in, we were deeply touched by your heartfelt intention to share yourselves and your stories with us and our readers. Many of these may be used in future volumes of *Chicken Soup for the Soul.* Thank you!

Because of the size of this project, we may have left out the names of some people who helped us along the way. If so, we are sorry—please know that we really do appreciate all of you very deeply.

We are truly grateful for the many hands and hearts that have made this book possible. We love you all!

Introduction

Welcome to *Chicken Soup for the Single's Soul*! For the first time in history, there are more single people than married people in our society. If you are reading this book, it is likely that you have never been married, or have become divorced or widowed.

This is a book that shares the love, the challenges and the unique joys of being single. Whether you are single by choice or by circumstance, these stories will show you that you are not alone.

When we started this book, our intention was to compile a collection of stories that would address the many types of single people—from the twenty-year-old never-married man or woman, to the fifty-year-old divorcée, to the eighty-year-old widower. And we discovered that the opportunities and challenges facing this diverse group of people are numerous and often inspiring.

For example, we included stories about being Single and Happy—an unprecedented trend in our country. For the first time, many people are choosing to remain single for a lifetime—something that was almost inconceivable even twenty years ago.

On the other hand, it's impossible to talk about being single without addressing the desires that so many single people have regarding relationships. Many single people want to have a relationship, and that's why we have included chapters on Dating and Finding Your Mate.

Still others are in the process of letting go of a relationship or grieving the loss of a love. The stories in Single Again deal with rebuilding life after divorce. The stories in Losing a Partner share experiences of healing after the death of a partner.

Then there are single parents! Thirty-three percent of all families in the United States are now headed by a single parent. We hope the stories in Single Parenting will touch the hearts of single mothers and fathers everywhere and encourage them on their journey.

One of the most rewarding aspects of working on this book has been discovering the strength and commitment many single people have to making their own lives fulfilling and enriching the lives of others. You will find their stories in our chapter on Making a Difference.

We have also included stories about the incredible support available in many ways for single people. In our chapter We Are Not Alone, we see the support that often appears when least expected or in miraculous ways. In the chapter called Friends and Family, we see the power of the support that comes from the deep bonds of family and important friendships.

Finally, there's love. Love is the most powerful force in the universe. While we often think of love in terms of a marriage or intimate relationship, it's very clear that love comes in many forms. And in a world where 50 percent of the population is now single, we recognize that love is not just for those in relationships. In fact, it is the common thread that binds the many different kinds of stories in *Chicken Soup for the Single's Soul.*

So in the spirit of love, we offer this book to single people everywhere. No matter what your circumstance in life as a single person, we hope these stories open your heart and give you a vision of life's possibilities. May your path be filled with joy and the magical touch of love—wherever you find it.

Share with Us

We would love to hear your reactions to the stories in this book. Please let us know what your favorite stories were and how they affected you.

We also invite you to send us stories you would like to see published in future editions of *Chicken Soup for the Single's Soul.* You can send us either stories you have written or stories written by others that you have liked.

Send your stories to:

Chicken Soup for the Single's Soul
P.O. Box 30880-SI
Santa Barbara, CA 93130
e-mail: *www.chickensoup.com*
fax: 805-563-2945

You can also visit the *Chicken Soup for the Soul* site on America Online at keyword: *chickensoup.*

We hope you enjoy reading this book as much as we enjoyed compiling, editing and writing it.

1

SINGLE AND HAPPY

A happy person is not a person in a certain set of circumstances, but rather a person with a certain set of attitudes.

Hugh Downs

"It's very sweet of you, Rick, but I'm afraid I've fallen in love with myself again."

Reprinted by permission of Donna Barstow.

Room at the Table

Have you ever noticed that dining room tables seat six, eight or twelve—not seven, nine or thirteen? I've been single all my life, usually not thinking much of it. But on holidays even the place settings conspire against me, rendering a silent rebuke against my single status.

You can endure holiday dinners two ways if you're single: 1) Bring someone you don't particularly care for; 2) hear the awful words "Pull up an extra seat," a euphemism for either a collapsible chair or one that is too high or too low for the table. Either strategy leaves you uncomfortable.

At Thanksgiving two years ago, while my calves cramped from straddling the leg of my brother's dining room table, Aunt Nell took the opportunity to ask for details about my love life, which was seriously lacking at the time. The event was excruciating.

Though I enjoy singlehood in the main, there have been times when I've worked myself into a mad frenzy looking for someone to fill a void I thought I couldn't satisfy on my own. Someone, anyone with a pulse would do. Over the years, I dated quite a few guys I liked—I was even engaged once, but "till death us do part" seemed a very long time. I was relieved to be alone again.

So holidays, especially with the Aunt Nells of the family leave me a little bereft. One day, noting my frustration a friend of mine suggested we try something different on the next such holiday.

"How 'bout you and I go down to a homeless shelter and help out? Then maybe we'll be grateful for what we have," she proposed.

I had a thousand reasons why this wasn't a good idea, but my friend persisted. The next Christmas I found myself in an old warehouse, doling out food.

Never in my life had I seen so many turkeys and rows of pumpkin pies. Decorations donated by a nearby grocery store created a festive atmosphere that uplifted even my reluctant spirit. When everyone was fed, I took a tray and filled a plate with the bountiful harvest. After a few bites, I knew what everyone was carrying on about; the food was really good.

My dinner companions were easy company. Nobody asked me why I didn't have a date. People just seemed grateful for a place to sit and enjoy a special dinner. To my surprise, I found I had much in common with my fellow diners. They were people like me.

My experience that Christmas brought me back to the shelter the following year. I enjoyed helping others so much that I began seeking more opportunities to serve. I started volunteering for the Literacy Foundation once a week. I figured I could sit in front of the TV, or I could use those evening hours to help others learn to read.

Caring for others has abundantly filled the void in my life that I had sometimes interpreted as a missing mate. When I stopped trying so hard to fit in, I realized I was single for a reason and found my own special purpose.

There is room at the table for a party of one. And sometimes "just one" is the perfect fit.

Vivian Eisenecher

The Professor and the Soulmate

The sounds of the wedding march filled the air. Jennifer and I, bride and groom, were radiantly happy as we stood at the altar. After decades of searching, I had found and married my soulmate. It was the most thrilling moment of my life.

There was only one thing wrong with this scene. It was taking place solely in my own mind. I was in fact pacing up and down my own living room in a state of exhilaration, as my cassette player belted out the familiar music. Being something of a classical music and opera buff, I had selected Wagner's opera "Lohengrin" because it contained the traditional wedding march, and it was really firing my imagination.

The real truth was that I'd just returned home from only my third or fourth date with Jennifer. We hardly knew each other yet, so I was, to put it mildly, jumping to conclusions.

This was a familiar pattern with me, having begun many years ago when I was a shy, sixteen-year-old boy growing up in England. I had a friend named Simon, and he and I would sometimes amuse ourselves by posing the question, "I wonder what my future wife is doing now?" Speculating idly on this unanswerable question allowed us to forget the unfortunate fact that since we attended an all-boys school, not only did we not have girlfriends, we didn't even know any girls.

It was at about that time that I began to entertain the notion of a cosmic soulmate, the one who would appear at some unspecified point in my future and miraculously supply whatever it was that I lacked. This soulmate had neither face, nor name, nor form, and yet she was somehow more real in my imagination than any of the flesh-and-blood girls that I was soon to encounter.

Throughout the ups and downs of my skirmishes with the opposite sex during my teens and early twenties, this belief in a soulmate showed no signs of abating, in spite of the fact that the soulmate chose—as soulmates do—to postpone her appearance indefinitely.

In 1981, when I was thirty-two and still single—and still looking, perpetually—I left England behind for America, where I was to take up a job as a professor of literature at a small liberal arts college in the Midwest.

Never having been to America before, I had little idea of what to expect. For a while, culture shock—everything almost the same, nothing exactly the same—spun me in a whirl of disorientation.

But that changed on my second day on the college campus. I was taking care of some business in one of the administrative offices. As I made my inquiry, a look of delight crossed the face of the attractive young lady behind the desk. "Where are you from?" she asked, smiling at me. "You have such a wonderful accent."

So it was true! Americans really *did* say that when confronted with a perfectly ordinary BBC voice. I began to sense that living in America might have advantages that I had not hitherto suspected.

Thus emboldened, I plunged into a decade of Serious Quest for Soulmate. After all, she was there, somewhere in this New World. She must be. I certainly looked. At faculty meetings, for example, my eyes would dart around the room for clues, as if American Soulmate, Ph.D., might, in a mystical moment of recognition, disclose herself by look, word or gesture understood only by me.

One thing I did notice was how much psychic energy this took, and how restless and unhappy it sometimes made me, particularly when my relationship with Soulmate *du jour* would fall apart after only a few months.

Take Jennifer. Jennifer, in my eyes, had class, dignity, intelligence, beauty. And reservations.

"It doesn't feel quite right to me," she said to me over dinner one night.

"Would you like some more pasta?" I replied.

"I think you have too many expectations."

"No, I don't," I shot back, demonstrating my finely honed ability to deny the obvious.

A few more hops and skips, and Jenny and I had reached the familiar conclusion: tension-filled silences followed by angry outbursts, culminating in Jennifer's *coup de grace,* "I don't think we should see each other again."

And so the long-running play continued. A series of unsuspecting women found themselves filling a position they neither asked for, nor (with some exceptions) wanted. And often in the background, my tapes of "Lohengrin," as well as the Mendelssohn wedding march from his "Midsummer Night's Dream" music, would rotate merrily around their spindles. Still the real soulmate eluded detection.

One morning a few years ago, I had just returned from the gym, which I had found to be an interesting, if so far unproductive, place to scout for Soulmate-in-Skimpy-Workout-Gear. It was spring and the lilacs in my yard were in bloom. I sat on the deck with a Styrofoam cup of coffee in my hand, looking out on the display of nature's greenery. It wasn't the high from the workout or the coffee that did it, but I gradually became aware that everything in that moment was perfect. Everything was exactly as it should be. Nothing else was needed. Nothing added or subtracted from that minute could possibly "improve" it. This certainly wasn't the way I normally felt, having conditioned myself to believe that what every minute really needed was a quick infusion of Soulmate.

And yet that moment shifted something inside me. I don't know how or why, but I do know that it has continued, that there is a tranquil "place" inside me, that is no place at all, because it is everywhere and nowhere, and it is still and silent and has neither beginning nor end and is not alien or foreign to me or outside of me. After years of searching, I have found my soulmate, and it is myself. The bachelor is content. Oh, he still dates women from time to time, and he listens to the wedding marches sometimes, too. But only because he likes them.

Bryan Aubrey

Is Fire Goddess Spelled with Two Ds?

Happiness depends upon ourselves.

Aristotle

When I was eight years old, I saw a movie about a mysterious island that had an erupting volcano and lush jungles filled with wild animals and cannibals. The island was ruled by a beautiful woman called "Tandaleah, the Fire Goddess of the Volcano." It was a terrible, low-budget movie, but to me it represented the perfect life. Being chased by molten lava, bloodthirsty animals and savages was a small price to pay for freedom. I desperately wanted to be the Fire Goddess. I wrote it on my list of "Things to Be When I Grow Up," and asked my girlfriend if "Fire Goddess" was spelled with two Ds.

Through the years the school system did its best to mold me into a no-nonsense, responsible, respectable citizen, and Tandaleah was forgotten. My parents approved of my suitable marriage, and I spent the next twenty-five years being a good wife, eventually the mother of four and a very respectable, responsible member of society. My life was as bland and boring as a bowl of oatmeal. I knew exactly what to expect in the future: The children would grow up and leave home, my husband and I would grow old together and we'd baby-sit the grandchildren.

The week I turned fifty my marriage came to a sudden end. My house, furniture and everything I'd owned was auctioned off to pay debts I didn't even know existed. In a week I'd lost my husband, my home and my parents, who refused to accept a divorce in the family. I'd lost everything except my four teenaged children.

I had enough money to rent a cheap apartment while I looked for a job. Or I could use every penny I had to buy five plane tickets from Missouri to the most remote island in the world, the Big Island of Hawaii. Everyone said I was crazy to think I could just run off to an island and survive. They predicted I'd come crawling back in a month. Part of me was afraid they were right.

The next day, my four children and I landed on the Big Island of Hawaii with less than two thousand dollars, knowing no one in the world was going to help us. I rented an unfurnished apartment where we slept on the floor and lived on cereal. I worked three jobs scrubbing floors on my hands and knees, selling macadamia nuts to tourists and gathering coconuts. I worked eighteen hours a day and lost thirty pounds because I lived on one meal a day. I had panic attacks that left me curled into a knot on the bathroom floor, shaking like a shell-shocked soldier.

One night, as I walked alone on the beach, I saw the red-orange glow of the lava pouring out of the Kilauea volcano in the distance. I was wading in the Pacific Ocean, watching the world's most active volcano and wasting that incredible moment because I was haunted by the past, exhausted by the present and terrified of the future. I'd almost achieved my childhood dream—but hadn't realized it because I was focused on my burdens instead of my blessings. It was time to live my imagination—not my history.

Tandaleah, the Fire Goddess of the Volcano, had finally arrived!

The next day I quit my jobs and invested my last paycheck in art supplies and began doing what I loved. I hadn't painted a picture in fifteen years because we'd barely scratched out a living on the farm in Missouri and there hadn't been money for the tubes of paint and canvas and frames. I wondered if I could still paint or if I'd forgotten how. My hands trembled the first time I picked up a brush, but before an hour had passed I was lost in the colors spreading across the canvas in front of me. I painted pictures of old sailing ships, and as soon as I started believing in myself, other people started believing in me, too. The first painting sold for fifteen hundred dollars before I even had time to frame it.

The past six years have been filled with adventures: My children and I have gone swimming with dolphins, watched whales and hiked around the crater rim of the volcano. We wake up every morning with the ocean in front of us and the volcano behind us.

The dream I'd had more than forty years ago is now reality. I live on an island with a continuously erupting volcano. The only animals in the jungle are wild boars and mongooses and there aren't any cannibals, but often in the evening, I can hear the drums from native dancers on the beach.

Well-meaning friends have tried countless times to introduce me to their uncles, neighbors, fathers and even grandfathers, hoping I'd find a mate to save me from a lonely old age. They use phrases like, "a woman of your age . . ." and "You aren't getting any younger . . ." to push me into blind dates.

I gently point out that "a woman my age" has paid her

dues. I enjoyed being a wife and mother and believe in my heart that I was a good one. I did that job for over a quarter of a century. And now at my age, I have grown into the woman I wish I could have been when I was in my twenties. No, I'm not getting any younger, but neither is anyone else, and honestly, I wouldn't want to be young again. I'm happier than I've ever been. I can paint all night and sleep all day without feeling guilty. I can cook or not cook. I can live on cream puffs and Pepsi for a week at a time and no one will lecture me on the importance of a balanced diet.

It took a long time to find myself, and I had to live alone to do it. But I am not lonely. I am free for the first time in my life. I am Tandaleah, the Fire Goddess of the Volcano, spelled with two Ds . . . and I'm living happily ever after.

Linda Stafford

Stone Soup. ©1999 Jan Eliot. Distributed by Universal Press Syndicate. Reprinted by permission.

Lessons from Aunt Grace

Nobody trips over mountains. It is the small pebble that causes you to stumble. Pass all the pebbles in your path and you will find you have crossed the mountain.

Source Unknown

The day we moved away I hit bottom. Saying good-bye to my friends and to the house I had loved made me feel as though my moorings had been ripped loose. Now, in what my husband kept calling "our new home" (it wasn't new, and it wasn't home), I was so awash in self-pity that I almost ignored the white leather book I found while unpacking an old trunk. But something prompted me to examine it.

The gold Victorian script on the cover spelled *My Diary.* Opening the book, I recognized the spidery handwriting of my great-aunt Grace, who had lived with us when I was a little girl. Aunt Grace belonged to a species now extinct—the unmarried, unemployed gentlewoman forced to live with relatives. All the cards had seemed to be stacked against her. She was plain-looking; she was poor; she was frail.

Yet the thing I remember about her was her unfailing cheerfulness. Not only did she never complain, but she never seemed to lose her gentle smile. "Grace always looks on the bright side," people said.

I sank down on the rolled carpet to read her diary. The first entry was dated 1901; the last was the year of her death, 1930. I read casually at first, and then with riveted attention.

Three years have passed since my dear Ted was killed at San Juan Hill and yet every day is still filled with pain. Will I ever be happy again?

Ted? I thought of Aunt Grace as the complete old maid. She once had a sweetheart! I read on:

My unhappiness is a bottomless cup. I know I must be cheerful, living in this large family upon whom I am dependent, yet gloom haunts me. . . . Something has to change or I shall be sick. Clearly my situation is not going to change; therefore, I shall have to change. But how?

I have given much thought to my predicament and I have devised a simple set of rules by which I plan to live. I intend this to be a daily exercise. I pray that the plan will somehow deliver me from my dismal swamp of despair. It has *to.*

The simplicity of Aunt Grace's rules-to-live-by took my breath away. She resolved every day to:

1. Do something for someone else.
2. Do something for myself.
3. Do something I don't want to do that needs doing.
4. Do a physical exercise.
5. Do a mental exercise.
6. Do an original prayer that always includes counting my blessings.

Aunt Grace wrote that she limited herself to six rules because she felt that number to be "manageable." Here are some of the things she did and recorded in her diary:

Something for someone else. She bought three calves' feet, simmered them for four hours in water, with spices, to make calf's-foot jelly for a sick friend.

Something for myself. She trimmed an old blue hat with artificial flowers and a veil, receiving so many compliments that she thought the thirty-five cents well spent.

Something I don't want to do. She "turned out" the linen closet—washed three dozen sheets by hand, sun-bleached them, and folded them away with lavender sachet.

Physical exercise. She played croquet and walked to the village instead of going by horse and buggy.

Mental exercise. She read a chapter a day of Dickens's *Bleak House,* "which everyone is talking about."

To my surprise, Aunt Grace had trouble with number six. Prayer did not come easily. "I can't concentrate in church," she wrote. "I find myself appraising the hats." Eventually she discovered a solution: "When I sit in solitude on the rock overlooking our pasture brook, I can pray. I ask the Lord to help me bloom where I am planted, and then I count my blessings, always beginning with my family, without whom I would be alone and lost."

When I put down Aunt Grace's diary—aware now that "cheery Aunt Grace" fought the battle against darkness that we all fight—tears filled my eyes. But at first I ignored her message. I was a modern woman who needed no self-help crutches from a bygone era.

Yet settling into our new life proved increasingly difficult. One day, feeling totally depressed, I lay in bed and stared at the ceiling. Should I try Aunt Grace's formula? Could those six points help me now?

I decided I could continue to be a lump of misery, or I could test Aunt Grace's recipe by doing something for someone else. I could, for instance, phone my eighty-five-year-old neighbor who was ill and lived by herself. One of Aunt Grace's sentences echoed in my head: "I alone can take the initiative to escape from 'the sarcophagus of self.'"

The sarcophagus of self. That did it. I would not be buried by my own ego. I got up and dialed Miss Phillips. She invited me for tea.

It was a start. Miss Phillips was delighted to have someone to talk with—and in her musty parlor I listened to details of her illness. Then I heard her say something that snapped me to attention.

"Sometimes," said Miss Phillips, "the thing you dread doing is the very thing you should do, just so you can stop thinking about it."

I walked home, turning over that insight in my mind. Miss Phillips had cast a new light on Aunt Grace's third rule. *Do something I don't want to do that needs doing.*

Ever since we moved, I had avoided organizing my desk. Now I made up my mind to get the blasted pile of papers in order. I found a file and folders, and every paper on my desk went into one of them or into the trash.

Two hours later I put down a new green blotter and a small philodendron plant. I beamed. I had done something I did not want to do, and it made me feel good.

At first, "doing a physical exercise" wasn't quite so successful. I signed up for a jazz-exercise class and hated it. I tried jogging, until it dawned on me that I hated it, too.

"What's wrong with walking?" my husband asked. He offered to join me each morning before breakfast. We found walking to be wonderfully conducive to communication. We enjoyed it so much that evening walks eventually replaced our evening cocktail. We felt healthier than we had in years.

At "doing something for yourself" I excelled. I began with Aunt Grace's idea of bath therapy. "A bath should be the ultimate place of relaxation," she wrote. "Gather fresh lemon balm, sweet marjoram, mint, lemon verbena, lavender and rose geranium. Steep the dried leaves in boiling water for fifteen minutes and strain into the tub.

Lie in the bath with your eyes closed, and do not think while soaking."

Miss Phillips happily supplied me with herbs from her garden. I put the herbal mix in the tub, turned on the water and stretched out to let the tensions of the day melt away. It was sensational.

Soon I started an herb garden of my own and made herbal sachets for Christmas gifts. Doing something for myself had turned into doing something for someone else.

The "mental exercise" was more of a challenge. I couldn't decide what to do until I read about a poetry course at the local community college. The teacher was a retired college professor who made poetry come alive. When we reached Emily Dickinson, I went into orbit. I read all 1,775 of her poems and was enthralled. "I dwell in Possibility," wrote Emily. Marvelous.

Our professor was big on memorizing, which turned out to be the best mental exercise of all. I began with "I'm Nobody! Who are you?" and progressed to more difficult poems like "I felt a Funeral, in my Brain." How I've enjoyed recalling these poems while waiting in supermarket lines or at doctors' offices!

Aunt Grace's prayer assignment was the most helpful of all. I try now to make up a short prayer every day, and I always include some thanksgiving in it. Writing a prayer isn't easy, but it's a valuable spiritual discipline. I don't have Aunt Grace's meditation rock, but I do have a peaceful village church where I can attend to that inner voice.

I don't worry how *well* I fulfill Aunt Grace's six rules, so long as I do them *daily.* I will give myself credit for just one letter written, or one drawer cleaned out, and it's surprising how good feelings about a small accomplishment often enable me to go on and do more.

Can life be lived by a formula? All I know is that since I started to live by those six precepts, I've become more involved with others and, hence, less "buried" in myself. Instead of wallowing in self-pity, I have adopted Aunt Grace's motto: "Bloom where you are planted."

Nardi Reeder Campion

Seeing 20/20

Springtime in New York City—my first apartment, a good-paying job and a great-looking girlfriend. It couldn't get much better than that. I had my life figured out. In fact, I felt so good, so magnanimous, that I decided to share my happiness with others. Helping someone less fortunate seemed the noble thing to do. Following a friend's example, I volunteered with the Lighthouse for the Blind.

The friendly volunteer coordinator explained they needed help with an outreach program for the elderly—recently blinded shut-ins. Telling myself I'd bring a little joy to some poor, unfortunate senior citizen, I agreed.

The night before my first meeting with the "shut-in," my girlfriend and I had a major fight. She stormed out; I sulked. The next morning, I struggled to open my eyes. I had spent most of the night reliving the fight. I was cranky, saturated with self-pity. I dragged myself out of bed to do my volunteer work, but my generous mood had evaporated. I didn't want to visit some old blind man.

Charlie lived in a rough section of Manhattan: the lowest section of the Lower East Side. Dodging delirious winos, occasionally crossing the street to avoid desperate-looking drug addicts, I trudged toward our first meeting. I tried to imagine what Charlie looked like. The coordinator said he was very old. At twenty-three, as far as I was concerned, anyone over sixty-five was at death's door. He was definitely over sixty-five, I'd been told. *Probably senile, too,* I thought to myself.

Well, I'd wasted this Saturday morning, I thought, but I can call the Lighthouse early Monday morning and take myself off the list of volunteers. I climbed the crumbling steps to Charlie's run-down building and began the ascent to his sixth-floor apartment. No elevator.

Shuffling sounds signaled Charlie's approach; a face appeared from behind the graffiti-covered apartment door. I gasped. *This guy's older than God,* I thought. Cataract-clouded eyes, wispy white hair. He was ancient. Charlie wasn't just sixty-five; he was sixty-five years older than I was. He was eighty-eight.

He ushered me into his surprisingly tidy apartment. I couldn't help noticing it looked neater than mine, and I wasn't blind. Sitting on a slightly musty sofa, Charlie told me how he'd lost his vision and wife of more than fifty years, all in the previous ten months. He told me the past without a trace of self-pity.

I tried to imagine the tragedy of his life, thinking that I'd be suicidal if I was blind and alone. Charlie interrupted my thoughts. He was telling me how fortunate he'd been to have such a wonderful marriage for so long. He smiled at me gently, as if sensing my discomfort.

That first day, Charlie and I visited his barber and walked—more than he had walked since his wife's funeral. As we walked, Charlie talked. Charlie had outlived everybody. All his friends and relatives were gone, with the exception of a son in California. He told me tales of his younger days at sea, his service in World War I and his wonderful wife. Time slipped by. My agreed-upon one-hour visit stretched to three hours. Charlie was a great storyteller, but he was more than that. No matter what life event he shared, he never complained. Never. He was always able to find something positive to say about what had happened to him.

Eventually, Charlie needed a nap, and I left him as his clouded eyes were drifting off to sleep. As I left, I thought that Charlie's eyes may have been fogged over, but his perspective was 20/20. Just spending a day with him corrected my distorted view of life. I saw all my problems plainly, and my self-pity vanished as I headed home.

Visits with Charlie became the high point of my week; his stories always put things in perspective for me. It's been a long time since I've had to struggle to wake up on a Saturday morning. Life's full of surprises, Charlie often said on our visits. It was true, I knew; no event was as surprising as my reluctant visit that Saturday morning many years ago, when an aging blind man opened my eyes.

Bill Asenjo

Have Freedom, Will Travel

The man who goes alone can start today; but he who travels with another must wait until the other is ready.

Henry David Thoreau

I had a ticket. I had my passport. And he had cold feet. I might have known fairy tales don't come true.

Seven months out of my marriage, I had met the "great love of my life." We dated a year. I'd always longed to see Europe, and, with my divorce final, we planned the trip together. Then two weeks before takeoff, he took off. Having piggybacked two breakups, I felt as if I'd been through a double divorce. Here I was, thirty-nine years old, with two small children, and facing my ultimate fear: a life alone.

Was I ready to spend a month in Europe by myself? I had a hard time going to a movie alone! But it did seem now or never. The kids would be with their dad, the money came as part of my property settlement, and I had a job waiting when I returned. Okay, if I was going to be lonely for the next few years, I might as well start by being lonely in Europe.

The highlight of my journey was to be Paris, the city I'd always wanted to see. But now I was frightened to travel without a companion. I steeled myself and went anyway.

I arrived at the train station in Paris panicked and disoriented. I hadn't used my college French in twenty years. Pulling my red suitcase on wobbly wheels behind me, I was shoved and pushed by perspiring travelers reeking of cigarette smoke, different diets and not nearly enough deodorant. The roar of many languages bombarding me seemed unintelligible—just babble.

On my first Metro ride, I encountered an incompetent, clumsy pickpocket. I melted him with a look, and he eased his hand from my purse to fade into the crowded car. At my stop, I hauled my heavy suitcase up the steep stairs and froze.

Cars zoomed helter-skelter, honking belligerently. Somewhere in this confusing city my hotel was hidden, but the directions I had scrawled suddenly weren't legible.

I stopped two people. Both greeted me with that Parisian countenance that said: "Yes, I speak English, but you'll have to struggle with your French if you want to talk to me." I walked up one street and across another. A wheel broke off my suitcase. When I finally found the hotel, my heart was pounding, I was sweating like a basketball player and my spirits drooped. They flattened altogether when I saw my room.

I couldn't stay. Could I? The wallpaper looked like it had been through a fire. The bedsprings creaked. The bathroom was down the hall, and the window looked out onto the brick wall of another building. Welcome to Paris.

I sincerely wanted to die. I missed my friend. I was entering my third week away from home and my kids, and I had arrived in the most romantic city in the world, alone. Alone and lonely. Alone, lonely and petrified.

The most important thing I did in Paris happened at

that moment. I knew that if I didn't go out, right then, and find a place to have dinner, I would hide in this cubicle my entire time in Paris. My dream would be foregone, and I might never learn to enjoy the world as a single individual. So I pulled myself together and went out.

Evening in Paris was light and balmy. When I reached the Tuileries, I strolled along a winding path, listening to birds sing, watching children float toy sailboats in a huge fountain. No one seemed to be in a hurry. Paris was beautiful. And I was here alone but suddenly not lonely. My sense of accomplishment at overcoming my fear and vulnerability had left me feeling free, not abandoned.

I wore out two pairs of shoes during my week's stay in Paris. I did everything there was to do, and it was the greatest week of my European vacation. I returned home a believer in the healing power of solitary travel. Years later, I still urge divorcing or widowed friends to take their solo flight in the form of travel plans.

Those who have gone have returned changed—even by a four-day weekend in Santa Fe, an Amtrak ride up the coast or an organized tour of Civil War battlefields. Traveling alone redeems itself by demanding self-reliance and building the kind of confidence that serves the single life well.

Certainly Paris became my metaphor for addressing life's challenges on my own. Now when I meet an obstacle I just say to myself: *If I can go to Paris, I can go anywhere.*

Dawn McKenna

Have freedom, will travel

Reprinted by permission of Donna Barstow.

The Visit

What a lovely surprise to finally discover how unlonely being alone can be.

Ellen Burstyn

Slowly I walked down the aisle of the empty church. It had been a while since I'd stopped by for a visit. After many years of attending Catholic schools I'd slipped into the category of "lapsed." Whatever spiritual juice I'd felt as a young boy growing up had evaporated years ago.

I looked around before slipping into a pew and kneeling down. It was pretty much the same as I remembered. I glanced up toward the altar and noticed the flickering candle that symbolized God was present, though invisible. "So," I whispered, "maybe you're here and maybe you aren't. We'll see." Somewhere along the line I'd lost faith in whatever had sustained me in my earlier days.

I blessed myself, sat back on the hard wooden pew, gazed ahead and continued to address the God whose presence I doubted. "Anyway, if you're really here, I need your help. I've tried everything I can think of. Nothing works. I feel totally helpless. I have no idea what else I can do. I'm thirty-three, healthy and fairly successful. You probably know all this. But I'm lonely. I have no one to share my life with, no special woman to love, no one to start a family with. My life feels empty, and I have nowhere else to go. I've taken eighteen seminars in as many months, learned how to access my feelings, release past hurts, complete old relationships, communicate my needs, understand and respond to what my partner wants. But still I'm alone. I can't seem to find the right woman, the one who feels right deep inside. What am I missing?"

I sat still, listening. There was no reply to my question, no still small voice. Just the occasional car horn outside, or the sound of a bus passing by. Just silence. I shrugged. Continuing to sit quietly, I let the silence wash over me.

Day after day I repeated this routine. I sat in the same pew, on the same hard bench, uttering the same plea to a flickering candle, in the same silence. Nothing changed. I was as lonely as I had been on day one. There were no mystical answers, no hidden messages.

I continued to live my life, managing to laugh and have some fun. I went on dates and enjoyed myself, whether I was dining out, dancing or at the movies. I also prayed. Day after day, I took an hour away from my regular activities, emptied myself and asked the same questions again and again.

One morning about six weeks later, I awoke and knew that something had shifted. I looked around. Something about the slant of light through the clouds, the fragrance of newly bloomed jasmine, the warm beach breeze, was different. I couldn't quite put my finger on what it was, but I felt it. On my way home that afternoon, I stopped by the church as usual. Instead of my usual whining, I knelt and smiled at the candle.

Then I conveyed my thoughts to God. "I'm not quite sure what happened, but I feel different. Something has shifted inside. I don't feel lonely anymore. Nothing's changed 'out there,' but it all feels completely different. Would you happen to know anything about that?"

Suddenly, I was struck by the foolishness of the question, and I laughed out loud. My laughter echoed off the high ceilings and the stone walls, and then there was silence once more. But even the silence felt different. It no longer conveyed a feeling of emptiness and desolation. On the contrary, it radiated a wonderful serenity and tranquillity. I knew in that moment that I had come home to myself. I felt full, complete inside. I bowed my head, took a deep breath and exhaled.

"Thank you," I whispered. "I have no idea what you did but I feel this happiness comes from you. I know that. I haven't done anything new or different. So I know it's not from me. Who else could it be from?"

I continued to sit in the silence, alone, content, happy. Then I spoke again to God. "I surrender to not knowing. I surrender to you being in charge. I surrender to my life being an expression of your will instead of my will. And I thank you for this feeling, this change or transformation or whatever it is."

In the days and weeks that followed, my sense of fulfillment grew and expanded. I looked at everything from an entirely different perspective. Rather than looking for my "missing piece," I simply enjoyed life. Gone was the angst, the stifling urgency to find the "perfect woman" for the rest of my life.

The shift in my viewpoint expanded into other areas as well. Instead of trudging through life I glided. I embraced being single. It felt wonderful. As long as I maintained my connection with my inner self, I brimmed over with happiness, excitement, joy, fulfillment. There was nothing to fear. If it was God's will that I should marry, then I would. If not, that was fine, too. I no longer held onto any preconceived notions of how my life should turn out. Every day was a new and wonderful adventure.

Four months later, I bumped into Kathy—again. We'd met years ago, but I'd forgotten all about it. She was sweet, bubbly, cute and lots of fun. We hit it off instantly. Her marriage was over and she was still mourning its passing, even though her brown eyes twinkled whenever we got together. There was something powerful that I couldn't ignore about this bright Irish lass.

Her laughter was infectious, her heart as big as the endless sky. Every time we were together, time stood still. We finished each other's sentences, giggled like school kids, brimmed over with excitement and delight. I felt protective of her. She was everything I'd ever dreamed of, everything that I'd stopped looking for months ago.

Once again, I surrendered to something so much more powerful than myself. We were in love.

One afternoon on my way back from the beach, I made a quick visit to the church. It was still just as silent, and the wooden bench was as hard as ever. The candle still flickered on the empty altar. Full of joy and mirth, I raised my eyes.

"Thanks," I whispered. "Again. For bringing us together. For helping me let go of all the baggage I was carrying, all the stuff that prevented me from seeing what was already there inside. Thanks for showing yourself to me in her smile, in myself, in the summer breezes, the cool evening sky, the curling waves, the seagulls, the sun and the rain. I couldn't have done it without you. But you always knew that, didn't you? I was the one who had to learn. Thanks for not giving up on me like I had on you. Thanks for hanging in there with me. I promise I'll never forget."

C. J. Herrmann

Fascination with Dree

You cannot be lonely if you like the person you're alone with.

Wayne Dyer

Aunt Dree is my favorite aunt, indeed, my favorite person. The highlight of my summers as a child was not that my mom, dad, younger sister Lillie and I headed out from St. Louis to Myrtle Beach, South Carolina, but that we stopped off along the way at Aunt Dree's house in Atlanta, Georgia. I knew I was in store for three days of splendid fun.

It usually started off with a magnificent dinner planned by Aunt Dree, which Dad and Mom helped prepare in the kitchen, with flour and spices flying everywhere. Lillie and I were always a part of the process—we were never in the way or too young, according to Aunt Dree. And once the dinner was ready, we didn't just sit down, but went off and dressed in our finest; Dad in a handsome suit, Mom in a sequined dress, and my sister and I in lacy socks and flower-print dresses usually reserved only for Easter. We'd sit down to a classy spread, complete with fine china and crystal goblets and warm, glowing candles. We'd make a most grown-up toast to our wonderful time together. Aunt Dree knew how to make the most ordinary of times most fascinating.

If it rained, we'd spend afternoons playing canasta, a card game Aunt Dree taught Lillie and me, and listening to Patsy Cline or Billie Holiday tunes on her ancient record player. I knew all the words to those songs sung on those lazy afternoons. Often, a card game would be interrupted as the three of us mouthed the words into our soda bottles and gave emotional concerts to imaginary yet worshiping crowds.

If the weather was nice, we'd play croquet with Aunt Dree's friends and neighbors. While Aunt Dree wore an actual pair of knickers, she helped us achieve the look by tucking the cuffs of Lillie's and my pants into knee-length socks, and giving us jaunty hats to wear. She taught us the fine art of sophisticatedly leaning against our croquet mallets while waiting for the others to take their turns tapping the colorful balls rolling about the lawn.

Aunt Dree would treat us to high tea, where we wore white gloves and talked in very stiff upper-lipped English as we delicately raised pretty teacups to our lipsticked lips (compliments of Aunt Dree's makeup bag). As we pretended we were members of the Royal Family, Aunt Dree went about filling our teacups, often taking the role of the maid or a butler and announcing, amid our giggles, the arrival of some very proper English gent.

There were cocktail parties where my sister and I got to carry silver trays of tiny cucumber sandwiches or goblets of amber-colored liquid. As we did our serving, complete with white cloths over our arms, Aunt Dree's animated friends would pat our curled hair and pinch our rouged cheeks and exclaim, sincerely I believe, that they loved it when we came to town because Aunt Dree always threw the most marvelous parties just for us. I never remember spilling a single goblet. Aunt Dree always had a way of making me believe I was in another world, another time, capable of doing and being anything I wanted.

Lillie and I slept with Aunt Dree in her huge bed with a soft feather mattress and what seemed like hundreds of pillows. She would begin a story of some fabulously rich character in some faraway country and with her coaxing, Lillie and I would finish the story to Aunt Dree's most profound applause of how creative and brilliant her two nieces were. "We'll send that story to Hollywood!" she'd say. "It's an Oscar nomination, for sure!" and we'd fall asleep curled next to her with images of movie premieres flashing through our dreams. Oftentimes, we were awakened in the middle of the night, beckoned by Aunt Dree to come to the window seat and look out past the flowering gladiolas and the statuesque pine trees up to the silver white moon high in the summer sky. With her arms squeezed about us, we'd look with wonder upon what had been a very ordinary moon back at my house in St. Louis. "Don't you wish we could bring it down to the yard and play kickball with it?" Aunt Dree would suggest. "A glow-in-the-dark dodge ball," she'd say with a grin. I could have lain in her arms all night.

During one visit, I remember Lillie exclaiming that she wanted to grow up to be just like Aunt Dree. I was old enough then to catch the exchanged glances from my mother and father. I knew my father loved his sister, but Aunt Dree was, after all, single and living alone—not exactly the life parents would want for their daughter. And despite my wonderful times and loving feelings toward Aunt Dree, I had to admit I slightly agreed. I mean, after all, she was alone.

I remember lamenting about this to my grandmother, Aunt Dree's mother, once. "I'm afraid that she might be lonely," I confessed to Grandma. "I worry about her. She's all by herself."

"Oh, my dear," Grandma said. "Dree may be single and may often be alone, but I suspect she is never lonely. She has so many friends and family members that love her so much. And she's so charming that I don't believe she's ever met a stranger. And best of all, God has given Dree that most wonderful of talents—she is able to appreciate and enjoy her own company. Now isn't that a wonderful thing!"

And I knew that it was a wonderful thing. And with Grandma's wise words, I never worried about Aunt Dree again. Aunt Dree did not need my sympathy. She was most fervently enjoying her journey, and it was most certainly not a journey that she traveled alone. I decided then and there that I, too, wanted to grow up to be just like Aunt Dree.

Megan Martin

I Don't Even Know Your Name

I'm Nobody! Who are you?
Are you—Nobody—Too?
Then there's a pair of us?
Don't tell! they'd advertise—you know!

How dreary—to be—Somebody!
How public—like a Frog—
To tell one's name—the livelong June—
To an admiring Bog!

Emily Dickinson

When I mailed my registration for a teachers' conference in Louisville, Kentucky, I also ordered a ticket to a local play about the life of Emily Dickinson. Being single, I'm used to doing things alone, and mostly I enjoy my own company. The conference was good. But after days of wearing a nametag and conversing with strangers, I was more than ready to spend a quiet evening with "The Belle of Amherst." And I was looking forward to doing so alone.

After dinner at my hotel, I asked for directions to the theater. Too far to walk, I was told. But it was on a bus route, so I headed up the street to the corner. My bus came right away. I took a seat up front, across from the driver, and she agreed to tell me when to get off. Out the window, I watched the riverfront tourist area turn into blocks of department stores and offices. Then, we were on narrow streets of old, close-set apartments.

As the streets grew more deserted, I began to feel a little anxious. Here I was, doing just what *The Single Woman's Guide to Travel* said not to do. On my way to see a show about a reclusive poet, I was venturing out alone, at dusk, into unknown territory.

As I slipped into this worst-case scenario, the driver said, "Here's your stop. The theater is over there, three blocks down."

And she pointed down a shadowy side street. Trying to appear purposeful, yet nonchalant, I walked that street fast.

The theater was small with no real stage—just a place up front where the chairs stopped. Individual folding chairs, maybe forty in all. I took a place in the front row, second seat in from the middle aisle.

Mostly in pairs, other people filtered in. But not very many. There were still more seats empty than full when the lights flickered. I was the only one in the front row on my side of the aisle. This was fine with me. I like breathing space, and I had been sitting beside strangers making small talk all week. But as the lights dimmed, a man rushed in, stumbled in the dark and plunked himself down in the chair on the aisle, right next to me.

With all that space in the theater, even in the front row, I thought, a bit irritated. But then "Emily Dickinson" appeared not five feet in front of me and started speaking, and all annoyance disappeared.

When the lights came up for intermission, neither the man nor I rose with the others to head for the tiny lobby.

We both just sat there, each looking straight ahead, deep in silence. For me, a big advantage to going places alone is that I can absorb the experience—my own experience—without hearing someone else's version right away or being asked to talk about it, or worse, about something else.

I was absorbing Emily Dickinson when the man turned and asked, "Are you from Louisville?"—skipping a few letters in the name and pronouncing it the way the natives did.

"No, I'm from Iowa," I responded, pleasantly enough, but obviously—or so I hoped—not an invitation for further chatter.

"Iowa. I lived for some years in Des Moines. Is your home close to there?" he asked.

"Not too far. About 120 miles southeast." But at the mention of "home," I started thinking about my hotel. I wasn't looking forward to walking those three long blocks to the bus stop, especially when I realized it would be pitch dark on the return trip. Then, I had a truly unnerving thought.

"Do you know how late the buses run?" I asked the man. He didn't. Then, the lights dimmed.

After the show, I sat there, mesmerized. Most of the audience left immediately, but I was suspended somewhere beyond time and space. I had forgotten my plan to rush out quickly. I had forgotten about the bus ride. I didn't want to move quite yet for fear of breaking Emily's spell.

That's when the man beside me said, "Did you come here on the bus? I could give you a ride home." I turned toward him, ripped from the world of Emily Dickinson, probably looking a bit disturbed.

"Don't worry," he said. "I'm a safe person. I'm an English teacher, in town for a conference." With that, he pulled a nametag from his jacket pocket. The border on it was familiar, but I couldn't make out his name.

"I'm at the same conference," I said. "Yes, thank you, I would appreciate a ride home."

In the parking lot, we approached a minivan with Ohio plates. He opened the door for me as if it were second nature and asked what hotel I was staying at. I told him, and we were off, with none of the awkwardness you might expect in a situation like that. No small talk. No details of our everyday lives. Gender was not an issue.

He asked, "What's your favorite Dickinson poem?"

When I responded, "I'm Nobody," he recited the whole thing, with me chiming in on the last lines. After that, we talked almost nonstop the rest of the way home—real conversation about the things that mattered to us most. After a while, we stopped being surprised by the discovery of yet another similarity or coincidence and accepted the fact that, appearances to the contrary, we were as close as old friends.

When the van pulled into the hotel driveway, the bright lights were startling. I felt like I was coming back to Earth from another realm. All of a sudden, I felt awkward. For me, the world in the van had been fulfilling, and I didn't want any more than that. But perhaps he was thinking something else?

He also seemed a bit uncomfortable. I opened my door quickly and thanked him once again. As I was about to leap out, the man yelled, "Wait," just a little too loud.

I froze. Then, he continued, much more gently, "After all this, I don't even know your name."

I wanted to say "I'm Nobody, there's a pair of us, don't tell." By ordinary standards, we had gotten to know each other backwards, and to introduce ourselves now, I thought, would break the spell. But how could I refuse to answer?

"It's Jean."

"I'm Tom," he said. We looked at each other, and started laughing. Saying our names seemed so absurd when we already knew each other so well. And then there was that line from the poem about saying your name to an "admiring Bog."

We never spoke another word. Both of us still laughing, I jumped out of the van, shut the door, and he drove away. As I walked into the hotel, I was happy to be a Nobody who had crossed paths with someone who loved being a Nobody too.

Jean C. Fulton

Surviving the Shipwreck

Most folks are about as happy as they make up their minds to be.

Abraham Lincoln

I folded up into a clump in the center of a sea of boxes, holding my knees tightly to my chest, and sobbed. This was a shipwreck of cosmic proportions. I had floundered from there to here, and I didn't even know where "here" was. "There" was my beautiful old home in the Hollywood Hills, where I had been floating serenely with my husband, our two sons, a veritable ark of pets, tons of friends, laughter, holidays, theater, movies. That was my life. That was my anchor.

And now? Now I might as well have splashed down into the Bermuda Triangle, thousands of miles from my home. I had become a victim of the Hollywood I had lived in: promised scripts of a lifelong marriage that didn't happen and other women that did. I was thrashing in uncharted waters. My sons were grown and gone, and I was bankrupt and betrayed.

I came to shore in Northern California, an eerie desert

island of mist, sea and forest. I rented a tiny basement apartment and surrounded myself with my two birds, two dogs and two cats—two of everything to weather this storm—but only one of me. I hadn't been single since I was a child. I didn't know anything about myself, but I did know that I couldn't make it. I curled up in my apartment, drowning in sorrow, and waited to die.

To my shock, I kept my head above water. I endured getting a box of bank checks with only my name on them, grocery shopping for one, starting a sentence with "I" instead of "we," circling "divorced" on job applications. When I survived those first waves of despair, I gained confidence to head into others.

I began dating—major uncharted waters—and found the strange creatures there humorous: the guy who assured me he was "one of the Great Ones" in his past life (maybe that explains why he was one of the Great Jerks this time around); the fiery Russian sculptor who loved his own body more than anything else; the vagabond carpenter who loved his dog more than anything else; the intense writer who loved his own words more than anything else; the radio producer tuned into the hypochondriac channel who was too worried about dying to love; and the predatory Peter Pan, who preyed on a woman until she fell in love with him before he mad-dashed-it back to his pack of Lost Boys.

And there were some gentle, sweet men friends who held me up when I was tired, and many wonderful women friends who taught me the beauty of the female soul. Through all of them, I began to learn about myself: what I liked, what I didn't, what I deserved.

I learned that I could support myself. I banquet-served at a huge Monterey hotel, freelanced articles for a Salinas hospital and sat in on surgeries. I wrote radio spots and worked for a security systems company. (Be careful what you pray for: I prayed for security and learned that God is very literal.) I helped an aging millionaire write his memoirs. I wrote a book.

I learned to love this sea that had first seemed so tempestuous. In fact, I began to enjoy the silence of being alone. At night, I lit candles in my new little cottage, breathed and surrendered myself to chance, not to someone else's script.

One day, out of the blue, a young man asked me if I was happy. The question, to which I would have answered a resounding "no" not long before, made me pause. And when I answered him, "Yes, I really am," I knew that it was true. The stormy seas that had so deeply frightened me had also been my healing waters. As Helen Keller said, "Life is either a daring adventure, or nothing." I wasn't divorced and drowning. I was delivered, and I had finally come up for air.

Cara Wilson

"No, Richard, I won't be coming home for dinner tonight, tomorrow or the next day. We've been divorced for six months, remember?"

Reprinted by permission of Martin Bucella.

2

DATING

Take a chance! All life is a chance. The man who goes the furthest is generally the one who is willing to do and dare.

Dale Carnegie

"Our company has finished programming the computer and we'll have your perfect mate in just a minute."

Reprinted by permission of Randy Bisson.

A-Head of the Game

A friend of mine had been suffering from a lack of self-confidence after a particularly difficult breakup. He was a bit wary of returning to the dating world, worried that he had "lost his touch" with women.

Unfortunately, soon after ending his previous relationship, he began to lose his hair, and he saw this as a sign from above that he was doomed to be alone forever. "Who the heck is going to want to date some bald guy?" he said to me one night as we commiserated over large yummy cups of cappuccino. The eternal wit, he was convinced that good hair was the ticket to a successful relationship. "What will she run her fingers through now?" he exclaimed discouragingly. "My scalp?"

As he started asking women out, he only took them to locations where a baseball cap was acceptable—playing Frisbee in the park, walking the dog, a baseball game or any other faintly sporty event where he could successfully hide his thinning top. This worked out fine for a while, but there are only so many sporting events to go to, and only so many sunny days to toss the Frisbee and walk the dog.

Also, one huge aspect of my friend's personality was

that he absolutely loved going out for a nice dinner. We had enjoyed many nights in college spending too much money on bottles of wine, hors d'oeuvres and warm chocolatey desserts at the most upscale restaurants. Unfortunately, none of these restaurants would allow a baseball cap, no matter how nice it may be. This started to discourage him and again his spirits dropped, until he received notification in the mail that he had won a free dinner for two at an exclusive restaurant downtown.

"Congratulations!" the letter read. "You and a guest have been chosen to sample and savor our elegant cuisine and ambiance. Please find the enclosed gift certificate for fifty dollars!" He was thrilled. Jumping up and down with enthusiasm, he thought out loud about what to wear, what to order, when to go, and . . . uh oh . . . who to take. He couldn't wear a hat into this new restaurant. But who could he take who wouldn't be shocked by his barely covered head? His brow furrowed in disappointment and he collapsed on the nearby couch. After a few minutes of silence, he shouted out, "Aw, phooey. I'm going." Leaping from his seat, his face took on that all-too-familiar glow and he quickly breezed through his index of possible dates, finally landing on Sarah, the woman whom he had been admiring from afar for months. He sat down in his favorite chair, dialed her number confidently and asked her to accompany him—and she gratefully accepted. A few nights later, dressed to the nines and beautifully bareheaded, he and Sarah shared a perfect evening and have been wonderfully in love ever since.

And I'll tell you this: That was the best fifty dollars I've spent in a long time.

Katie Mauro
Submitted by Eileen Lawrence

Bowled Over

"I know it's the last minute," Carl said timidly when I answered the phone, "but I, um, need a date for tonight." A date? Carl had never once mentioned the "D" word to me before, and it left me speechless. "I hope you're available," he added.

I glanced at the clock. It was after four. How many other numbers had he dialed first? He probably thought, maybe I'll try ol' reliable Jan. She's usually home on a Saturday night.

"It's my company party—a bowling party," he said. *He needs a date for bowling?* "Okay, sure," I replied.

When I hung up the phone my thoughts drifted back to two years ago when Carl first joined our church singles group. He wasn't what you'd call a hunk and didn't have a sparkling personality, but there was an instant tug at my heart. It wasn't his steel blue eyes, the premature gray hair or warm smile that attracted me, but an obvious strength of character. I wanted to know this man.

After the singles meetings, a few of us would meander over to the coffee shop. I'd linger around, making sure I found myself alone with Carl. One night we talked until the late hours, conferring about everything from childhoods to politics to the Bible.

"You have firm opinions, and you're not afraid to state them," he told me. "I like that." Feeling as flimsy as a soggy piece of toast, I gazed longingly at him, but I received only congenial smiles in return.

Every week my heart fluttered at his warm "Hello." *I know he must be attracted to me, too, but this guy guards his heart like a sentry over the crown jewels.*

A few months later at our group's annual country hoedown, Carl and I square-danced together most of the night, twirling, tripping and laughing like teenagers.

He offered to drive me home after we cleaned up. "I have a view of the valley from my deck," I said, nudging Carl through the front door to the backyard. "Come and see." As we stood close together, watching the city lights flicker, I thought my anxious heart was about to explode like a pan of sizzling popcorn. *This is the perfect moment to sweep me into his arms.* Then, abruptly, he said, "I've really got to go now."

"He's driving me crazy," I later told my best friend, Jeanne.

"Could you be misinterpreting his attentions, just a bit, Jan? He's still healing from a recent divorce. He's got to test the single waters and see which way to steer his boat."

"But, but . . ." I was about to counter with *He likes to be with me, and we have so much in common, and doesn't he realize I'm perfect for him?* What was the matter with me? I'd been single again for ten years. A mature, professional woman, a singles group leader, not a schoolgirl dizzy with her first crush.

Jeanne piped in. "Earth to Jan—remember that seminar on dating and healthy relationships? The tricky little 'I' word?"

Infatuation, the chemistry that turns the sensible into silly. Yes, and it's the mystery, the uncertainty that keeps the fires of infatuation going.

"I must be imagining things that just aren't there."

"You're in love with the idea of falling in love."

I suppressed some tears. "I feel like a fool."

"Let it go, Jan. The timing is wrong," Jeanne urged.

Yes, and if Carl was the right man for me, it would happen in God's time with no plotting on my part. I asked myself, do I care about Carl enough to want the best for him, even if it is never me? I wrestled with it all night. How is it possible to have a platonic relationship while a medley of feelings dances on my heart?

"Give it to God," Jeanne said. She was right, but why do fantasies feel so comfortable, like a soft, cuddly lamb's-wool rug in front of a warm fire? It was hard to let go, but even harder to spark a romance with only one flame.

Carl was a popular guy in our group, friendly with everybody, and in the next year he had his share of women chasing him. He did have some dates, but none with me. He was like a cat with a dish of cream, lapping up strokes to his self-esteem. He was in his single heyday. Finally content to be his pal and cheerleader, life went back to normal.

But then came the telephone call, and that "D" word. I raked over my closet trying to find the perfect bowling outfit. *Oh, here I go again, feeling all giddy. After all this time? Get a grip, girl.*

We met for dinner at Garcia's, a Mexican restaurant near the bowling lanes, and before the fajitas stopped sizzling, the atmosphere shifted. This was not our usual "Let's grab a bite to eat." This was a lingering-over-the-meal, his-eyes-riveted-on-me, soaking-in-my-every-word-as-if-I-hadn't-existed-before kind of thing. This was a real date! And to cinch it, he paid for my dinner! While I didn't make any strikes later at the bowling alley, there was a telltale twinkle in his eyes that showed me I'd made a big strike with him. Bowled over, my emotional alarm clock started to go off.

Jeanne was half asleep when she picked up the phone at midnight. "What are you so afraid of?"

"That old floating-on-a-cloud feeling. I don't want to go back there."

"I like you better sane, myself."

Three weeks went by and no telephone call from Carl. *It figures. He's probably back at Garcia's sampling the chili rellenos with somebody else. That's fine. At least I got a nice dinner out of it.*

It was time for our singles Saturday social: a trip to San Francisco, a bike ride in Golden Gate Park and an optional dinner cruise on the bay. We rendezvoused at the grocery store parking lot.

"Lover Boy just showed up," Jeanne announced as Carl began to unload his bike from the back of his car. I bolstered myself up. *Be mildly sociable, but aloof. Let him come to you.* After biking along the beachfront, ten of us changed into dinner clothes and boarded a blue-and-gold double-decker boat. As it headed out in the choppy waters, we all stood on the lower deck, watching the blazing sun slip under the Golden Gate Bridge, coloring the sky like a dream. I was spellbound by the lights emerging from the bridge. I barely noticed the music starting to signal dinner being served. I saw Jeanne and the group go below, and suddenly the deck was empty. Except for me and Carl.

As the boat began to circle, a cold blast of sea breeze made me shiver. Carl slid his long arms around my shoulders. This was no benign hug. Suddenly, I froze like a petrified tree.

Gently, he lifted my chin and looked down at me. *He's going to kiss me. In the most romantic place in the world he's going to kiss me. Wait a minute. I have a few questions. . . .* But I closed my eyes, slipped my arms around his neck and just let it happen.

"I knew you wanted me to do that long ago," he finally said, "But I couldn't. I was nowhere near ready for a committed relationship, and it wouldn't have been fair. I needed time—to become the right man for a woman like you."

Eleven months later we were married. During our wedding vows, Carl said, "Thank you for waiting for me, Jan." When it was my turn, I shared something I'd tucked away in my heart. It was from one of those dating seminars: "Love is a friendship that has caught fire."

Jan Coleman

Reply to Box 222B

Was it loneliness, the call of adventure or just plain insanity that made me answer that newspaper ad? I paced back and forth through my house, telling myself it was a really stupid thing to do. But like a jeweler crafting a priceless, one-of-a-kind brooch, I composed my reply to the tantalizing ad.

I actually answered a lonely hearts ad. Am I really that desperate for a man?

I'd always believed that only born losers advertised for a companion or answered the ads of those who did. Surely you had to be dying of loneliness, ugly or really dumb!

That's what I am, I thought, *really dumb!*

What would my children think? Would they understand that the bold, black letters just leaped out at my unsuspecting eye? *"Christian Rancher. 6′ tall, 180 pounds, 50+. Hardworking, clean-cut, healthy, good physical condition. Enjoys fishing, camping, cross-country skiing, animals, dining out. Wants to meet sensible and sincere lady, 40–50, attractive, neat, loving, honest, for meaningful relationship. Box 222B."*

Mama mia! What loving, sensible, honest and *lonely* woman could resist? Well, maybe not sensible.

"Fifty-plus what?" my letter began. "I'm a healthy,

hardworking woman who loves to cook, sew, travel, pray, and walk in a desert sunset or barefoot on the beach."

I didn't say I could meet all the requirements in his ad, but I didn't give him any reason to think that I couldn't. But could I?

I was already past fifty, questionably attractive, not always neat and very uncertain about pursuing a meaningful relationship. What I really wanted was a friend. Had I been dishonest not to tell him so?

Holding the letter heavenward, I asked God, "If you want me to meet this man, will you bring him to me?" Then I set the stamped envelope on the desk for the following day's mail.

During the next few weeks, I found my hands getting sweaty every time the phone rang. Could it be him? What if he didn't like me? What if he showed disappointment as soon as he set eyes on me? Could I handle that?

Contriving excuses to be away from the telephone became a game I played with myself. At the car wash one afternoon, towel-drying the finish and shining the windows, I found myself fantasizing about every man who came in to wash his car. *Look at him; I bet he's 50+. He's almost bald, has floppy jowls and a big stomach. Oh, dear, he's wearing a cowboy shirt and boots. I'll just die if that's my Christian rancher!*

I didn't see even one man there who I hoped might be Box 222B. Damp and discouraged, I went home to shower, questioning my motives, suppressing my loneliness. Dressing before the mirror, I turned from side to side, surveying the ravages of fifty-plus years on this Earth.

I studied my face, hollow and gaunt, perched atop muscular shoulders and arms. Large, sturdy hands that never knew what to do with themselves. Twenty extra pounds, a thick waist, stalwart thighs above husky calves and large, scrawny feet. I remembered the boy in the fifth grade who told me I was built like a brick outhouse:

strong and useful but not much class.

Tears began to flow freely as I slumped to my knees beside my bed. "Oh, God, look at me, I'm a mess. Why did I send that letter? Please forgive me for misleading that man, for communicating the woman I want to be, not the woman I am."

It was a Sunday evening a few weeks later when I invited my friend, Jeanette, for waffles after church. As we were leaving the service, she introduced me to a friend from the singles group she sometimes attended. Impulsively, I asked him if he'd like to join us for waffles and he said yes.

We spent the next three hours stuffing ourselves, laughing and talking. Jim was divorced, had several grown children and raised alfalfa for cattle feed. He was a likable man, tall and handsome, considerate, and seemingly ambitious. I felt sad for him as he talked about his loneliness.

Shutting the door behind them after a delightful evening, I began to clear up the clutter. I'd dumped my past few days' mail on the big maple desk in the dining room, and it seemed like a good time to sort it out. I tossed the junk mail in the trash and filed some bills for payment. Then I stared in astonishment. There was the letter! My reply to "Christian Rancher" had never been mailed. All that emotion and self-doubt for nothing.

Then a suspicion crept into my thoughts. Pieces started to fall into place. Jim wore cowboy boots and a western shirt; he was a rancher; he was lonely. Could he and the Christian rancher possibly be one and the same?

I rushed to the phone to call Jeanette. "Do you think he ever put an ad in the newspaper for a woman? Do you suppose he'd call himself a Christian rancher?"

Jeanette roared with laughter. "Yes, everybody at the singles group knows he did that. I guess he's gotten some seventy or eighty answers by now. Some real lu-lu's, too."

I hung up the telephone feeling a trace of excitement, a

bit of foolishness and a lot of awe at a God who would arrange for a letter that I never mailed to receive an answer. And God and I were the only ones who knew about it.

Several days passed before I picked up the telephone to hear Jim's voice suggesting that we go to the state fair for the day. "I'd love to," I said. *Wow! A real live date with a guy who had seventy or eighty women to choose from!*

A warm toastiness cradled me as I hung up the telephone. Then I raced to the bedroom, my heart pounding with excitement. What would I wear? In front of the mirror once more, I observed a middle-aged woman, still awkward and overweight, with a skinny face and bony feet, but she wasn't afraid anymore. "What you see is what you get," I chuckled.

The next day I stepped out into the sunshine to begin a new friendship with a Christian rancher.

What happened that day at the fair? We had fun together. Did we see each other again? Yes. Did we marry? No. But that didn't matter. My self-confidence soared, and I learned something else too: If you're destined to meet a particular person, whether future friend or spouse, it *will* happen, as surely as the sun rises every morning. And it'll happen even if your perfectly crafted letter sits gathering dust on an old maple desk.

Barbara Baumgardner

New Year's Eve Dilemma

New Year's Eve was only a week away, and I didn't have even the prospect of a date for that important beginning to the New Year. Was the rest of the year going to be like this? Sitting in front of the television with my mother and younger brother watching other people enjoy themselves?

Six months ago, I had moved from the lush southeast coast to this desolate part of west Texas, in order to live with my mom while I recuperated from a serious motorcycle accident. Now that I was able to work again, I planned to hightail it back to God's country as soon as I was able to save enough money.

In the meantime, here I was, a twenty-one-year-old with a possible New Year's Eve at home looming in front of me. "Don't just sit there," an inner voice prompted me. "Do something." Usually, the thought of a blind date would have made me shudder, but I was determined not to spend the night in front of the TV.

I picked up the phone and called Penny, someone I'd met here who seemed to know a lot of people in town. Penny said she'd give the matter some thought and get back to me if anyone came to mind.

Two days later, she called back. A former coworker, who didn't know she was recently engaged, had asked her out for New Year's Eve. When she explained that she was no longer available, he asked if she had a friend to whom she could introduce him. "He's divorced with custody of his two kids, pretty clean-cut, and doesn't do drugs," she told me. Nervously, I accepted—then spent the next week regretting my impulsiveness. Several times, I almost picked up the phone to cancel.

But I made it through the week, and, finally, the night arrived. Now I couldn't decide how to dress. Would he expect casual or a dress and heels? About thirty minutes before he was due to arrive, I called Penny in a panic. What should I wear? Penny said she didn't think he was the "formal type." What did that mean, not the formal type? Now I was really confused. I finally settled on what I considered to be a happy medium, slacks and a sweater.

The doorbell rang. Should I answer the door myself, or ask my younger brother Jerry to get it? I sighed as I walked to the door, mentally composing various excuses that would allow me to exit the evening gracefully should it prove disastrous. Fixing a smile on my face, I opened the door.

I stopped short and stared as I took in the Stetson hat, western shirt, long blue-jeans-clad legs, and pointed-toe boots. A cowboy! My date was a cowboy! Then my gaze swept back up to his face, and I found myself looking into the greenest eyes I had ever seen, eyes full of laughter at the expression on my face.

I stuttered "hello" and politely held out my hand. Jerry struggled to contain his laughter, while I struggled to regain my composure. We chatted briefly, and suddenly I didn't care where we went or what we did.

Over dinner, we never seemed to run out of things to talk about. And I found my eyes kept coming back to those green eyes and that smiling mouth. After dinner, he took me to an action movie. I forgot to warn him how actively I participate in action adventures. He laughed as I screamed, hid my eyes and cowered in my seat, and lifted my feet off the floor when insects or rodents appeared on the screen. I think the really big adventure for him was watching me react to the show.

When the movie was over, he said he had to get home. I wondered if this was a brush-off. I also wondered if he would kiss me good-night on this first date. He had been such a perfect gentleman the entire evening, he'd probably just shake my hand, and maybe I'd never see him again. I realized how much I wanted that good-night kiss. Would he think I was too forward if I kissed him first? Would it drive him away, or bring him back? Once again, I was in an agony of indecision!

When we arrived at my house, he walked me to the door, came in for a moment, then turned to leave. *What the heck?* I thought to myself. *Go for broke.* I followed him out to his car and asked for that good-night kiss. He obliged, and, lightheaded, I floated back to the house, hoping I would hear from him again.

I did. The next morning, early, he called. He liked me, too! Fifty-six days later, we became husband and wife. That was twenty-one years ago, and even after all these years together, his kisses still make me lightheaded.

Never underestimate the power of a blind date.

Judith L. Robinson

Dave Barry's Guide to Finding a Mate

At the risk of generalizing, I would say that the basic reason men and women have trouble getting along can be summarized as follows:

WHAT WOMEN WANT: To be loved, to be listened to, to be desired, to be respected, to be needed, to be trusted, and sometimes, just to be held.

WHAT MEN WANT: Tickets for the World Series.

So we can see that men and women do not have exactly the same objectives in mind. In getting into the field of marriage, one very important decision you must make is who, exactly, will be your spouse. I am not saying this is the most important decision. It is certainly not as important as selecting the right wedding caterer. But you should definitely give it some thought.

The Singles Scene

The singles scene is located in bars that are so dark and loud it's impossible to see or hear anybody else. You can meet, fall in love and get engaged without ever getting a clear view of the other person, which can lead to a situation where you arrive at your wedding, with all your friends and relatives, and you discover that you are betrothed to a cigarette machine.

To avoid this kind of embarrassment, you should do what other smart singles do: Before you sit down, go around the room discreetly shining a police flashlight into the other singles' faces. Once you have selected a likely looking one, you should sit down near this person and get into a spontaneous conversation.

How to Get into a Spontaneous Conversation

In the old days the way people got into conversations was the woman would take a cigarette out of her purse and pretend to look for a match, which was the signal for six or seven available lurking men to lunge toward her, Zippos flaming, sometimes causing severe burns.

Smoking, however, has pretty much lost its glamour, which is a shame, really, because men are deprived of the chance to feel bold and masculine and necessary in the hostile bar environment. It would be nice if we had a modern bar-meeting ritual. Like maybe the woman could come in with a jar of relish, and she could sit there pretending she couldn't get the lid off, and the man could come along and offer to help, and soon they would be engrossed in a fascinating conversation. ("Are you fond of relish? Huh! I am fond of relish myself!")

But for now, we are stuck with the system where one party has to boldly walk right up to the other party and, with no real excuse, attempt to start a conversation. At one time this was strictly the man's responsibility, but now, what with Women's Liberation, it is still strictly the man's responsibility.

Men, this is nothing to be nervous about. After all, why do you think the woman came to a singles bar, if not to meet a guy like you, only smarter and more attractive? So go to it!

The trick is to know some good "opening lines" that are guaranteed to get a woman's attention and make her realize you are a caring and sharing kind of guy who has things on his mind such as international politics and great literature, and who doesn't just want to grope her body.

Here are some good opening lines:

- "How about those problems in the Middle East?"
- "How about those Brothers Karamazov?"
- "I don't just want to grope your body. I mean, not here in the bar."

Meeting People Through Personal Ads

These are those little paid advertisements that people take out in magazines or newspapers. A lot of people laugh at these ads, but in fact this is the way top stars such as Johnny Carson and Joan Collins get most of their spouses.

If you want your ad to be effective, however, it must have certain characteristics:

1. It should say you are profoundly attractive. Nobody in the personal ads, nobody, is ever "average-looking." If, for example, you had Elephant Man's Disease, you would describe yourself as "rugged."
2. It should be extremely specific. For example, if you're a man, you don't just say you're looking for "a nice woman." You say you're looking for "a 5'8" twenty-three-year-old blond Capricorn woman of Croatian ancestry weighing 109 pounds and having a degree in cultural anthropology from Duke University." This

lets everybody know you are in a position to pick and choose, and not some semi-desperate schlump who has to advertise for dates.

3. It should say you like "candlelight dinners and long walks on the beach." All personal classified ads contain this phrase, not because anybody really wants to take long walks on the beach, but because people want to prove they're Romantic and Sensitive. The beaches of America are teeming with couples who met because of personal ads, staggering along, sweating and picking sea-urchin spines out of their feet, each person afraid to reveal to the other that he or she would rather be watching a rental movie.

Dating

"Dating" simply means "going out with a potential mate and doing a lot of fun things that the two of you will never do again if you actually get married." Dating is a very important part of the mate-selection process throughout all of nature. Some sectors of nature, such as insects, date for only a few seconds; birds, on the other hand, perform an elaborate Dating Dance.

Human beings dated as far back as ancient times, as is shown by the biblical quotation: "And Balzubio *did* taketh Parasheeba to a restaurant, and they *did* eateth potato skins." The next recorded date was between Romeo and Juliet, a young Italian couple who went out despite their parents' objections, and just about everybody involved ended up either stabbed or poisoned.

After this tragedy, there was very little dating for several centuries. During this time, marriages were arranged by the parents, based on such things as how much cattle the bride and the groom would each bring to the union. Often the young couple wouldn't even meet until the wedding, and sometimes they were not strongly attracted to each other. Sometimes, quite frankly, they preferred the cattle. So now we feel that dating is probably a better system.

Falling in Love

When two people have been on enough dates, they generally fall in love. You can tell you're in love by the way you feel: your head becomes light, your heart leaps within you, you feel like you're walking on air, and the whole world seems like a wonderful and happy place. Unfortunately these are also the four warning signs of certain diseases, so it's always a good idea to check with your doctor.

Dave Barry

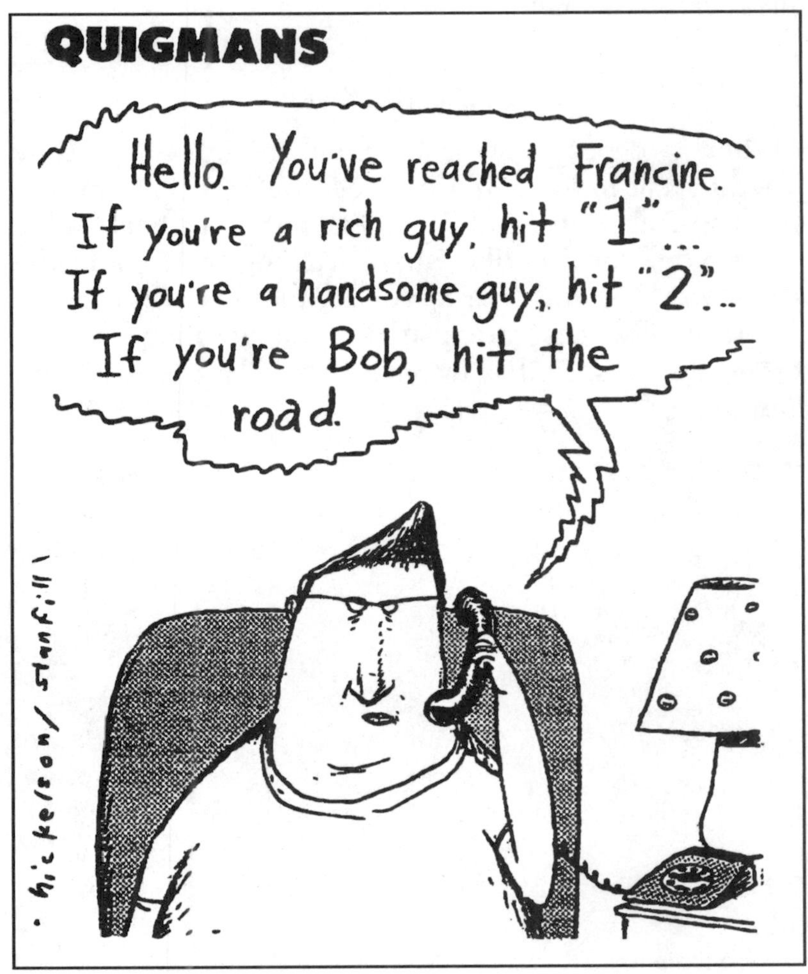

Buddy Hickerson. ©by Los Angeles Times *Syndicate. Reprinted by permission.*

On the Rocks

The view high up in the Colorado Rocky Mountains was breathtaking. All around us the mountains were snow-capped, even though it was July.

I was on an outing, but it was not a pleasant one. My girlfriend, Paula, was upstream; I was downstream. I should have been delightedly skipping flat stones across the stream, but instead I sat on a huge boulder watching the crystal-clear water rushing over the rocks. And that suited me just fine.

Once, it had been so much fun to be together—I thought that I might be falling in love. But today Paula was acting strangely. This was supposed to be a wonderful, exhilarating date—the surroundings were spectacular. Yet I agonized over Paula's silent treatment of me. It seemed that a wall of ice had been building between us, and I couldn't melt it.

Confused and feeling rejected, I pulled a small pocket edition of the Bible out of my back pocket. I wanted to read something to get my mind off my pain. The previous day I had stopped reading in the middle of a chapter. Heaving a sigh, I found the place where I had stopped reading. Half-heartedly I continued: "Love your enemies."

Enemies? I perked up as I read. That's Paula. Look how she was acting toward me! It went on to say, "Do good to those who mistreat you." Yes, she sure was mistreating me. Her rotten behavior toward me made me want to withdraw. Who needed that kind of pain?

As I continued reading, this verse really caught my attention: "Give and it will be given to you . . . for with the measure you use, it will be measured to you."

My focus had been on myself. I felt justified in my anger. Paula had made it plain to me by her coldness that our relationship was over. After all that I had done for her, she was putting our relationship into a deep freeze.

"Give, and it will be given to you." As the mountain stream cascaded over the rocks, thoughts rushed through my mind about the nature of true friendship. Even when hurt or misunderstood, a true friend reaches out to bridge the gap. A true friend is a giver, not a taker.

I was appalled at my own self-pity. My focus had been on "enemies," but now I realized it was better to focus on "love." "Melt that ice—starting from my side of the wall," I mumbled to myself. It would definitely be difficult to begin acting kindly toward Paula. She may totally reject me or hurt me even more. I decided the risk would be worth it.

More than an hour had elapsed since we had parted. As I searched for her, I finally saw her way upstream, sitting on the rocks near the loud, gurgling water. She didn't notice me because she was facing the other way, and the roar of the rushing stream drowned out my steps.

When I got within ten feet of her and looked at the back of her head, I thought, *I am too nervous to open my heart to her.* I retreated to the trees along the bank. My nervousness was eating me alive.

I tried approaching her a second time, but retreated to the trees again with my self-respect at an all-time low. But the verse kept flooding my mind: "Give, and it will be given to you." That gave me courage, but not quite enough. I knew that if I tried a third time, I would chicken out again. Then it hit me—get her attention from a distance. If she sees me, I will have to go talk with her.

I shouted, rustled some trees and banged some branches. Have you ever tried to make a noise louder than a roaring mountain stream? It's impossible. So I decided to throw some stones—not at her, but near her so she would turn around and see me.

It worked. When she turned and noticed me, I ventured out onto the rocks where she was sitting.

"Hi," I said. The lump in my throat felt as big as the boulder I sat down on next to her. "Mind if I join you for a few minutes?"

"No, I don't mind," she replied with a surprised look on her face.

"What have you been doing?" It was awkward, but I couldn't come up with anything better.

"Oh, thinking. What have you been doing?"

"Reading. May I show you what I read?" I was sure that she could hear my heart pounding in my chest.

"Sure."

I pulled out my Bible and began to read: "Love your enemies." I wanted to make some comment, but I was afraid I would lose my composure. "Give, and it will be given to you." I cleared my throat.

I stammered, "For the past few days, whenever I tried to communicate with you, I felt as if there were a wall of ice between us. You may never want to see me again, but I want to let you know my innermost feelings toward you. I care a lot about you and want to be your friend. If you don't want to date anymore, I'll be disappointed, but I still want to be your friend."

I paused, waiting for an angry rebuttal. What I received was a surprise.

"Would you like me to tell you what I have been thinking?" Paula asked.

"Yes! What have you been thinking?"

"I have started to like you, but I was afraid that you would reject me. My former boyfriend really hurt me, and I did not want to go through that kind of pain again. So, to protect my heart, I have been keeping you away. I'm sorry. Will you forgive me?"

Right there on the rocks we began to break through our barriers of fear. The wall of ice melted. Oh, how easy it is to think the worst about someone, and so difficult to think the best. Building the foundation of a close relationship takes courage, but the lesson I received next to that mountain stream was this: Seek to be a trusted friend, and keep taking the risk to communicate with honesty and humility.

Our experience on the rocks was wonderful. So wonderful that six months later, sitting in a romantic restaurant in Atlanta, Georgia, I asked Paula to marry me—to be my best friend for life.

On our wedding day, we exchanged rings. Inscribed inside each of our rings are the words, "Give, and it will be given to you."

Whenever I look at my ring, I am reminded to be a giver, not a taker. And that simple thought has made all the difference in our sixteen years of marriage.

Dick Purnell

"Of course our marriage is on the rocks—
where else would it be?"

Reprinted by permission of David Howell.

A Good Catch

My friend Nancy is smart and self-sufficient. She's someone a lot of women might aspire to be. She's thirty-nine, pretty, confident. She works as a casting agent for movies, so she knows a lot of people. All in all, Nancy is what's known as a good catch.

So why was no one catching her? This was the question she pondered. This is the question a lot of women I know ponder. Women who don't need a man in order to feel whole, but would certainly prefer sharing life with a partner to going it alone.

"I'm too nice," Nancy would say. "Guys like women who are mean." I am not sure where she developed this theory, except perhaps from a famous celebrity that Nancy once cast in a movie, who reportedly behaved like a dragon lady toward every man on the set. Such behavior, also reportedly, only encouraged the males in their drooling.

Nancy tried to be just like her. She would try to say something rude to the man of her desire, try to refuse his calls, try to stand him up, but she'd end up listening to his troubles and making him a fancy roast with rosemary potatoes.

And the man would leave. The way Nancy saw it, this *pas de deux* was all her doing. She thought the trick to love was learning how to change yourself into the right kind of person. She would see lovers behaving like friends and wonder how in the world they ever got that way.

"What about Jack?" I said to Nancy about nine months ago.

"Who?"

"Jack," I said. "The guy who treats you like an actual human being?"

"Oh, him," she said, and then: "Do you think I should get my hair cut?" She mentioned the latest object of her affection, a six-foot-two blond banker who played a lot of hockey. "He would just die if I cut off all my hair."

"Oh, him," I said. The hockey player was Nancy's latest Prince Charming. He would sweep her off her feet, for an evening, and she would do the roast-and-potato thing. Afterward he'd promise to call, forget to call, go out with someone else, go back with Nancy, forget to call. All of which, of course, only made Nancy's desire keener. Nancy had an entire history of guys like this.

"I don't think you should cut your hair," I said, and tried to swing the conversation back to Jack. He and Nancy had known each other for a long time, until he got married and dropped out of the circle. After a few years, he got divorced. Now he was trying to reconnect.

Jack was the one who brought flowers to greet Nancy at her new apartment, who unpacked boxes until midnight, who hooked up her stereo while she sat by the phone waiting to hear from the hockey player.

"Jack is too nice," Nancy said.

I said maybe. Maybe people just have to keep striving for the unattainable until they're ready to attain.

It wasn't too long after this conversation that Nancy had more to think about than the boy-girl thing. She found out her mother had bone cancer. She began shuttling back and forth between work and her parents' house, three hours away.

The hockey player said he would call.

A few months later, Nancy found out her father had bone-marrow cancer.

The hockey player forgot to call.

And there was Jack. Jack's own mother had died in his arms; he knew a lot about saying good-bye. Jack was trying to make it as a single father; he knew a lot about the sacrifices you make to care for others. He would talk to Nancy. He would invite her over to his house, to dinner, to a movie, to a concert, to a . . . hockey game.

Nancy had a hard time not looking around for the hockey player.

Shortly before Thanksgiving, Nancy's mother was hospitalized with pneumonia. For a while there, they didn't think she'd pull through. Nancy began spending more time at her bedside than at her father's.

Jack called and offered to make Thanksgiving dinner for the family. Nancy accepted, and then told her mother about him.

They sent Nancy's mother home in an ambulance. They put up a hospital bed in the room next to the one her father's hospital bed was in. Nancy's mother asked her to change the pillowcase, to bring in her makeup and to help her with her hair. All fixed up, she said, "Okay, now please bring Jack in."

Jack sat with Nancy's mother a long time. Then he watched football with her father.

Nancy and Jack cooked the turkey together and somewhere in those moments Nancy let go. She thought, *Oh, this is how it works; some lovers are friends first.* She didn't have to change anything to be loved; she just had to be.

Nancy's parents are hanging on, to life and to each other. Nancy and Jack are, too.

The hockey player called a little while ago. Nancy didn't call him back.

Jeanne Marie Laskas

Reprinted by permission of Creators Syndicate, Inc.

The Surprise Date

Ever had your grandmother set up a blind date? My friend Annie did.

The nephew of her grandmother's bridge partner called. He was in town and would Annie join him for dinner? She accepted, resigning herself to a dull evening, that is until Date arrived at her front door. Talk about hunk with horsepower! The man could have earned a decent living as a cover model, even without the Porsche.

Grandma deserved a thank-you letter.

Except the man drove too fast and brushed her knee every time he changed gears . . . but the inside of the car was cramped, and his elbow couldn't really help bumping hers as they turned around sharp corners, could it? As they parked, his hand sort of fell onto her leg . . . and stayed, but a flash of a smile and "I hope you like Italian" had her semi-convinced it was an accident.

Italian? Yes. The neighborhood spaghetti palace? No. This was fine cuisine. A smiling maître d' called Luigi. Obsequious waiters in white jackets and bow ties. Verdi playing in the background. Subdued lighting. Orchids in silver vases. Starched linen. And a charming date who listened as much as he talked. He ordered in Italian and told witty stories that had her chuckling as she ate crabmeat ravioli and sipped Frascati. This was all very well, but when he ordered a second bottle with the veal, Annie began to worry about driving back. Until Hunk mentioned he was staying . . . nearby. Okay, he could walk back, and she'd get a cab with the emergency money tucked in her bag.

"It's a good hotel," he said with assurance. "I've got a double room. With a king-sized bed and a Jacuzzi."

Poor Annie almost choked on her saltimbocca. "How nice." This was the best she could manage with eyes watering.

"You'll enjoy it."

She wouldn't. "I've got to get back." Not exactly a lie—her roommates were waiting.

"Oh, come on!" A flash of anger in his eyes half worried her as she repeated her refusal, but he smiled and shrugged. "If I can't persuade you, we'd better order dessert."

She chose tiramisu. He ordered strega with his espresso and then excused himself. Her pocketbook fell as he passed, but he caught and replaced it with a smiling apology. Dessert arrived before he returned. Annie sneaked a chocolate curl. She wouldn't actually eat until he got back; manners were manners after all. Several minutes passed. Annie tried a mouthful of whipped cream. And another. Had he fainted? Dropped dead? Been kidnapped? Nonsense! She was thinking like her mother. He was far too young for a heart attack and people didn't get abducted from respectable restaurants.

Halfway though the first layer of coffee and Marsala-soaked lady fingers, she decided she was her mother's daughter after all and summoned a waiter. Saying "Please check the bathroom for the man who was sitting here" wasn't easy, but processing the reply was harder. He was nowhere in the building. Abducted by aliens seemed possible after all.

"I believe the gentleman has left," the maître d' informed her with a chill in his voice.

"Wait!" Leaving her half-eaten tiramisu, Annie rushed through the restaurant and out the front door. A pale gray Mercedes was easing into the space where they'd parked. Whipped cream curdles fast under stress. Annie wanted to throw up, but she had enough trouble already. They'd picked the best dishes plus wine, and all she had was a cab fare home. She wondered how long she'd be washing dishes.

"He's gone." The maître d' nodded as she returned. "It happens."

Brother, would she have something to say to her grandmother—if she ever got out of this. "Look. I'm afraid I don't have much money with me, I wasn't expecting. . ." Her voice faltered.

"Neither were we," Luigi replied, a grim smile on his wide mouth.

Her bag still hung over the chair, gaping open. She found a torn page from a diary tucked in the pocket where she'd kept her emergency money. "Sorry, love," it said in a scratchy handwriting, "I need gas money."

Now she really did want to upchuck. She'd be walking home after doing the dishes. Her eyes misted, and worry thundered in her ears. A strong hand clutched her arm. She wobbled. Another hand caught her shoulder. "Come on." Two strong hands propelled her toward the back of the restaurant. Not toward the kitchen and a mound of dishes but into a small, cramped room. A confinement cell for nonpayers? She eased into a chair and looked up at dark eyes and a wide mouth. "Are you okay?" Luigi asked.

She could have handled anger or complaints. Concern undid her. Between sobs, sniffles and a couple of good nose blows, Annie spilled her guts and soaked a perfectly good linen handkerchief. Luigi offered a second handkerchief. "Just a minute," he said and slipped out. Annie half-expected to be locked in while he summoned the law, but he left the door ajar and returned minutes later with a steaming mug. "Cafe Sambuca." Luigi smiled as he handed it over. "Drink it."

Too worn down to argue, she drank. The sudden influx of sugar, caffeine and alcohol on her rattled sensibilities left her wobbly and fragile, but alert to the fact Luigi sat mere inches away. If he were to start anything. . . . Panic flared though her.

"Don't worry," he said, as if reading her mind. "Want another coffee?" She shook her head, and he took the empty mug with gentle fingers. "Feeling better?"

She nodded. "I can mail you a check."

Luigi interrupted with a shrug and a smile. "Forget it. It's not the first time someone skipped out without paying. We've had them leave coats and umbrellas as they flit, but never their partners. Feel well enough to go home? I'll call a taxi—on the house."

She couldn't accept. "Look, I'll send the money, at least for my share." Paying to feed Hunk Rat was going too far.

Luigi's dark eyes twinkled as he shook his head. "It's the cost of doing business." A minion called a cab, and Luigi walked her through the restaurant and out into the street.

"Look, thanks. I mean, sorry about the bill. The meal was wonderful . . . at least until. . . ."

"That peasant showed his true colors?"

She half-chuckled at that. "That's an insult to decent peasants." She held out her hand.

Ignoring the outstretched hand, Luigi hugged her tight, whispering, "A woman like you should choose her dates more carefully."

Not at all sure what to make of that, Annie vowed she'd be old, gray and desperate before she had another blind date.

Next morning, she returned to repay her half of the debt, and was graciously refused, or at least her money was. She came back smiling.

It wasn't long before Annie did write to her grandmother . . . to announce her engagement to Luigi.

Rosemary Laurey

"It says I forgot my wallet."

Reprinted by permission of Martha Campbell.

A Cure for Cold Feet

You can discover more about a person in an hour of play than in a year of conversation.

Plato

Winter finals were over, and the entire campus was ecstatic with relief. No more cramming, caffeine highs, tension headaches and cramped desks. We were free! We left campus en masse in the unusually crisp Seattle night, light on our feet, letting our hair down and our shirttails out. We were all going to the local dance club, the only place in the area that could accommodate a few hundred post-finals students who were ready to let loose. We squeezed ourselves into tight jeans and miniskirts, exposed some legs and bellies, and virtually wriggled with excitement. The music was loud and provocative, the figures on the dance floor sensuous, wild. The electricity was heart-stopping.

I looked pretty heart-stopping myself, poured into a bare-backed white satin pantsuit with three-inch heels and a rose in my hair. Unfortunately, it wasn't my date's heart that was stopping. It was mine. More specifically, it was being bored to death. My date was Dumbe, a native of Cameroon, West Africa. Granted, it was our first date, so I hadn't really known anything about him, but I had thought we would at least enjoy the rhythm on the dance floor.

Multicolored strobe lights flashed over the table in our booth, and we had to yell to make conversation over the DJ's voice. I was bobbing and swaying to the music, frantic to get out on the dance floor—and Dumbe was telling me about his plans for the next few days: going to the bookstore to get a head start on his reading for next semester. I began to think maybe this wasn't going to work.

"It's important to get the majority of your science classes out of the way before you go on to the university," Dumbe yelled over the thumping on the dance floor.

It's important for me to get out of here, I thought. By now it was midnight, and even the shy kids who didn't know how to dance had finally jumped out on the dance floor. Dumbe and I were still talking about college credits.

"Let's go," I called out. Dumbe looked surprised.

"Are you sure you want to leave?"

Apparently, the look on my face was answer enough. This was definitely not working.

Dumbe politely drew open the door to the dance club and let me out. To our surprise, a three-inch blanket of snow had fallen, and our ears buzzed from the sudden change from the noise of the club as we stepped out into a soft, quiet wonderland.

It was beautiful. It was cold. And I was wearing three-inch heels with thin stockings.

The winter weather had caught the city by surprise; no buses or cabs were running. Dumbe didn't have a car, so with an exasperated sigh, I pointed the way home and we started our slippery trek through the streets. Dumbe shoved his hands deep into his pockets to keep them warm. I, in my bare-backed suit and flimsy heels, looked like the snow queen within fifteen minutes. I stumbled, and Dumbe reached to catch me.

"This, too, is not working," I said, laughing at the fiasco.

Dumbe looked up and saw a tiny restaurant that was still open. A rush of warmth blew at us when we opened the door. The customers were huddled close together, talking in hushed tones that matched the weather outside.

Dumbe ordered two hot chocolates, and we sat down. *Ah, now we can talk a little more about scholarly habits,* I thought morosely. I looked ridiculous in my outfit, and I was still frozen solid. Dumbe, however, didn't start any conversation this time. He watched me swallow a few, steamy sips, and then asked me to take off my heels.

I did, puzzled. He pulled his chair up close to mine, lifted my blue feet into his lap, and gently began to rub them between his hands, easing away the numbness and ache of the cold. I watched him, speechless.

"There, that should feel better," he said. He looked into my eyes and didn't say a word about classes or books. "You look beautiful," he said.

I smiled, and flushed a little, pulling away.

"Wait a minute," Dumbe said. He threw some napkins on the floor, then gently set my feet down on them. He slipped off his own boots, and took off his thick, warm socks. They were still dry.

He slipped the socks onto my own feet, then stood up and draped his sports jacket over my shoulders. The look he gave me when he smiled thawed me from the inside out.

"Come on," he said, turning to leave. "Hop up on my back. I'll give you a ride, and you can keep those pretty feet of yours dry."

I was so stunned I did what he said, and we stumbled our way up the four or five hills back to my dorm. By the time we got there, we were both laughing, talking freely about ourselves. I had completely forgotten about the dance. All I could think about was how gentle Dumbe was, yet strong, how quiet he was, yet full of dreams.

Before Dumbe left me in the lobby of my building, I reached down to return his socks.

"No," Dumbe said. "I'd feel a lot warmer knowing they were still on your feet."

He gave me a hug, waved good-bye, and moved slowly down the street. I stood there in his socks, virtually pulsating warmth, watching him till he was out of sight.

It's a routine we've kept for eighteen years now, Dumbe and I. That first night was four college degrees ago for the two of us, but no matter where my husband, Dumbe, is going, I follow him to the door, hug him, and stand there in his socks, watching him move down the street till he's out of sight. It warms me down to my toes.

Pamela Elessa

"This is only our first date.
Let's not spoil it by being ourselves."

Dating Again

When my husband Edgar committed suicide, a lot of people looked at me, Joan Rivers, with pity and thought: widow. And, to tell the truth, that's the way I thought of myself at first: part of Hallmark's gloomiest section.

Our marriage had been of the kind you rarely see in Hollywood: genuine, deep and abiding. We loved each other and our daughter, we loved the life we built for ourselves. I knew I was going to miss that partnership, that sense of knowing someone so well that I could finish his sentences.

For a while I was tempted to stay mired in memories and regrets. But step by step I began to rebuild my social life. Eventually I knew I wanted to start dating again, because I missed the feeling of belonging with someone. I missed the pleasure of sharing the silly details of my day with someone who actually cared how that day had been. I missed the comfort of having someone to kiss my forehead when I was sick or someone whom I could take care of when he was sick or down. Some anthropologist once said that one of humanity's strongest needs is to know that there is someone who cares whether you've come safely home.

And equally sweet is having someone to make the trip with you. As a song in *The Golden Apple*—a 1954 musical based on Greek mythology—perfectly says:

It's the goin' home together
When the day is done.

But *dating?* When the Marine Corps refers to "a few good men," it is also referring to what's available to a suddenly single woman. *Dating?* After twenty-two years of marriage, I had no idea how to start. The last time I'd been dating, I used to ask the guy, "What's your major?" However, when you're over fifty, if you ask a guy where he went to college, he may not remember.

Nevertheless, I began to meet a few single men. Although none seemed right, I began to accept their invitations, reminding myself that I wasn't going on dates to have a great time. I was going on dates to meet someone I liked well enough so I could stop going on dates.

In spite of this somewhat unromantic approach, I was surprised to discover that, even in middle age, even after twenty-two years of marriage, I still got crushes. I found myself nervously waiting for phone calls. I found myself trying on forty-six different dresses before each dinner date. In the restaurant, I would wonder: Am I talking too much? Am I talking enough? Am I being charming? Am I being too loud?

In my first few months as a single woman, I felt awkwardness and disappointment, and I even shed a few tears. But whenever I thought of giving up, I also thought how nice it would be to have someone with whom I could share a midnight snack in the kitchen.

In the fall following Edgar's death, I encountered some nice men at business meetings in New York; and when I was looking for an apartment there, I met a real estate mogul who was both charming and funny. Although we became good friends, I wasn't in love with him. The problem for him and me wasn't the wit, it was the fit: Our styles and priorities were simply too different. Nevertheless, I will always be grateful that my first beau after Edgar's death was a man whose warmth eased my way back into the scary world of old-boy-meets-old-girl.

My next romance, however, was one that made me wonder if there was something else a girl could meet. I met a man who instantly impressed me with his culture and polish, but as the months went by, I discovered that he had neither generosity nor warmth. Cheap and cold is not a combination that Jerome Kern wrote about.

One night at a dinner party, after this man had ignored half my friends and insulted some others, I looked in the mirror and said to myself, Joan, you could get this from Don Rickles, but there would be laughs. It's better to be by yourself than to be with someone who's going to make you angry all the time. Although it was nice to have an escort, someone with whom I could take a walk in the park, it was better to go it alone than to be in the company of a man who felt that having a heart was optional.

After I sailed away from this iceberg, I spent many months dining out with groups of my girlfriends. I knew that I could live alone for as long as I had to. And then, as if rewarding my self-sufficiency, the gods sent me a very special man who is kind, witty, generous and loving.

"When they are together," says my old friend, Tom Corcoran, "they're always laughing and joking. I look at him sometimes, and he is just beaming."

Your first relationships after the loss of a love may not be successful, but those early, groping tries will slowly move you toward the sweet permanence that you deserve.

Joan Rivers

"She may be a single woman to you, but to me, she's MOM! . . . Be home by nine."

Reprinted by permission of Randy Bisson.

Loving Henry

A child's hand in yours—what tenderness and power it arouses. You are instantly the very touchstone of wisdom and strength.

Marjorie Holmes

"I don't want to! I don't want to!" he screeched.

In his Red Wings hockey jersey, Henry glared up from underneath the kitchen table. His wild, blond hair pointed in six different directions; his chin was raised and hardened, his six-year-old face forming a mask of defiance.

"Please, darling," Pauline implored him. "Mommy wants to talk with her friend. Won't you go out and play with Zach?"

Henry decided he apparently hadn't made his point clear. He pounded the table with his walkie-talkie.

"No! No! No!" he screamed again.

"You're going to have to leave," Pauline said, but not to Henry. She was speaking to me. "I'm sorry. He's jealous, and he won't settle down as long as you're here."

This did not bode well. Pauline and I had just reunited after eighteen years. Long ago, we had toyed with the idea of marriage, but I had backed out, suffering from inability-to-commit disease. Pauline had married someone else, but divorced ten years later. As soon as I heard she was single, I called. One of Pauline's first questions was whether I was married. When I told her no, she said she wasn't either. "There's just me and Henry," she said.

Who was Henry?

"My six-year-old. My one true love."

This was a problem. I had a reputation for not doing well with children. In fact, when I called my brother in Denver to tell him the news about Pauline and her son, he laughed. "How many times have you said you couldn't live with a child?" he asked.

"I know that," I said, "but I care for his mother, and maybe I was wrong."

"Maybe not," he said before he hung up.

At first, I thought I would prove my brother wrong. Loving Pauline was easy and natural—she and I instantly fell back into our familiar ways. How could loving Henry not be as simple? And when Pauline told me Henry's birthday was April 11, the same day as mine, my hopes were confirmed. Of course I would love her son who was born on the same day as I!

Henry's tantrum greeting squelched those hopes, and any uneasiness that Henry had around me was equaled by what I felt toward him. I couldn't control him, and his high-pitched voice set me on edge.

Every encounter produced more evidence that Henry rejected me, and the more I saw of him, the less I could imagine myself as his father.

Still, my love for Pauline spurred my efforts. I invited her and Henry over for dinner, making my specialty: creamed zucchini soup with asparagus spears on the side. Maybe this evening would form a special bond between us. As soon as Pauline and Henry saw my gourmet meal, they went into a huddle. When they broke, she turned to me and grinned. "You don't know much about kids, do you?"

"What do you mean?" I said, on the defensive.

"There isn't a kid on the planet who would eat that stuff." She rummaged through my cupboards for a box of Cheerios and parked Henry in front of the TV. So much for a bond.

Not long after that evening, I was sitting on the sofa at Pauline's when Henry came and sat next to me. "Mom said you used to be a soldier," he blurted.

"I was in air defense," I told him. "They shoot missiles at enemy aircraft."

"Did you carry a rifle?"

"An M-14. In basic training." I didn't reveal that I had been a clerk typist for most of my Army career.

"All the other guys in the condo have rifles, but Mom won't let me have one," he complained.

"Oh, you should have a rifle!" I vowed, with absolutely no authority to do so. I was grasping at any chance I could find to ingratiate the child to me.

Henry was thrilled. Pauline was mad. "You promised him something you can't deliver," she accused, her voice drowned out by Henry's pleas: "Please, Mama, please." Now I had managed to alienate both mother and child.

As the weeks progressed, my stock with Henry vacillated wildly. At the family picnics we attended, he seemed happy to be able to produce me for the father-and-son games, like the two-legged races. But when Pauline and I would link hands during our walks, he ran between us, breaking our hold. Clearly he didn't want us together, but Pauline said: "He must like you. At least he doesn't run over you with his tricycle, like he did my last boyfriend."

Well, here at last was a good sign. Still, I was uneasy about Henry, and not just because of him. Our reluctance to accept each other was mutual, and that failure was only magnified by the complete success Pauline and I were having. We were already discussing marriage. But what kind of father would I make?

After supper one evening, Pauline surprised me. "Henry asked what he should call you after we marry," she said quietly. "I asked him if he would like to call you 'Terry.' He said he wants to call you 'Dad,' but not until we're married." I was pleased. If only I could feel like "Dad."

A few days later, as I was walking to the supermarket, I passed Henry playing outside. He spotted me and asked to tag along. He pranced by my side, explaining to me the intricacies of day care, and when we reached a busy intersection, he instinctively grabbed for my hand. *A natural response,* I told myself; *children depend on adults for security.* But his small gesture touched deep inside me, in a place I didn't know existed. Suddenly, I understood what an enormous act of faith it is for a child to offer you his hand. In mine, his hand felt tiny and needy, and that vulnerability somehow broke within me an unknown flood of paternal feelings. Henry wanted a father; he wanted me to be that father. I suddenly was aware I never wanted to violate his trust. For the first time, I understood what a child's love meant—and what it meant to love Henry.

Two months later, Pauline and I married, with Henry as the ring bearer. No sooner had we marched down the aisle after the ceremony than Henry ran and threw his arms around my leg. Looking up at me with approving eyes, he said, "Hi, Dad!"

My voice was husky as I replied, "Hi, Son."

Terry L. Fairchild

The Last Date

When I first laid eyes on Rob, I whined to my girlfriend, "Why don't I ever meet anyone like that?" Even at a distance he just seemed so . . . right.

Then I got to know him. Up close, it was a different story. He still looked great, and in some ways he turned out to match my ideals perfectly: He was a talented engineer, owned a nice house, was kind to old folks and animals, and drove a car as if he was Steve McQueen. But if ever two people came from two different planets, it was us. We had a heck of a time finding anything to talk about, much less agree upon. He was a scientist who grew up on a farm in the Midwest, a Republican, a pilot, an orderly, efficient, methodical person. I was . . . something else. We needed a language that hadn't been invented yet to speak to each other. The one time we discussed politics, I got so mad I opened the door to leave—and we were in a car doing thirty miles an hour!

But we had both been here before. You see, we were both forty years old, and neither of us had ever been married. Oh, we had dated a lot. In fact, we had both made a pretty thorough canvass of our small town. But something was always not quite right. Somehow, the motivation to commit just hadn't been there. And people were starting to see us coming. When I told a friend I was dating Rob, she said, "Watch out. They've got his picture in the dictionary next to 'fear of commitment.'" And my friends were starting to refer to my dates as "interviews," as in, "How'd he do in the interview?"

We went out a few times over the course of several months. Our dates were always awkward, and we never felt we knew each other well enough to even kiss goodnight. But still, I had a vague feeling that, if it weren't for so many things being wrong, this would be just perfect. There was the compelling fact that he was just like my dad, whom I adored. But my dad and I had never needed to fill long evenings with conversation. Conversationally, Rob and I were marching to drummers in two different parades in two distant universes. I'd start talking about some novel I was reading, and Rob would chime in with his thoughts on the structure of orbital vectors. He'd tell a joke, and I'd defend the blond.

Still, we kept dating every now and then. Did I mention that the first gray hairs had been found? That we were, after all, old enough to be pushing grandkids in a stroller?

Finally, we felt our lack of enthusiasm building to a grand crescendo. At the same time, we later found out, we both decided to give it just one more date. Rob already had theater tickets, and he made reservations for dinner at a nice Japanese restaurant. I put on something slinky and blow-dried my hair for half an hour. We were dutifully going through the motions.

It was pleasant, quite pleasant. But we later discovered that, sitting silently in the buzzing theater during intermission, we had once again been thinking the same thing. This time it was, "Let's call the whole thing off." On the ride home we didn't bother to go into the details of exactly how wrong the other was in his or her thoughts about the radically feminist play we had just seen. What did it matter? Soon there would be other fish to fry.

We drove up the long driveway to my house. Rob turned off the car, and we sat for a moment in silence. Rob later said, "I knew it was our last date, and I had a sense of relief about it. Freedom! But, I thought, I'd always wanted to kiss this woman."

And so . . . he kissed me. It was our first kiss. It was a long kiss. We had time to make a leisurely trip from our distant planets, surveying the whole of creation along the way and landing gently in my driveway, different people. I had no thought for a long time, but then, as we slowly pulled apart, I had one enormous thought that was bigger than I was. This is what I have waited for all my life.

Today, we talk about the latest cute thing the cat did, the menu for supper, the reason the garbage is still in the basement. Sometimes we reminisce about the happiness on our mothers' faces as we walked down the aisle six years ago. Sometimes we talk for hours about matters closest to our hearts. And sometimes we don't talk at all.

Actually, I've come to think that talking isn't all it's cracked up to be. It's even occurred to me that the Republicans have a point sometimes. Why fight it? Sometimes love puts on a funny disguise just to give you a lovely surprise.

Cindy Jevne Buck

Reprinted by permission of Donna Barstow.

3

FINDING YOUR MATE

To touch the soul of another human being is to walk on holy ground.

Stephen R. Covey

Reprinted by permission of Andrew Toos.

The Invitation

It doesn't interest me what you do for a living. I want to know what you ache for, and if you dare to dream of meeting your heart's longing.

It doesn't interest me how old you are. I want to know if you will risk looking like a fool for love, for your dreams, for the adventure of being alive.

It doesn't interest me what planets are squaring your moon. I want to know if you have touched the center of your own sorrow, if you have been opened by life's betrayals or have become shriveled and closed from fear of further pain. I want to know if you can sit with pain, mine or your own, without moving to hide it or fade it or fix it.

I want to know if you can be with joy, mine or your own, if you can dance with wildness and let the ecstasy fill you to the tips of your fingers and toes without cautioning us to be careful, to be realistic, to remember the limitations of being human.

It doesn't interest me if the story you are telling me is true. I want to know if you can disappoint another to be true to yourself; if you can bear the accusation of betrayal and not betray your own soul; if you can be faithless and therefore trustworthy.

I want to know if you can see beauty, even when it's not pretty, every day, and if you can source your own life from its presence.

I want to know if you can live with failure, yours and mine, and still stand on the edge of the lake and shout to the silver of the full moon, "Yes!"

It doesn't interest me to know where you live or how much money you have. I want to know if you can get up, after the night of grief and despair, weary and bruised to the bone, and do what needs to be done to feed the children.

It doesn't interest me to know who you know or how you came to be here. I want to know if you will stand in the center of the fire with me and not shrink back.

It doesn't interest me where or what or with whom you have studied. I want to know what sustains you, from the inside, when all else falls away.

I want to know if you can be alone with yourself and if you truly like the company you keep in the empty moments.

Oriah Mountain Dreamer

How David and Lily Got Together

This is the story of how David and Lily got together, or at least, what they always told us. We didn't learn the truth till many years later.

Some years ago a good family moved into the third-floor apartment of the tenement where we lived in the Bronx. David was the son, and he was going to medical school. He was also an avid reader, so he spent most of his free time in the library.

The librarian there was a pretty, soft-spoken young woman named Lily. We kids all loved her. If we couldn't find a book, she would stop whatever she was doing, smile at us warmly and launch a search to find it for us. She was a hard worker.

She also secretly admired our new neighbor, David. Whenever he entered the small neighborhood library, Lily's eyes lit up and observed his wandering path through the stacks of books. She never struck up a conversation with him, though. She was much too shy, and in those days, a woman didn't talk to a stranger without a formal introduction.

One evening, as Lily was closing up the library, her assistant bent down near the desk to retrieve an unopened envelope off the floor. She showed it to Lily, and they noted that it was sent from a major city hospital.

"It looks so important," the assistant said. "Some poor person is probably looking for it frantically. It must have fallen out of his pocket or book."

Lily glanced at the address of the recipient and was surprised to see it was for the building right next to hers. She took the letter so she could drop it by the man's apartment on her way home.

She turned out the lights, locked up the library and hurried home, where she quickly set down her bags. Clutching the envelope, she ran across the way, entered the front lobby next door and scanned the mailboxes. She found a "Gordon," the same last name listed on the envelope, and rang the bell for that apartment.

"Who's there?" called out a woman's voice over the scratchy intercom.

"I'm the librarian," Lily answered. "We found a letter on the library floor addressed to a David Gordon. Does that name mean anything to you? The letter looks important."

After a pause, the voice replied: "Yes. Could you bring it up for me, Apartment B3? I fell a few weeks ago and can't walk the stairs."

Lily walked up the three flights of stairs and was greeted at the door by a sweet, older woman who was leaning on a crutch.

"Oh, thank you so much," she said. "As you see, I really can't walk the stairs."

Lily smiled. "I understand. Well, here's the letter. Is David Gordon your husband?"

"Oh, no," she answered. "That's my son. We were wondering where that letter went." She looked Lily up and down. "You say you found the letter at the library?"

"Yes," said Lily. "I'm the librarian there, but I live in the building next to you, so it was no trouble to bring you the letter."

"Well, look at us standing here like strangers," the woman said, smiling brightly. "Come and sit for a moment and have some tea. Please."

As she motioned Lily to a chair, the lady talked about the letter. "When I get mail for my son, I always put it on the kitchen table so he can find it when he comes home. This letter was important, so I stuck it in his book. You see, he is going to medical school to be a specialist," she said proudly.

Just then, the door opened, and in walked her son, David. Upon seeing that he was the young man she had admired so long, Lily felt her heart beat faster. His mother excitedly explained to him what had happened to the letter.

David looked at Lily in astonishment. "Gosh! You're from the library. Thank you! I was looking high and low for that letter." He turned to his mother. "You see, I was accepted to the hospital's medical program."

Then he turned back to Lily and smiled shyly. "Thanks again, Miss, errrr, I didn't get your name."

"Lily," she said, smiling her warmest smile. Her heart was still pounding, and she felt sure her cheeks were flushed.

Meanwhile, Mrs. Gordon was hobbling around, setting the table for tea and cookies. "Sit! Sit!" she urged the young couple.

"Have you decided which branch of medicine you want to specialize in?" Lily asked David.

"Cardiology," David answered, still smiling. "And this is the letter that will start me on my career. I was really worried when I hadn't heard from the hospital. I was considering going out west someplace, but I'd much rather stay at this hospital, here in the city."

And then, out of the blue, David blurted: "Would you care to go to a movie with me Saturday night?"

Before Lily could catch her breath, Mrs. Gordon grabbed her hand and said, "Oh, yes, Lily! Please say yes!"

Lily laughed. "I'd love to!"

And so began Lily and David's life together.

But now for the whole story. After they'd been married twenty-five years, he told us the truth about the letter. David was a cardiovascular specialist by then, and his dear Lily, the mother of their three children, was sitting by his side as he told us.

You see, David wasn't that avid a reader, as it turns out. He just wanted to see that pretty young librarian. He told his mother about the girl at his local library, but he was shy and didn't know how to approach her. His mother devised a scheme. Every time David went to the library, he was to drop an envelope addressed to himself on the floor. David's mother hoped Lily would retrieve it for him, call him over to the desk and give him a chance to strike up a conversation. So David dutifully dropped a letter each time he visited the library, but each time, someone would see the envelope fluttering to the floor and rush to reclaim it for him. "Oh, sir!" he'd hear someone cry out, but when he turned, it was never Lily.

On the day he finally met Lily, David waited till no one was left in the building but Lily and her assistant. Once again, he dropped his letter by the desk. The next day, he hoped, he could come back and ask Lily if she had found an envelope with his name on it. The plan worked far better than he imagined when Lily showed up in person to deliver the letter.

While David was telling this story, his beautiful wife Lily began laughing hysterically.

"David," she said, when she caught her breath. "You didn't seal that envelope very well. We opened it at the library. I saw that there was nothing but a blank piece of paper inside. I was dying to figure out what you were up to, so I played along. David, you were a terrible actor!" She turned her twinkling eyes to her husband's.

"But, oh, David! I loved you so!"

And that is how David and Lily really got together.

Arnold Fine

The Moment It Happens

You'll always miss 100 percent of the shots you don't take.

Wayne Gretzky

I know when it happened. . . . the exact moment.

Houston Intercontinental Airport, 11:30 P.M.: My flight was three-and-a-half hours late. I sat in a phone station in the baggage area to check my business messages, and like a bolt of lightning, it hit me. If I fell over dead at that very moment, no one passing by to get a rental car, or to get their suitcases, or to greet loved ones would know who I was, where I was coming from or where I was going. No one would know I was missing for quite a while. It was an odd, lonely and very important moment in my life. I then decided to find someone significant who would miss me if I failed to arrive.

After making that decision, I had dinner with a long-time friend who listened to my complaints about trying to "find someone." I said there were no decent men "out there" to find. Without hesitation, or even looking up from her salad, she asked what I had done about my search that very day. When I said, "Nothing because it's been a busy day for me," she said, "Either do something about it every day, or shut up."

After that "put up or shut up" encounter, I decided okay, but *how!?* I talked to myself about where "they" (decent men) were. The old conventional ways that everyone talked about—bars, classes, meetings, friends, blind dates, etc.—seemed uncomfortable and not for me. After all, it seemed I was doing some of that anyway in my regular day-to-day life and "they" just weren't there. So, my inner voice said, "Try something new."

I picked up my newspaper and read one hundred personal ads of women searching for "them."

The free five-line ads all seemed to say the same things. And I wanted to be different.

I called the newspaper and discovered the ads were free at that typical size but if I wanted a bigger one, it would be costly.

I have always believed if you want something, go all out. So I did.

A friend and her mother helped me write the ad that would end up changing my life. After seventeen drafts, I wrote *the* ad. It was twenty-three lines, expensive and really described me. I also recorded a voice-mail message that every one of "them" would hear.

The ad ended with "I miss being called 'Honey'," and it spoke the truth.

In the next two weeks, I had 104 replies. The messages they left for me told of delightful-sounding, accomplished men, in my area and in my age group, who were also tired of the tried and not-so-true methods of meeting potential mates. They had also grown weary of bars, groups, socials and the like. They were all intrigued with someone wanting to be called honey, and most of them, through nervous laughter, used that word somehow in their message. I made a long prioritized list on a legal pad. Three stood out. An FBI agent, a business owner and a firefighter. The firefighter turned out to be delightful on the phone, but reluctant to go any further. The FBI agent met me for lunch and was concerned about *my* motives in looking for him. I reminded him that he had answered my ad. I finished my lunch quickly and that name was crossed off the list.

In my recorded message, I had said the best movie I had ever seen was *The Day the Earth Stood Still* (still my favorite). The third man on my list, the business owner, left this reply: "Michael Rennie, Patricia Neal, Hugh Marlow, Sam Jaffe, Billy Gray, call me!" He had listed the major cast members of *The Day the Earth Stood Still.*

Because I was leaving town on a rush flight, time prevented me from answering his call immediately. Upon returning, I heard his second message. This time he listed all the cast plus the director, producer and key moviemakers. And he recited the key phrase in the movie ("Klaatu Barada Nikto") and said, "Call me." That was the phrase that Patricia Neal said to Gort, the robot, to get him to come to the aid of Michael Rennie, who was being destroyed by the frightened people on Earth.

Again fate stepped in and I couldn't get back to him immediately, so when I returned home this time, there was a message on the voice mail from his entire office staff chanting in unison, "Please answer this man—he is driving us nuts."

I learned later that upon hearing my voice message, this man had played it for his brother in California, who said, "If she ever answers you, you are going to marry her."

Finally we did talk, scheduled lunch and chose to see a movie. When he approached the restaurant (I was there first so I could see him), I knew I would marry him. His look, his swagger and his élan told me this was "him."

In the middle of lunch, he put down his fork and said,

"I think we are going to be married." I smiled.

Because I come from a self-sufficient generation, I told him at lunch that I would like to buy the movie tickets. He smiled and pulled them out of his pocket, saying the Italian side of him wouldn't let me pay, and that he knew I was going to offer.

We dated for nine months, planned a wedding, had the ceremony under a huppa in a temple and took an Italian honeymoon.

Upon returning, he presented me with a gift. On the table at our home was a square of Lucite with our crushed wedding glass reconstructed. The inscription on the Lucite square was the date of our wedding and the words to Gort, "Klaatu Barada Nikto."

He said, "They were true in the movie, and they are true for me."

Loosely translated: "You saved my life."

Carol A. Price-Lopata

QUALITY TIME. ©1999 Gail Machlia. Reprinted by permission of UNIVERSAL PRESS SYNDICATE. All rights reserved.

The High School English Teacher

Grandma Sophie was working in her kitchen when her granddaughter came home from school. The teenager leaned over and kissed the old lady. "Hi, Granny," she said. "Watcha making?"

"Dinner. How was your day in school?" the old lady replied as she bent over to return the kiss.

"Grandma, I'm in love."

"And with whom may I ask? That cute young man you were doing homework with last week?"

"No," Jeannie said with a lovesick sigh. "I'm in love with my English teacher. He is so young and gorgeous! He's brand-new to the school. He has such beautiful features, I just sit in class all day and can't help but look at him. And he speaks beautifully. He sounds like a radio announcer."

"Well, that's wonderful that you can admire a teacher as much as you do," Grandma exclaimed.

"He read one of Elizabeth Barrett Browning's poems today," she sighed. "I can listen to him read all day long. He has such a deep and warm voice. When he read that poem, *How Do I Love Thee,* I honestly felt he was reading it directly to me."

"Well," Grandma smiled, trying to break the mood. "Do you have any homework?"

Jeannie sighed once more. "I have some math and I have to write a composition for English."

"Well, Darling, hop to it. Get your homework out of the way, and then you can help me set the table for dinner before your mother comes home."

Jeannie, still star-struck, turned to her grandmother and asked, "Granny, were you ever in love?"

The old lady started to chuckle, "You bet your life! I was even a baby at one time." She leaned over almost whispering to the youngster and added, " . . . and I too fell in love with my English teacher. Oh, gosh, was he young and handsome."

Jeannie pulled up a chair and started to smile, "Tell me more. Please tell me what happened."

The old lady rinsed her hands under the running water in the sink, dried them on a towel and had a broad grin. "He was such a handsome man. Well, what I did was, I went home, and I wrote him a love letter."

"You didn't," the youngster asked incredulously.

"Yes I did. I told him how handsome I thought he was and how magnificently he spoke. The next day I put the letter on his desk when no one was looking. The bell rang, and we all went on to our next class."

Jeannie was all eyes with a smile from ear to ear.

"The next day," the old lady continued, "when I came into class he looked at me. Oh, so lovingly. I knew my letter had reached him. I wondered how he felt about me. Then as he conducted the lesson, he picked up some papers from his desk and distributed them to the students. He handed me a paper and I realized it was the note I left on his desk. I looked at the paper and almost died. He corrected it! There were red corrections all over the place. He wrote, 'Miss Goodman, your theme is excellent, but your grammar and punctuation are terrible. I had to fail you for this exercise. Please try to do better.'"

The old lady was smiling as she was reminiscing. "I was totally destroyed. On the other side of the paper he added another note. 'Please make these corrections and turn in your paper tomorrow.'"

Jeannie grabbed her grandmother's arm and started to hug her. "What happened then?"

The old lady began to laugh. "I went home in tears. How could he do this to me? I loved him so. He actually marked my love letter to him. But I sat down and rewrote the letter with all the corrections he had wanted me to make. My tears dripped all over the page as I wrote. The ink smears were so obvious. I was really hurt," the old lady explained.

"The next day in class I turned in the rewritten letter. He nodded his acknowledgment when he saw the letter on his desk. That was all there was to it. Would you believe he even flunked me in my first year of English in high school! But I got even with him."

The old lady got up from her chair and started toward the stove. "I was so blinded with love. And so the years passed and I graduated high school and went on to college. On the subway one day, lo and behold, who got on and stood in front of me? It was this wonderful gentleman. Oh, was he gorgeous. I didn't know if he recognized me, but I recognized him. I said, 'Excuse me, are you . . . ?' He looked at me and began to smile. 'Oh my goodness,' he smiled. 'You must be that pretty little girl who wrote me those wonderful notes when I was teaching my first year in high school.'

"I was so embarrassed," the old lady exclaimed. "But I nodded sheepishly. He then said, 'I owe you an apology. Can I make it up to you Saturday night? I have tickets to the Shakespeare festival. I'm sure you might enjoy it.'"

The old lady smiled. "And that is how it began. I really got even with him. I married your grandfather fifty-one years ago. Even to this very day he calls me his child bride."

The old lady took a deep breath and added, "And to this very day would you believe, he still corrects my spelling and grammar? Come, let us finish setting the table," the old lady exclaimed. "Grandpa will be back from his walk in a few minutes."

Arnold Fine

Perennials

Let your lawn be your home's velvet robe and your flowers its not-too-promiscuous decoration.

Source Unknown

If flowers can be promiscuous, then my yard is a little tramp. Honeysuckle and snows-in-summer border my lawn. Gigantic flower beds spill over with white hollyhocks, purple daisies and multicolored asters. Even some of my trees sport flowers for two weeks of every spring.

And I have a rose garden, which no one ever promised me.

My addiction to flowers started right after I left home for college. I discovered that gardening was a great way to relieve the stress of going to school while working full-time. I'd come home from work at ten o'clock at night, too wired to study or sleep. So I'd go outside in the dark and pull weeds in my flower garden. It rejuvenated me. After an hour or so of barehanded digging in the dirt and smelling the heady aromas, I'd feel like a new woman, ready to take on the world. Or Political Theory. Or whatever.

It was always different dirt because I changed residences often. When I was growing up, we moved so much that my sister and I pretended our olive skin was due to gypsy blood. Make-believe was preferable to the truth—that our Hispanic father said "Adios" before we hit kindergarten, and my mother hitched our lives to a stepfather who promised her stability, something they moved around constantly trying to find. By the time I was eighteen, I had lived in fifteen different places and attended seven different schools.

Out on my own, life was more of the same. I lived with a series of roommates, but whenever there was a disagreement, I packed my things and moved. I learned to pack in less than five hours, and the post office sent me a change-of-address kit every six months, whether I asked for it or not.

The one constant in my life was my flowers. I must have planted thousands of blooms during the four years I was in college. In ten different places.

It was always a different canvas—ceramic pots or driveway flower beds, but my medium remained the same:

Annuals.

The flowers that don't come back. "Why bother with perennials," I said to myself. "I won't be here long enough to enjoy them. Nothing has ever lasted long in my life. Why get my hopes up?"

Each spring I would just buy more annuals. Replanting was fun. Easy. And—most of all—safe.

After college I got a good job, but I kept up my old habits. Live somewhere six months. Plant annuals. And move again. Fresh soil. Clean carpets. No ties.

Then I met John.

John was another annual. On our first date he said, "I'll never get married, and I'm perfectly content to live alone, so don't get too attached."

I admired his honesty. This was not a man who would tell me he loved me just to get me into bed.

We played that game for about two years—him living alone in his apartment, and me living in a new place every few months. We both had our space, and we took a long time to get acquainted. I learned he was a man who greatly valued his alone time, and I learned not to take it too personally when he needed to escape inside himself for a few days. I continued to plant truckloads of one-shot flowers, unwilling to risk perennials.

During those two years, I slowly learned to trust. Despite his warning, John was there, spring after spring. The same touch. The same smile. The same guy.

And then, one hot summer day, when I was knee-deep in a batch of petunias, John asked me that magical question.

"Would you go halves with me on a house?" He paused. "Because I can't afford to buy the one I want all by myself."

Neither of us was in a hurry to marry, but we both knew what he meant. Neither of us would live together unless it was going to be permanent.

We moved into our brand-new, twenty-five-hundred-square foot house two weeks before Thanksgiving. The first few months we spent moving our meager furniture around and around, trying to fill up the space. During the cold winter I never thought much about flowers.

It happened on the first warm day in February. I always caught spring fever in February, even though I knew it would probably snow the next weekend. Normally I would content myself with reading garden catalogs and visiting home stores. But I discovered something magical on my first trip to the home-supply store as a bona fide homeowner:

Roses.

Roses are perennials, but you can plant rose bushes when it's still cold outside, because they are dormant. And they will bloom the first year you plant them.

I was a woman possessed. I had an acre of dirt at my disposal, and I could start planting immediately. I bought twelve rose bushes, or maybe I should say rose "sticks," for $1.99 each. They resembled very small TV antennas coming out of the ground, and I planted my very first rose garden. It was the first permanent mark in the soil of my new home.

That spring I went wild at the nursery, spending truckloads of money on flowers—sweet williams, johnny jump-ups, candytuft and fragrant phlox. I was amazed at new breeds and colors I had never seen before, all because I had never bothered to look in the perennial section. I realized there might be a lot of things just waiting to be discovered, if I opened my eyes and looked.

The first spring John and I worked in the yard together tested the limits of our relationship. I discovered what true love was when I tried to build a planter box with the help of the finickiest man on the planet—a man who not only reads all the directions before starting a project, but who goes to the hardware store and buys all the recommended tools. I'm a woman who is content to pound nails into the wall with my shoe.

Summer arrived with our love intact and plenty of perennials planted everywhere. We made it through three more springs before completing the landscape of our front yard, and then we decided to make our relationship legal. We figured if our love could survive the planting of a two-hundred-square-foot lawn and the construction of a granite patio, it could survive anything.

We were married three years ago—in the spring, naturally—and have experienced both the joy and frustration that come with a marriage license. I no longer read the apartment ads whenever we have a fight, and he leaves the door open when he goes into his private reverie.

My love affair with flowers is a tender one. But the

difference between flowers and people is that people can choose to be annuals or perennials.

Sometimes when I am working in the garden, I look across at John, and I have no doubt that the two of us will keep growing together, year after year. We are perennials.

Jackie Shelton

QUALITY TIME.

Hope Is Where the Heart Is

Donna Cleszykowski was born with kidneys that were too small. She didn't know it until she was almost twenty and began having terrible headaches. Tests revealed kidney problems as well as high blood pressure.

In 1981, she started dialysis, and soon she was going to the hospital twice a week for treatments. Although dialysis kept her alive and able to work at a bank, it was not the sort of life Donna had envisioned. She was beginning to realize that because of her shaky health, her dreams of meeting a wonderful man, getting married and raising a family would probably never come true. And although she tried to be grateful for the blessings she did enjoy, especially her family, sometimes life seemed hard indeed.

One of the bright spots in Donna's life was Kathy, another dialysis patient. Sick since childhood, Kathy had been on dialysis for six years when Donna met her, and she seemed resigned to it. Donna, however, still hoped for a way out.

"Have you ever considered a kidney transplant?" Donna asked Kathy one day.

"Yes," Kathy answered slowly. "In fact, my younger brother Ray told me on my wedding day—when he was sixteen—that he'd give me one of his kidneys any time."

"That's wonderful! Are you going to do it?" Donna asked.

Kathy shook her head. "Transplants aren't foolproof. I've known dialysis patients who died after receiving a kidney. And what about Ray? Would it be fair for him to take this kind of risk for me?"

"Maybe he'd want to take it, if it meant you'd be well," Donna pointed out. Ray Pokorny sounded like a great brother. But Kathy shook her head. She had thought about it, but she was too afraid to take the chance.

Donna knew there were complications with transplants. At least on dialysis, she was alive. And yet, she often wondered, what kind of life was she having? She had always been close to God, and she had asked him many times for a healing. He had said no—at least she assumed he had—and she could live with that. But should she, if there was something she could do to change the situation?

Donna continued her dialysis, but her condition worsened and she had to quit her job. Her health continued to deteriorate, and on Christmas Day, 1984, she looked around at her loved ones with a sinking heart. The longer she stayed on dialysis, the worse she was probably going to get. Would she even be here next Christmas? Her uncle Johnny, carrying out a Polish custom of sharing blessed water, had just wished Donna "health and a transplant." But she hadn't even put herself on the list. Should she try for a miracle?

Yes. Somehow it seemed right. She had prayed, and she had endured. If God had anything else in mind for her, she was willing to try it.

In September 1985, Donna received a new kidney. The operation was a complete success, and when Kathy came to see her, she could hardly believe her eyes. Donna had lost a large amount of weight. "You're so tiny!" Kathy exclaimed. But Donna was healthy too—everyone could see that. And life began to change for her, almost immediately.

She had a lot more energy and couldn't remember ever feeling so well. She could eat foods that had been forbidden before, so she gradually gained weight. She was able to return to work. And she started another habit as well, reciting each day a petition she had found in a little book. "Prayer for a Good Spouse," it was called. And why not? If the Lord had restored her health, he might have other blessings in mind for her too.

One unexpected benefit from her own surgery was the change in Kathy. Reassured by Donna's rapid recovery, Kathy finally overcame her fears. She asked her brother if he remembered volunteering his kidney all those years ago, and he said, "Sure—let's go for it."

Just a few weeks later, Kathy underwent surgery, with the same positive results. Ray too recovered with no difficulties. *What a fine brother Ray was,* Donna thought. To risk something like this for love. She hoped she'd get the chance to meet him someday and tell him so.

Christmas 1985 was far different than the one before. It was Donna's parents' turn to host the extended clan for Christmas Eve, so Donna bought champagne for a celebration toast. She thought for a long time about what to say, how to express her gratitude for their love and support and for all the prayers that had been answered. In the end, she simply raised her glass and thanked them all.

By the time Uncle Johnny came to her with the traditional blessing of water, most of the guests were weeping. "Donna," he said simply, "for you I wish continued good health, and whatever you wish for."

Whatever she wished for. . . . Despite the joy of this day, Donna still held some fear in her heart. Was she truly cured, or might her kidney problems recur? Would she always be alone, or would there be a special someone in her life one day?

A few weeks later, Kathy invited Donna to a family gathering at her mother's house. The two hadn't seen each other since Kathy's surgery, and they wanted to share transplant experiences. Donna found the apartment and rang the bell. No one answered. She rang again. Did she have the wrong address, or the wrong date?

Suddenly, a young man wrenched open the door, his hair still wet from the shower. "Hi!" he grinned. "You're . . . ?"

"Donna Cleszykowski." She put out a hand. "I'm a friend of Kathy's. . . ."

The young man took her hand, his eyes warm. "I know who you are," he said. "I'm Ray Pokorny."

Donna does not say that it was love at first sight, although Ray might disagree. (To this day, he remembers exactly what she was wearing that night.) But he proposed just a few months later. And she didn't have to consider very long. "Ray," she asked him one day just before the wedding, "did you ever ask God for anything in return, after you decided to take the risk and be a donor?"

Ray looked somewhat abashed. "I asked God to use my kidney to give Kathy a long healthy life," he answered, "and . . ."

"And . . . ?"

"That if he gave me anything, it would be a woman for me to love and marry."

Donna has long since passed the "Prayer for a Good Spouse" on to someone else, and she and Ray are enjoying the additional blessing of their adopted son, Stevie. God had not said no to her at all, she has discovered. He had simply said, not yet. There were events that had to happen, love that had to be given before her own answers could come, and the plan sometimes proceeds more slowly than we understand. But it does proceed, for God is never late. The Pokornys can attest to that.

Joan Wester Anderson

The Letter

In the fall of 1942 I agreed to fill in for a friend on a blind date and met Jack, a Canadian soldier. I was twenty-two. I'd been working as a receptionist at London's Hospital for Sick Children for six years. For three of those years the world had been at war. But for a brief time the bombing of London had eased. Jack and I began to date and only occasionally did we hear the wail of the air-raid siren, or interrupt an evening to dive into the nearest air-raid shelter.

When I finished work at five he would meet me, and off we would go on another adventure. We went to Madame Tussauds, the London Zoo, the museum. We saw Gracie Field and Vera Lynne in concert at the London Palladium. And sometimes he would whisk me off to an out-of-the-way restaurant he had discovered that served ham sandwiches or maybe even a steak, rare treats in severely rationed England.

It was all quite lovely, and it wasn't too difficult to imagine myself falling in love with this dear, sweet man.

But threaded through my happiness was the reality that across the English Channel the war raged on. Any day now, Jack would be posted overseas, to where the fighting was. I knew that he wouldn't even be able to tell me where he was going, when he was going. One day, he would just be gone. And by and by perhaps I'd get a letter from somewhere in Europe, stamped with the Censor's mark of the Canadian Armed Forces. Or even worse, a telegram beginning with the words: "We regret to inform you. . . ."

And if he did come back . . . then what? If I married him I would be bound for Canada, leaving my family, friends and life as I had known it for twenty-two years.

I made arrangements to take two weeks off work and visit my parents in the north of England. And I wrote Jack a letter, explaining all of the very good reasons that I would not see him again. The next day, on my way to Victoria Station, I mailed it. Jack was stationed at Brighton, about forty-five miles from London. I knew the letter would be in his hands tomorrow, the next day at the latest.

At home, my parents fussed over me. I played with my younger siblings, visited my grandmother, went to the cinema with my cousins. Three days passed; a week; nine days. By now Jack would have gotten the letter. . . . Soon, I would go back to London. Had I made the right decision? It was a moot question. I would never see him again.

One rainy afternoon there was a knock at the door.

Must be one of the neighbors, popping in to say hello, I thought as I went to answer it. But it wasn't a neighbor. It was Jack.

"I got a three-day leave," he said. "I thought I'd come up and visit you."

I stood, stunned, staring at him as dozens of thoughts raced through my head. He must have gotten my parents' address from one of the girls at work. But, why had he come? Surely he had received the letter. It had been ten days.

And yet, there he was, standing on my mother's white-washed front step, grinning at me—asking me if I was going to invite him in. I had never been so happy to see anyone in all of my life. I couldn't stop smiling.

I had known Jack only a few months, but I knew he would not go where he wasn't wanted. If he had seen the letter, if he had thought there was even the slightest chance that he wouldn't have been welcome, he would never have come. I knew that he couldn't have received the letter.

He was the same sweet, funny Jack he had been in London. He chatted with my mother and father. He teased my younger sisters and brother. Even the cat loved him.

Before I knew it the three days were gone, and I was seeing him off at the railway station. Down the line the train's whistle sounded, then died away as the London locomotive chugged its way up to the platform. I thought of all the trains and ships and the horrible war that would take us away from each other over the next months, perhaps years. I thought of all the impediments that lay before us, all the problems we would certainly encounter, the heartbreak that could be around the next corner. And it didn't matter, it didn't matter, it didn't matter. I knew that I couldn't live without him.

"When you get back to Brighton, there'll be a letter waiting for you," I told him, as he swung up onto the train, "a letter from me. Don't read it. Rip it up and throw it away. I should never have written it."

Sure enough, the letter was waiting. It had finally arrived. He didn't rip it up. He read it.

And years later, on a little farm in Saskatchewan, every once in a while he would tease me about the "Dear John" letter I had written him so long ago—the letter that mysteriously, wonderfully, miraculously had taken ten days to travel forty-five miles.

Doris Byers
As told to Shirley Byers Lalonde

"I guess I'm confused. I sent him a Dear John letter, but I put a love stamp on it."

What's Your Sign?

There is no instinct like that of the heart.

Lord Byron

While my mother changed the sheets on my little sister's bed, I lounged on mine, soaking up the article in my teen magazine, "How to Recognize Your True Love Mate."

"Mom," I said, closing the magazine, "how did you know you loved Daddy?"

She smoothed the wrinkles out of the sheets, and looked at me as she made neat hospital corners. "I just knew."

Swinging my legs over the side of the bed, I sat up. "No, Mom, I mean did you hear bells? Or violins? Or did you feel dizzy or anything?"

My mother laughed. Annoyed, I stood and cried, "Come on, tell me how you knew."

She wrestled a pillow into a fresh slip. "Honey, when you love someone, you'll just know."

I sighed, rolled my eyes, and fell backward onto my bed, staring at the ceiling in frustration. I couldn't believe my mother. Why was she giving me these cryptic answers?

With a quick flick of her wrist, she snapped the bedspread

into the air. It billowed over the mattress like a parachute and slowly settled on top of the blankets. After tucking it in place, she walked to my bed, leaned over and stared down into my face. "The only other thing I can tell you, Sweetheart, is: If you have to ask if it's love—it's not."

Oh, great. That's a big help, I thought. Usually my mother issued simple, direct commands like "Clean your room," "Hang up your coat," or "Get off the phone." Suddenly, she was speaking in riddles like some Zen master. She grabbed the laundry basket and headed across the hall toward my brothers' room.

I closed my eyes and steeped in adolescent impatience, while the words, "You'll just know," repeated in my mind like the refrain of an annoying song. *She's wrong,* I thought. *There has to be something concrete, something definite, a tangible sign. When you're in love, there must be some telltale clue or identifying mark. A special alignment of heavenly bodies would do nicely,* I thought. *Or birds and butterflies flitting around your head like Disney's* Snow White *had would be fine, too. There just has to be some indication that you have passed beyond the veil to the other side where people in love reside.* Heck, I would have even settled for something as corny as a gleam in the eye.

So with the words "You'll just know" as my only weapon, I ventured out into the world of love. Fortunately, my teenage romances never progressed past the point where I cared whether or not if it was love. Even with my lack of experience in affairs of the heart, I recognized my adolescent liaisons as nothing more than crushes, passing fancies or just the need for a warm male body to escort me to a dance.

With the onset of my twenties, however, romance became a much more serious subject. The stakes were higher. Bet on the wrong man, never see the winner's circle. Already I had friends whose marriages had just left the starting gate and were pulling up lame. Cautious,

I planned to thoroughly study the field before I placed my wager.

It was with this mind-set that I accepted a blind date with an older man named Ed. He was twenty-five, a full five years older than I—positively middle-aged. He had graduated from college, had worked for three years and had his own apartment. In my mind, I envisioned a tuxedo-clad Dean Martin in a penthouse swilling a martini. All the men I had ever dated were still in school. This was a breed I had never encountered before. He could be a serious prospect; I would scrutinize him carefully.

On a chilly November night, the bell rang, and I opened the door to find Ed's warm, handsome face smiling at me. He wore a corduroy jacket, striped pullover sweater, jeans and suede shoes—not a tuxedo. I breathed a sigh of relief.

During our first few dates, I learned he preferred beer to martinis, only wore tuxedos when in a wedding and shared an apartment with a friend. The apartment was not a penthouse by any stretch. His couch, missing a leg, had been propped up with a brick, and his wall decorations consisted of a Steelers calendar and a dime-store rendition of the *Mona Lisa* in a gold plastic frame. It hung over the toilet; at least he had an appreciation for the arts.

Ed was kind and decent and, unlike other blind dates that I had gone out with, not in rehab, on lithium or out on parole.

We were quite compatible, and a great friendship blossomed that soon deepened into something more. But what was that something more? Was it merely affection? Was it love? I respected and admired Ed. But then again, I respected and admired the Pope, and I certainly had no interest in him as a future mate.

Throughout the next few months, that question, How do you know if it's love? nagged me. Taking refuge in

Alexander Pope's famous words, "Fools rush in where angels fear to tread," I spent most of that winter hanging back with the heavenly host awaiting "the sign" that it was okay for me to rush in.

Near Valentine's Day, Ed and I were invited to a party. A heavy snowfall forced me, a fashion-conscious female, to do something unthinkable—wear snow boots. We skidded in his green Toyota over slick roads and trudged through snow drifts to get to the party.

When we arrived, Ed took our coats and left to add them to the mountain piled on the host's bed, while I took off my boots. Or I should say tried to take off my boots. Clinging to the wall for balance, I stepped on the heel of my boot with the toe of my other foot. The boots wouldn't budge. I tried bending over to pull them off, but my dress was too tight. So I alternated, back and forth, between feet, stepping on the heels like I was doing some sort of strange folk dance.

Ed came back and saw me struggling. "Here," he said, grabbing my hand and leading me to a nearby chair, "let me help you." And then he knelt down before me, and I watched this kind, sweet man pull and tug and nearly sail across the room as my boot came flying off. As he dusted himself off and knelt to pull the other boot off, he laughed and looked up into my eyes.

And then I knew.

No pixie dust fell, no violins played, no fireworks exploded. But I knew right then and there that it was love. Love!

All along, I expected to find love's signs in the spectacular and extraordinary. But I never found them in dozens of roses, heart-shaped boxes of candies or flowery lyrics of sonnets. For me, love slipped into my heart, without notice, without fanfare, without ceremony, and it quietly set up housekeeping only to reveal its presence in a common, simple kindness.

How do you know if it's love? As my mother said, "You'll just know."

Janice Lane Palko

An Educated Woman

My grandfather, Stavros Economy, had come to America from Greece at the turn of the century seeking to make a better life for himself. Rather than settling on the East Coast, as so many other Greeks had done, Stavros heard that men were being hired to work on building the railroad network in the West. So he headed off to the desolate, arid country around Rock Springs, Wyoming, to eke out a living through backbreaking labor.

With money in the bank, the time finally came for Stavros to get out of Rock Springs and settle down. He headed to Chicago and told relatives there that he was looking for a wife. An arranged marriage was a common custom among immigrants, who learned to love each other later. "What kind of woman do you want?" asked his cousin George.

"A woman from a good Greek family," he said. "And someone who is educated." Stavros had taught himself how to read and write English. He loved the opera and studied the great Greek poets and philosophers: Homer, Plato and Socrates. He wanted a wife with whom he could share his love of learning.

"I think I know just the woman," said George. "She is the youngest daughter of the Mallieris family. Her name is Stavroula. She is very beautiful, and I am sure she is quite well-educated." And so, a date was set to introduce the two.

Stavroula sat in the chair in the parlor wearing her Sunday finest. Her father was very anxious to marry her off. After all, he had four daughters to support. "Here," he said, handing her a newspaper. "He wants an educated woman. Read this when he comes through the door."

"But Papa, you know I can't read!" Stavroula cried.

"Don't worry," he said confidently, "God will take care of the situation."

After the introductions with Stavroula's parents, Stavros approached the parlor to meet his prospective fiancée. He stood up straight, twirled the ends of his large handlebar moustache, smoothed out the lapel of his pin-striped suit and walked purposefully into the room.

The sight he beheld was more beautiful than he could have imagined. There sat an angel. Stavroula had a milky white complexion and delicate features. Long, thin fingers, a perfect little nose and plump, full lips. With her wavy blond hair, she almost didn't look Greek. Blue eyes, like a clear summer sky, peered over the top of the newspaper at him.

Completely mesmerized, Stavros knew he would have to look no further. Stavroula would be his bride. She was beautiful *and* educated. They would marry, move to Colorado and start a family—the first Greek family in Denver.

He bowed to greet her, taking her small, soft hand in his. He never noticed that the newspaper she held was upside-down.

Christine E. Belleris

Love at First Bite

Romance is like baking cookies. You start with rich ingredients, mix them together and apply heat. The result is love at first bite.

Christine Harris was a flight attendant for TWA in New York, who was perhaps much more famous for her ability to create beautiful embroidery on shirts and jeans than for her ability to make chocolate chip cookies. She learned to make those cookies from her mother, Ruth Harris, who held cooking school in her kitchen for all the neighborhood kids. She was known as "The Chocolate Chip Cookie Mom."

Wally "Famous" Amos was a talent agent living in Los Angeles, twenty-five hundred miles away from Christine. In his work he booked such talents as Paul Simon, Art Garfunkel and Dionne Warwick. He, too, was just a boy when he learned to make chocolate chip cookies from his Aunt Della, a happy woman, so full of love and goodness that her cookies became the symbol of love to Wally. During a low time in his life, he started making Aunt Della's chocolate chip cookies to lift his spirits, and he gave them away as a kind of calling card.

Christine regularly flew back and forth between L.A.

and New York, and it was a coworker who put her in touch with Wally. "There's this guy selling chocolate chip cookies at Bloomingdale's," she said. "They're not as good as yours, but you should check them out."

The very next day Christine was working first-class on a flight from New York to L.A. when Wally himself boarded the plane. He smiled at Christine with his million-dollar smile. Six-feet-one and dressed in a smart business suit, he looked like a prince. He handed her an armload of his cookies.

"Here," he said, "share these with the crew."

Wally had just settled into his seat when another flight attendant stopped to chat with him. She pointed to Christine and said, "You know, you ought to talk to Christine about embroidering some cookies on your jacket. She could make you look fabulous! And, by the way, she makes terrific chocolate chip cookies!"

Wally and Christine talked in front of the L.A. airport and exchanged cards. Wally couldn't take his eyes off her as he spoke. "You should stop by my store in Hollywood," he sang out in his musical voice. "Maybe we could share some cookies and milk."

Christine laughed. "Sure." And, eyeing his jacket, she replied, "Maybe I can embroider a jacket for you."

And that was the extent of their friendship until three months later.

She was in New York when the phone rang. It was Wally. "Christine? I was just thinking maybe you would like to go to dinner with me?"

"Yes! Yes, I would like that very much."

When Christine hung up the phone, she got out her cooking utensils. "This would be the perfect time to offer him some really great chocolate chip cookies."

She whipped up a batch, picked up a bottle of champagne and drove to his hotel.

"Welcome to New York," she said, smiling, as Wally got into the car, but something in her voice was saying, "Welcome to my heart."

Maybe it was the milk and cookies or maybe the champagne or perhaps the funny faces Christine put on the cookies. Whatever it was, the evening was made in heaven.

It wasn't long before Christine and Wally were together so much that Christine had to take leave of her job to travel with him, promoting his cookies as if they were her own. She was helping to make him "famous." And together they were happy.

At Christine's suggestion, Wally shed his business-suit image in favor of Hawaiian shirts and Panama hats, embroidered with her colorful one-of-a-kind rainbows, hearts or suns. Even his socks and shoes bore her creative touch.

An artist at heart, Christine enjoyed giving Wally a sunny personality through his bright clothing, and she added her touch to those chocolate chip cookies as well. She created cookie characters, boy and girl cookies called "Chip and Cookie." She put them on a T-shirt that said "Love at First Bite."

The cookie business boomed, and they moved to Hawaii in 1978. When they married in 1979, the wedding announcement read, "Once upon a time there was this handsome chocolate chip—who met up with this cute little cookie. . . ."

And the rest is cookie history.

Christine Harris-Amos
As told to Cliff Marsh

A Chance of a Lifetime

Twenty years from now you will be more disappointed by the things that you didn't do than by the ones you did do. So throw off the bowlines. Sail away from the safe harbor. Catch the trade winds in your sails. Explore. Dream. Discover.

Mark Twain

"This is a chance of a lifetime," I declared to my friend Stacy as I locked the door of my office and left the restaurant I managed. "It's every twenty-seven-year-old woman's dream to live in New York City, and in a few months I'll know if I get the transfer."

I watched the moonlight glisten on the waters of Laguna Beach. "I'll miss it here, but living in the Big Apple is everything I've ever wanted—a dream come true."

We met a group of our friends at a local café, and I jabbered on about the possibility of my move. Laughter erupted from a nearby table. I watched as a handsome man captured the attention of his friends with his engaging story. His broad, warm smile and air of confidence held me in a trance.

Stacy nudged me. "You're staring, Michelle, and about to drool."

"Wow," I whispered. I watched the gorgeous guy push up the sleeves of his bulky sweater. Everyone at his table had their eyes fixed on him. "That's the man I want to marry."

"Yeah, right," Stacy droned. "Tell us more about where you'd like to live in New York, because we all plan to visit you there when you land this job."

As I spoke my gaze drifted back to the debonair man.

Three months later my friends and I gathered at the same restaurant. "To life in the Big Apple!" they cheered as we tapped our glasses together.

"My chance of a lifetime!" We talked for hours. I told them of my plan to save money by moving out of my beach cottage and renting a room for the few remaining months.

Our friend offered, "I have a fellow South African friend who is considering renting one of the four bedrooms in his house. His name is Barry. A great guy." He scribbled on a napkin. "This is his number. He's a forty-two-year-old confirmed bachelor. Says he's much too busy being a single dad to be a husband."

I made an appointment to see the room the same day. I approached the entrance of the spacious house, and the door opened. "You must be Michelle," he said. He pushed up the sleeves of his bulky sweater and flashed his handsome smile. It was the man from the restaurant months before—the man I wanted to marry.

I stood staring, my mouth gaping, hoping I wasn't drooling.

"You are Michelle, aren't you?" he said, coaxing me out of my trance. "Would you like to see the room?"

I followed him through a tour of the house, then accepted when he offered me a cup of tea. Barry had a sophisticated kindness about him and listened attentively as I chattered nervously about myself. His silver-rimmed glasses accented a few gray streaks in his dark hair. Soon, his warm, inviting smile put me at ease, and we spent the next two hours talking casually. Ultimately, I decided not to take the room and reluctantly bade him good-bye.

The months went by quickly while I busied myself with preparation for the move. I thought of Barry often, but couldn't consider calling him.

"I'm moving to New York in three weeks," I said to Stacy as we walked out of my office and into the dining area. "As much as I'd like to see him again, it would only complicate my life."

"Well, brace yourself for complications," Stacy muttered, then nodded toward the door.

Barry, with his big blue eyes and engaging smile, walked into my restaurant.

"Hello," he said softly. "Do you have time to join me for a cup of coffee?"

"Of course." I tried not to gasp.

We slid into a booth and our conversation picked up where it left off before. He, too, was making a career change and was moving back to South Africa. His departure date was one week before mine. Now I knew I had to calm my pounding heart. We obviously had no future together. He took my phone number and invited me to dinner sometime. I accepted, suppressing my sadness, knowing I would be leaving in two short weeks and the date would probably never happen.

But it did. He picked me up a few days later for a movie and dinner. We talked for hours about our lives, our hopes, our separate dreams—mine in New York, his in South Africa. Never had I spoken so freely, so comfortably, with a man. He reached across the table and took my hand. I thought I saw in his eyes the same love I felt swelling in my heart. He said, "I'm just sorry I met you only one week before I leave."

"We still have seven days," I said meekly.

"Then let's make the most of it." He helped me on with my sweater. Hand in hand, we strolled to the car and made plans for the next day and the next and the next. As he drove me home, Tracy Chapman sang, "Give me one reason to stay, and I'll turn right back around." Was his heart singing along like mine?

We spent part of every day together for the next week. I knew I was falling in love, but dared not speak it. I couldn't upset our chances for a lifetime.

"And I know he loves me, too," I moaned to Stacy over a cup of coffee in my near-empty restaurant. "We've even talked about trying to get together over holidays. He's meeting me here soon to bring me a gift to remember him by."

Just then, Barry strolled in. I stood to welcome his arms around me. We sat, sipping our coffee. "I will miss you so much," he said softly. "But I know you'll think of me whenever you hear this." He placed a Tracy Chapman CD on the table in front of me. Then he pointed to the song title, *Just Give Me One Reason.* "We can listen to the same music and remember each other."

I gulped my coffee to wash away the lump in my throat. "I'll never forget you, Barry. Ever."

"Oh, and one more thing to remember me by." He set a small box on top of the CD. The same awe I felt at our first meeting paralyzed me now. The love I saw in his eyes as we gazed across the table was gift enough for a lifetime. Finally I reached for the box and opened it slowly.

A diamond ring.

"Michelle, I have loved you from the first moment I saw you. On our first date, even before we had coffee, I knew you were the woman I was going to marry. I woke up this morning, desperate, thinking, it's May 3! In three days I'll lose my angel. Sure, my career in South Africa is a chance in a lifetime, but *you,* Michelle, are my dream come true. Please marry me."

"Yes, Barry, yes," I cried.

"I know what moving to New York means to you, but will you come with me to South Africa? I believe with all my heart, Michelle, that we were brought together on purpose. Nothing in my life is going as I planned it, but I know it's all a part of a bigger plan." Barry chuckled. "God has a great sense of humor, but a poor sense of timing."

Exactly one year later, on May 3, we were married under an African sky. Our dream come true. Our chance of a lifetime.

Michelle Wolins
As told to LeAnn Thieman

"Could you be more specific regarding the benefits program?"

liked to talk. There was talk I'd end up an old maid. We took that kind of thing seriously. I didn't say anything. I kept going out with him, but something stopped me from getting engaged. He wasn't the one. My mother was worried about me. I wasn't worried. I knew that there was someone, somewhere. I wasn't ready to settle."

She squeezed my hand.

"So, then I met your grandfather. He saw me out walking with my friends and found—who knows how—that he knew my cousin. In a few days, he managed to come calling with my cousin. I never saw the other man again.

"Six weeks later your grandpa proposed." She started laughing until tears gathered in her eyes. "He said he needed a wife to manage his money. He didn't have two dimes to rub together."

"Did you know that before you married him?" I asked, thinking of the tales I had heard about her well-off parents.

"Of course I knew that. I also knew he was the one I had waited for," she said. She looked at our faces in the ornately framed mirror. In my face she saw the young woman she had been; in her face I saw my future. I kissed Grandma's cheek, knowing I would never settle. I would wait for the right one, and now I was certain I would know him when I saw him.

Diane Goldberg

4

MAKING A DIFFERENCE

Life is not a "brief candle." It is a splendid torch that I want to make burn as brightly as possible before handing it on to future generations.

George Bernard Shaw

Mrs. Grodefsky

If the world seems cold to you, kindle fires to warm it.

Source Unknown

If anything in our immediate neighborhood ever happened, you could find out instantly from Mrs. Grodefsky, the lady who ran the corner candy store. Her husband had passed away shortly after they had opened the store, and she didn't have any children of her own, so she stood in that store from morning till night. It was her life, and the people from the neighborhood who passed in and out of the shop were her family.

Mrs. Grodefsky was the "News Bulletin" of our day—a walking newspaper. All she did was work behind the counter making up sodas. But in those years, no one in our neighborhood had a telephone except the corner candy store. So, if Mrs. Silverman got a phone call at the candy store and a doctor told her that her tests were positive, she would gasp, "Oy, doctor, that's wonderful. My husband will be so happy!" And Grodefsky would know a baby was on the way. If Selma Lieberman's boyfriend proposed over the telephone, when she left the booth, she would hug and kiss Mrs. Grodefsky.

How did Grodefsky relay these instant "bulletins" to the neighborhood in general? Simple! If someone gave birth, she would hang a little rubber doll in the store window. If someone got engaged, two huge boxes of chocolates went into the window with a sign that read "Mazel Tov!" Everybody in the neighborhood knew her signals.

Saturday night at the corner candy store was a must. We youngsters stood in front of the store from seven o'clock on, waiting for the "date" calls to come in. When a call came in, Mrs. Grodefsky would motion to one of us, give us the building address, and say, "Call Sarah Goldberg—it's her boyfriend—ah date—good for ah nickel tip. Yell loud!"

We would run to the designated house, stand in the hall, and bellow, "Sarah Goldberg! Telephone! It's your boyfriend! You're all set for tonight!" Sarah would come charging down the stairs all smiles, press a nickel or a dime—sometimes even a quarter—into our outstretched palm, and race for the candy store.

It was good business for Mrs. Grodefsky, too. If the boy didn't stop by for a box of candy, the next time he called we'd get orders to call his date to the phone "softly." If we got no answer, Grodefsky would say to the caller, "Her date from last week must have taken her out already. He bought a big box of candy for her. Listen, where were you? I had a box waiting for you!" The caller got the message—and the candy the following week—and the girl got her calls.

When the army years came upon us, Mrs. Grodefsky changed her window. She put up a big piece of cardboard and very neatly wrote on top of it in colored crayons, "Serving Our Country." Underneath she pasted the pictures of the fellows who went into the service. All the guys in the neighborhood sent her pictures wherever they were in the world. In fact, many of them put her name and address down on the army papers where it asked who to notify in the event of an emergency. They knew Mrs. Grodefsky was the one to break the news to the parents if there were ever an emergency.

Whenever a kid on the block was reported missing in action, Mrs. Grodefsky saw the Western Union boy pull up on his bike in front of the house across the street from her store. In those years, when you saw a Western Union boy, you knew it was bad news. So Mrs. Grodefsky would close the store and go up to the apartment where the telegram had been delivered. From the screams she heard in the hall, she knew already what the telegram contained. That night, the picture of the boy that hung with the others in her window would be bordered in black crayon. Within a very short period of time, the piece of cardboard that stood in her window had eight black-bordered pictures.

As each kid was reported missing, she literally sat *shiva,* the Jewish mourning ritual, for each one. They were her children! Every one! In fact, the kids often told her things they couldn't tell their own parents. She wrote to each one in her own inimitable style and always enclosed a stick of Wrigley's chewing gum so that the kids would remember the old candy store on the corner.

After the war was over, Mrs. Grodefsky took the cardboard out of her window and carefully took off the pictures of the boys who were lost in the war. She made up another cardboard and put a black border around it. She placed the eight pictures of the boys who were lost in the center, and every night for as long as I can remember, she lit a *Yahrzeit* memorial candle and placed it in front of the cardboard. It was her Eternal Light for "her boys."

The old lady kept that candy store for years, even after most of the people in the old neighborhood moved out.

The Puerto Rican youngsters who moved into the community continued to be "her boys." They loved that old woman.

When she passed away, I think it was the only time in history that more Puerto Ricans than Jews went to our old temple. They all went to pay tribute to that dear woman. Although she had no immediate family, at least a thousand people filled the streets as the hearse carried her to her final resting place.

Some who received word of her passing got together a short time ago and paid for perpetual care for her grave and placed a rather novel headstone on it. It had a *Yahrzeit* candle, just like the one she had lit in her window every night, carved into the stone. Underneath it simply said, "With her boys again."

I guess every neighborhood needs a Mrs. Grodefsky—someone who mothers the whole community. Someone to hold a nervous hand, caress a tortured soul or soothe a broken heart.

Arnold Fine

One Day at a Time

Kindness gives birth to kindness.

Sophocles

At some point in our lives we all go through a dark night of the soul, when our lives seem barren and pointless and painful. My dark night came in the aftermath of my divorce, and I felt it most keenly on the eve of my brother's wedding. It was the first wedding I had attended since the divorce.

While I felt proud of my brother and happy for this new step in his life, I felt the emptiness of my own. That night, as I tossed and turned in my bed in the hotel, I was assailed by so many griefs: broken dreams, the raw fear that I might never have children, and the coolness of family and friends who, while sympathizing with me, pulled their own families closer, as if divorce might be an infectious disease. I prayed, begged and cried, not understanding why I had to go through all this. Loneliness loomed before me, and I wondered if my prayers reached heaven at all.

After the wedding I returned to my job in Norristown, Pennsylvania, knowing that I had to take my life in hand.

I'd been renting a room from a very kind lady but wanted and needed my own kitchen, a place for my books, and maybe even a pet to share those lonely nights. I was tired of eating all my meals alone in diners or in my car. I might not have love in my life, but surely I could find a small place to call home.

Apartments were beyond my means, but I found a trailer—a dirty trailer—in a rundown park. With careful budgeting, I could afford it. I scrubbed from floor to ceiling, and beneath the grime and the trash I found the basis for a home. I sewed curtains from remnants and repaired the few pieces of broken furniture left by the previous owner. I bought a desk from a secondhand shop.

Wild roses, unplanned saplings and hedges long out of control bordered the overgrown yard. I clipped, mowed and weeded. Then one day, while planting mums, I looked up to find a dirty and ragged young boy in front of me.

"You live here, lady?" he asked. Before I could answer, another child ran up to us. There were more questions. Then more children emerged seemingly from nowhere. Soon an entire crowd—I counted fourteen children in all—gathered round me, all excitedly asking questions.

I soon learned that in that neighborhood, young children grew as wild and in some cases as neglected as the hedges I'd just pruned. But beneath dirty faces and stringy hair they grew far more lovely. And hungry. Hungry for food, warm clothes, shoes, guidance, attention and affection.

I could not supply all their needs but by the grace of God I did what I could. I bought flour in bulk and baked bread. The fragrance, steaming through open windows, drew them to my door. In exchange, while perched on kitchen counters or sitting cross-legged in my bay window, they colored bright pictures to decorate my refrigerator.

A few of the children could read, but they had no books. So I purchased a small bookcase from the second-hand shop and scoured flea markets and yard sales for children's books. Together we set up a lending library in my kitchen. The children loved writing their names on "library cards" and marching out my door, two or three books tucked under their arm.

We read by the hour together, refreshing ourselves with warm bread and cold milk. We talked about school, reading, God, death, divorce and prison—all things that concerned them and their families.

I learned that my life was not so hard after all, and it was no longer so lonely. At times my young community drained my finances and energies to the point of exhaustion. Often the children's parents took advantage of my generosity. But on snowy, icy days I sometimes found a path shoveled to my mailbox, or the windshield of my car scraped clean. And as long as I had childish arms around my neck and laughter in my home, I didn't worry. I had gained the shining light of trust from children's eyes and was able to share my great love of books and reading with the most appreciative audience in the world.

I didn't know then that one day I would find love and give birth to my own precious children, or that I would eventually become a school librarian and a lifetime writer of stories. But I didn't need to know. I needed only to do what was before me, extending my hand one day at a time. And gradually, that dark night of the soul passed. My prayers in that lonely hotel room had been heard after all, and I had been blessed many times over.

Cathy Gohlke

Can You Love Me?

The more faithfully you listen to the voice within you, the better you hear what is sounding outside of you.

Dag Hammarskjöld

The girl's image on the television flickered in front of me like a ghost, demanding my attention. "I need a mom who can help me become a young woman," the twelve-year-old on the television screen was saying. I was watching a segment called "California's Waiting Children," a show that interviewed older foster children who wanted to be adopted. I didn't know if I felt sorrier for myself or her. She was motherless, and I was childless, but I couldn't make the match for her.

I would be facing motherhood as a single woman, so I wanted to start with a clean slate, a new and innocent baby who could gently ease me into the trials and joys of parenting. That child on television, well, she'd already been through so many problems, I knew I couldn't handle caring for her alone.

Something in the girl's voice, though, made me stop

mid-chew. "I need a mom," she emphasized, staring not at the camera but at me. I looked in her eyes and was stung by her honesty. She knew no one wanted to adopt a preteen with a troubled past, a child who had problems far beyond those of a typical girl's. Yet she raised her voice in a challenge: I need you. Can you love me?

I sat straight in my chair and reached for the phone. I wanted to love her. Would that be enough? I took a deep breath and vowed to try. I dialed the number shown on the screen and surrendered myself to adoption: the red tape, the social workers' scrutiny, the endless waiting, and the uncertainty of whether I could love such a child, and whether the child could love me. The process took months, and by the time I'd fulfilled all the requirements, the girl I had seen that Thursday evening had already been adopted.

The call I finally got was for a boy, a much younger child, but his past. . . .

"Michael's not easy," the social worker warned. "His mother was a drug addict." She was calling from the hospital, where Michael had been admitted with a broken leg. "We think his foster mother is the one who broke his leg," she said. "He won't be going back to that home."

The next morning, I stood outside his hospital room, eyeing him. He was only four, with unkempt hair and a wary, world-worn gaze. His broken leg was balanced above him in traction. "Who's she?" he asked the social worker when he spotted me. I stepped back a little. Several months ago, I had vowed to love a child, but what if this child hated me? What if I discovered he was too difficult, that I couldn't love him?

"My name is Pam," I said, summoning my courage. "I've come to visit you for awhile. Would that be okay?"

I waited for a brusque answer, a suspicious glare at yet another adult drifting in and out of his life. To my shock,

Michael nodded his head eagerly. He was so excited he couldn't talk. We spent that morning and several others during the following week coloring, playing games, singing, talking. When the doctor came to put on his cast, Michael tearfully begged me—a stranger—to stay with him. He didn't know me, but he knew he needed me, and because of that, it was easy to give him my love.

Ultimately, it wasn't Michael I was able to adopt but his own younger brother and sister. The girl, my daughter, was born addicted to heroin; both she and her brother require medication just to behave normally; and they have seen more grief than someone three times their age. My house is loud and chaotic, my days exhausting and demanding. Sometimes I think maybe I can't make it alone.

Recently, though, the kids spent the night with a friend, and I faced something I hadn't in a long time: a quiet evening alone. As I savored a moment of peace, curled up on the sofa watching television, I smiled. Not long ago, a brave young girl on that television screen spoke for herself and thousands of other children like her. She asked me to meet the challenge of mothering, and I had been afraid I couldn't handle the pressure. Now, the house was so quiet I wanted to scream!

My kids are demanding, and I'm proud of it. They will get right in your face, screaming in frustration, then turn around and cling to you, arms squeezing the breath out of you. "I need you," they're saying. "Can you love me?" And I answer with satisfaction, "Yes, I love you."

Pamela J. Chandler

Christmas Is Coming!

I sat on the floor near Jeremy, my three-year-old, and handed him assorted ornaments to put on the Christmas tree. He stood on a holiday popcorn can to reach the middle section of the tree, which was as high as he could reach. He giggled with a child's pure delight every time I said, "Christmas is coming!" Although I had tried many times to explain Christmas to him, Jeremy believed that Christmas was a person. "Christmas is coming!" he would giggle. "And all of these presents are for Christmas when she comes!"

I was sitting back, watching him smiling to himself as he carefully placed each ornament on the tree. *Surely he can't know enough about Christmas to love it this much,* I thought.

We lived in a small apartment in San Francisco. Although the weather was usually mild, this Christmas season it was chilly enough for us to need a fire. On Christmas Eve I threw in a starter log and watched my son sliding around the apartment, sock-footed on hardwood floors. He was anxiously awaiting Christmas. Soon he couldn't stand it any longer and began jumping up and down. "When will she be here, Mommy? I can't wait to give her all these presents!"

Again I tried to explain it to him. "You know, Jeremy, Christmas is a time of year, not a person, and it will be here sooner than you know. At twelve o'clock, Christmas will be here but you will probably be sleeping, so when you wake up in the morning it will be Christmas."

He laughed as if I was telling a silly joke. "Mommy," he said, "will Christmas eat breakfast with us?" He spread out his arms over the gifts under the tree. "All of these presents are for Christmas! All of them!"

I tickled his belly and laughed with him. "Yes," I said. "They are all for Christmas!"

He scampered about the apartment until fatigue slowed him down and he lay on the rug by the tree. I curled up next to him and when he finally fell asleep I carried him into his bed.

I decided on a hot chocolate before bed and as I drank it I sat near the window looking down on the decorated streets of San Francisco. It was a beautiful scene. But there was one thing that disturbed me. Directly outside our apartment, in the spot where I usually left the garbage, was what looked like a crumpled heap of old clothes. But I soon realized what the heap really was. It was an old homeless woman who usually hung out near the corner store down the street. She was a familiar sight in the neighborhood, and I had tossed a few coins into her bag a few times after shopping at the grocery. She never asked for money, but I think she got quite a few handouts from passersby because she looked so helpless.

As I looked out on this Christmas Eve, I wondered about this poor old woman. Who was she? What was her story? *She should be with family, not sleeping in the cold street at this special time of year.*

I felt a sinking feeling inside. Here I was, with a beautiful child sleeping in the next room. I had often felt sorry for myself as a single mom, but at least I wasn't alone and living on the streets. How hopeless and sad that would be for anyone, let alone a woman who must be about eighty years old.

I went to my front door and walked down the steps to the street. I asked the old woman if she would like to come inside. At first, she hardly acknowledged me. I tried to coax her; she said she didn't want my help. But when I said I could use a little company, she relented and agreed to spend Christmas with Jeremy and me.

I arranged for her to sleep in the living room on our foldout couch. The next morning, I was awakened by Jeremy yelling at the top of his lungs. "Christmas is here! Christmas is here, Mommy!"

I quickly pulled on my robe and hurried to the living room, where I found a very excited little boy presenting a very surprised "Christmas" with gifts from under the tree. "We've been waiting for you!" he shouted joyfully. He giggled and danced around as she opened the presents he had given her.

I don't think "Christmas" had known a Christmas like this for a very long time. And neither had I. I also knew that it would have taken more than just one special day to lift the burden from that old lady's weary heart, but I was thrilled when she promised to come back the following year. I hope she will. And Jeremy knows she will.

Deb Gatlin Towney

Mama's Heart

I am beginning to learn that it is the sweet, simple things of life which are the real ones after all.

Laura Ingalls Wilder

Every Tuesday and Friday, my best friend Marilyn and I went to the foundling home behind the hospital. It was our volunteer job to help the three regular nurses change, feed and care for about twenty babies waiting for adoption.

We loved our job and constantly dreamed about adopting one of these babies. We each had our special favorites. But we were only eighteen, so it wasn't part of our immediate plans.

As we changed into our volunteer uniforms, I looked at our mirror reflections and thought how lucky Marilyn was. She had inherited all her mother's beautiful attributes and was so pretty. My mom was beautiful, too, but my brother had her dainty features, fair skin, curly hair and outgoing personality.

Everyone said that I looked exactly like my dad. I had his darker complexion, long nose, stringy horse's-tail hair, even his grainy voice and quiet, reflective manner. Dad was a handsome man, but his features on me fell far short of beautiful.

Mama was an absolute dynamo: a hospital volunteer, spotless housekeeper and neighborhood guardian angel, always helping someone. She'd rush out the door with a steaming casserole for a sick neighbor or fill grocery bags for a family temporarily out of work. She'd help toddlers into their "jammies" when they were our houseguests while their mamas were having babies at the hospital.

Her charity didn't end there. She rescued lost pets, kept them with our own until their owners were found and nursed injured hit-and-run wild creatures until they recovered. Her energy was endless.

One Friday, Marilyn and I arrived at the nursery, greeted all our precious babies, changed each one and began placing them on a mattress-covered floor with some toys. We worked together in our bed-stripping routine and fitted clean sheets on every crib.

The nurses seemed unusually preoccupied with a tiny baby in a cordoned-off area of the nursery.

"That baby's very sick," one of the nurses whispered. "Say a prayer . . . please. She may need surgery."

I said a quick prayer, but soon we were busy with our many duties: We helped prepare the bottles for the afternoon feeding and spooned warm baby food into tiny dishes for the older babies. After feeding, all the babies got clean outfits before being placed in their cribs for naps.

We used their nap time to clean up the nursery, sort and fold all the clean laundry, and fold dozens of cloth diapers. We normally would stay until everything was readied for the next feeding. Then we'd eat, change our clothes and our dates would pick us up at the nursery.

Suddenly, there was a flurry of activity in the corner.

Two doctors rushed out, and I heard one nurse crying softly. The head nurse hurried by.

"Hate to impose on you girls, but we're needed in the OR. The baby's going to surgery. Hold down the fort, okay?" She didn't wait for our response, and we were left alone.

"I'm only staying until Bruce comes," Marilyn wailed. "I know him. He'll go to the dance without me. I'm not letting one of those vampires get their clutches on my boyfriend."

Bruce arrived as we were preparing dinner for the babies.

"Call someone!" Marilyn shouted, and she took Bruce's arm and whisked him out the door, leaving me alone.

I was warming bottles when I felt a hand on my shoulder. It was Nick, my steady boyfriend.

"Where is everyone?" he asked, glancing around.

He blotted my tears as I recounted the predicament.

"Please, go to the dance without me. All the babies are hungry and I can't leave them. I really have to stay."

"Where do I wash up?" Nick asked, removing his football jacket. "I've never dropped a football, so a baby should be perfectly safe in these hands."

"Thanks," I whispered, hugging him.

"Can't dance without my favorite partner. No one else's toes could take such punishment," he said, laughing.

Soon, we were seated on the mattress-padded floor, surrounded by babies holding their own bottles, while we fed and burped the tiny ones. Nick paused for a moment to watch me rock and soothe a fussy infant.

"I know Marilyn is your best friend," he said quietly, "and you think she's so beautiful. But you have the best beauty of all," he said, kissing my cheek. "You have a pure and gentle heart. That's why I love you so," he whispered.

It suddenly occurred to me: Mama had given her good looks to my brother, but she had given her most precious gift to me.

Toni Fulco

The Angel at the Bank

Life's most urgent question is: What are you doing for others?

Martin Luther King Jr.

Some years ago on the Lower East Side of New York City there was a little *shteibel* (a small house of worship). If ten men gathered for prayer, it was standing room only. (It used to be a locksmith's store; really, how much room does a locksmith need to make keys?)

The old locksmith's store had stood vacant for many years, until Rabbi Seigel moved into the neighborhood and asked the landlord if he could use the empty store for his people and their religious services. He promised he would vacate as soon as the landlord found a tenant. The landlord, Morris Rabinowitz, realized the Jewish community in his neighborhood needed a place to pray, but these were the Depression years, and the congregation certainly could not raise enough money to rent even such a small store.

But Rabinowitz was a good man, and he let the people use the store. "Until I get a tenant," he reminded them.

"Then I will have to ask you to leave. I have to make a living also."

And so for many more years, the store stayed unrented, and the congregation met there every morning and evening for their prayers.

Rabinowitz had a good soul, and he liked to help others. Unfortunately, the Depression years were not kind to Rabinowitz either. He lost most of his properties that he owned and had only a few left, including the little *shteibel.* He lived alone, on very little money.

One day the wife of an old friend came to Rabinowitz to explain that her son had been arrested and that she needed $300 immediately for a lawyer. Would he help? Rabinowitz went to the bank and asked for his bank balance from the young teller. He had $532. He withdrew $300 and took it to the woman. She blessed him and promised to pay it back as soon as she could. He smiled and said, "Listen, when you have it you'll give it to me. Not before!"

A few months later another friend approached Rabinowitz and asked if he could have $500 for his daughter's wedding. Rabinowitz told him he did not have that much money, but would gladly give what he did have. He hurried to the bank, made out a withdrawal slip, and handed it to the teller. "You're my favorite teller," he told the young girl. "You see, I really need $500 to help Rosen, but give me whatever I have left in my account," he said good-naturedly.

The young girl smiled back and said, "Mr. Rabinowitz, you have $5,532 in your account."

"That is impossible!" he exclaimed.

The girl rechecked his account and said, "No, I'm right. You have $5,532 in your account."

"Okay," Rabinowitz said. "In that case, give me the $500 Rosen needs for his daughter's wedding."

The teller handed him the money, and he left, still quite puzzled. As he walked along, he thought to himself, "Maybe the good Lord jimmied their books so I could have enough money to give Rosen. Who am I to question the Lord's ways?"

A few weeks later, the rabbi from the little *shteibel* came to Rabinowitz. "Morris," he said, "I know things haven't been too good for you lately, but we are in desperate need. You know the Goldbergs who live on the corner over the grocery store? Their child needs an operation immediately. Could you loan them about $5,000 to save their child's life?"

Rabinowitz sighed. "I don't have a full $5,000, but I'll give you whatever I have. Saving a child's life: What could be more important?"

Once more Rabinowitz went to the bank. He presented his favorite teller with a withdrawal slip to close out his account.

"You don't have to close out your account if you want $5,000, Mr. Rabinowitz," she told him. "You have $10,000 in that account."

"Ten thousand dollars! I haven't made a deposit in weeks!" Rabinowitz cried.

The girl rechecked and smiled. "You do have $10,000 in your account."

"Are you sure?" Rabinowitz asked. "Are you sure? I don't want the bank running after me for the money."

The girl checked again and even called the bank manager over. He confirmed that the account contained $10,000. The girl gave Rabinowitz a bank check for $5,000, and he took it to the *shteibel* and handed the check to the rabbi.

But Rabinowitz never said a word about how money seemed to grow in his bank account.

Some time later, an elderly woman came to Rabinowitz and told him her grandson wanted to be a doctor; she didn't have the money to send him to college, though.

Rabinowitz smiled. "Let me see what's happening with my account. If I have it, the money is yours."

He went to the bank, approached his favorite teller, and asked her to close out his account so he could give whatever was left in it for the old lady's grandson.

"Fine," the girl said. "Do you want the entire $25,000?"

"Twenty-five thousand!" he gasped. "That is impossible! I haven't been to the bank since the last time I drew out money!"

The girl called over the bank manager. He confirmed the account balance was correct. Rabinowitz withdrew $24,000 and promptly took it to the old lady. "I have $1,000 left," he told her. "Come back when you need more."

And so throughout his life, Rabinowitz—who had no family and had never married—continued performing small miracles for his friends in the community, giving what he had to others instead of himself. The years passed, and he became frail. The young boy whose way he had paid through medical school tended to him day and night. When Rabinowitz grew worse, the young girl whose dowry Rabinowitz paid nursed him. The young boy who had needed the life-saving operation was now a man, a wealthy banker who saw that Rabinowitz wanted for nothing.

The building that housed the *shteibel* was given over to the rabbi, who, with Rabinowitz's help, managed to raise enough money to turn the building into a beautiful synagogue where the faithful could pray each morning and night. So Rabinowitz's life came to an end.

And what of the mystery of the growing bank account?

The young girl who had been Rabinowitz's favorite teller was the daughter of a man who had once been in serious financial trouble. Rabinowitz had helped the man. By pure luck, this man, who was not Jewish, purchased an

Irish Sweepstakes ticket and won millions. He invested the money wisely and had more than he could ever need. When he realized his daughter intended to continue working at the bank where Rabinowitz's account was, he had an idea. He deposited $1 million in the bank with orders to his daughter to see to it that Rabinowitz's account was always full. And because Rabinowitz always went to the same teller, she was always able to see to it that the money was there for whatever he needed it for.

Rabinowitz passed away without ever knowing any of this, though, and till he died, he considered the sweet, young teller to be an angel in disguise, sent to bless a poor, lonely man as he blessed others.

Arnold Fine

5

SINGLE PARENTING

Trust yourself. You know more than you think you do.

Benjamin Spock, M.D.

"You have reached the Single Mom's Support Line.
If you'd like to speak with a counselor,
please press 1 with your nose."

Reprinted by permission of Randy Glasbergen.

Hands to Go 'Round

Our children were a handful to begin with. There were five of them, all home-schooled, each pursuing his or her talents through a sport and a musical activity. That's what Steve and I wanted for them. Our home was filled with soccer balls, gymnastic leotards and ballet shoes, while the air rang with piano, violin, viola and recorder music. The children and their activities kept both Steve's and my hands constantly busy, but we enjoyed the pace. We were fulfilled watching our children grow and develop into strong, intelligent, competent people.

Then Steve died. Being a single parent of five children between the ages of six and seventeen seemed a Herculean task. My two hands were all there were to take children to lessons, to applaud at recitals, to bandage scraped knees. I was overwhelmed by the ten young hands of my five children reaching out to me. They needed their father, but he was gone. They needed me, but I couldn't see how I could provide for all their needs.

Added to the stress of trying to be both father and mother were the mounting financial difficulties. The music lessons and sports cost money. I worked several small part-time jobs, and in between, I constantly chauffeured someone to some place. I began to feel that I was hardly ever there for my children. I began to feel lost—lost in my own neighborhood, in my own home, in my life.

I turned to Terri, my close friend, who had been a great source of strength and comfort at the time of my husband's illness and death. But Terri had her own family to take care of, and I found her unable to help me now. I compared her situation to my own. She also homeschooled her children. They were involved in sports and various activities. Yet her life seemed to flow so calmly and peacefully, while mine remained in tumultuous upheaval. What was the difference in our lives? Perhaps she held the secret to running a smooth life.

One evening, I sat alone in my living room with a pencil and sketchbook, trying to find a way beyond words to express my desperation and pain. First I drew Terri's "ideal" family, sketching two stick-figure boys reaching out for love, help and guidance. Surrounding them I drew their caring mother, their strong and supportive father, their grandmother, their aunt. I suddenly realized these children lived with four loving adults. They had but to reach out their hands and eight, strong supportive hands reached back. Was Terri's "secret" simply having plenty of loving hands, four for each boy?

Comparing my family to Terri's devastated me. Life did not seem fair. Worse, my children were beginning to feel like the adversaries—a burden I was breaking beneath. I felt more alone and despondent than ever.

The following evening my children and I were gathered around the table, finishing dinner. I began to talk about hands, how my hands were so busy: providing for them, helping them, and taking them to their many activities. I described their friends, Terri's family and how many hands of support her boys received

Then I reached out my two hands and asked each child

to take hold. Ten hands shot out across the table. Each child found just two fingers to grab. There were so many of them and only one of me. We sat transfixed in stunned silence, as I realized there was no way I could meet all their needs.

A small voice broke the silence. "Mommy, if we all reach out to each other, we could each get a whole hand."

Releasing my fingers, sisters and brothers reached out to one another. Each person clasped tightly to two other supportive and loving hands. We began to smile.

Our days are still filled with home-schooling, dance lessons, gymnastics, ball games, recitals, concerts and the like. I'm still a single parent of five active, intelligent children. But my children have had to grow just a little bit stronger. They don't reach out solely to Mom for help; they reach for each other, as well. I still have only two hands with ten fingers.

But with those ten extra hands, our family is now a circle of help and support. We have enough hands to go around.

Linda Butler

Take Heart, Mom

For everything you have missed, you have gained something else.

Ralph Waldo Emerson

Being a divorced and very young mother in the late 1950s was not something to be celebrated. People were quick to judge. Although outwardly I put on a brave front, I was deeply hurt by the lack of understanding and support of my peers and loved ones. The isolation and desperate poverty it created were unbearable, and drove me more than once to the brink of ending it all. Facing this new life of motherhood in a disapproving world was terrifying.

Against all odds, we two "little girls"—for I was hardly an adult myself—grew up together, often more like best friends than parent and child. There were a lot of close calls as I nursed my little one through pneumonia, measles, raging fevers and all the other childhood traumas. Often I did not have enough money to take her to the doctor.

It broke my heart and hers to leave her with strangers at preschool, but if I was going to support us I had no choice. I had never worked for money in my short life, even after school, so this was another scary first. To make things more difficult we had no car, so we walked everywhere. I would often carry Cathy long distances, until I could literally no longer lift her off the ground.

In the earliest days of our tiny family of two, there were desperate times when our meager diet consisted of splitting an eighteen-cent hamburger or a lone box of Bisquick made any one of 101 ways, from pancakes to gravy.

I made plenty of mistakes. I was so afraid I wouldn't do it right—that she would die, or end up hating me—but I tried to do the very best I knew. Of course I felt terribly guilty about not giving her a "real family" and pretty things.

Throughout all this hair-raising turmoil I was determined to be a good mother and fulfill my dreams, no matter that I had been written off by my family and friends as "the Little Miss Artist Black Sheep"—a hopeless case. So when little Cath was not yet two and I was still under twenty, I went back to school to finish my degree.

One day my child psychology professor announced a class experiment. We were to observe two very young children, one at a time. The parent would leave the room and would watch unseen through the tiny door window.

The first child would come from a two-parent, well-adjusted, loving home and family, with all the normal middle-class advantages. The second child would be from a single-parent home (then referred to as a broken home) lacking in all the desirable privileges.

On the basis of what we had read in our textbooks, the class was expecting that child number one would display a sense of security when the parent left, a cooperative independence in the presence of strangers and the unfamiliar environment and an easy welcome or neutral response when the parent returned.

The second child was expected to display insecurity, marked by clinging, fearful or destructive behavior and possibly withdrawal and tears.

We were all curious to see what would really happen. Child number one was brought in and the father left the room. The child immediately headed straight for our third-floor windows and tried to climb out. He fought anyone who tried to coax him back and turn his attention to more creative pursuits. He would have none of it! His entire visit was a disruptive ordeal. In fact, his father had to be summoned back early to save us all from chaos.

As child number two was left to the class's care, she walked straight to the board, picked up the chalk, climbed upon the professor's chair and began to chatter away in baby English. She proceeded with confidence to teach her class, drawing and pointing to the blackboard, then looking back to her rapt audience. After an extensive "lecture," the tiny professor climbed down and placed the chalk back in the trough. She then wandered about the room holding intimate conversations, while happily digging into the mysterious depths of the girls' purses and displaying "her" treasures all over the floor.

Finally, our frazzled professor, who had just returned from having to take his own son home, asked the virtually unmissed mother to come back into the room.

As I entered and sat in my seat, little Cathy looked up from her play and climbed onto my lap as if I'd never been gone. She gave me a big hug.

The class began to laugh in sheer joy and delight. They got to their feet and gave us an ovation. I broke down and cried. After all, we were the unfortunate, the underprivileged; I was the second-class citizen and she was the number-two child.

As a result of this experiment, my dark days as a lonely student were over. Little Cath and I were invited out to lunches and dinners and outings with these new friends and families.

Over the years we came a long way together, Cathy and I. And always there were new challenges. Many years later, in our comfortable California house in the pines, by the sea, Cathy was going through one of her difficult and lonely rites of passage as a teenager. I said to her, "You of all people in the world deserve the ideal family life, with two loving parents, brothers and sisters, the whole lovely dream. But it isn't that way for us. I am so sorry. I love you more than anything in the world and I am doing the very best I know. It's just you and me. When we accept it as it is, we can create a truly magical life, from who we are and with what we have."

Cathy looked deep into my eyes and said, "Take heart, Mom, you're the best."

Hugging, crying and laughing in our cozy kitchen, that night we had one of our many candlelight dinners together, just the two of us. After all, we're best friends.

Cielle Kollander
Submitted by Eileen Lawrence

A True Christmas

I plopped the last of the ready-made cookie dough onto the cookie sheet and shoved it into the oven. These standard-issue chocolate chip cookies would be a far cry from the bejeweled affairs I'd baked for the past twenty-six years, but the only reason I'd even summoned the effort was because my youngest son, Ross, had opened and re-opened the cookie jar four times the previous night, saying with fourteen-year-old tact, "What? No Christmas cookies this year?"

Since today was the twenty-third, and his older siblings, Patrick and Molly, would be arriving Christmas Eve, Ross informed me that they would be "big-time disappointed" if there wasn't "cool stuff" to eat. This from the same kid who had never watched a Christmas TV special in his life and who had to be dragged into the family photo for the annual Christmas card.

I never considered a family picture this year. A big piece of the family was now missing—or hadn't anybody noticed?

All my friends had been telling me the same thing since the day of the funeral: "Pam, the first year after you lose your husband is the hardest. You have to go through the first Valentine's Day without him, the first birthday, the first anniversary. . . ."

They hadn't been kidding. What they hadn't told me was that Christmas was going to top them all in hard-to-take. It wasn't that Tom had loved Christmas that much. He'd always complained that the whole thing was too commercial and that when you really thought about it, Easter seemed a much more important Christ-centered celebration in the church.

The phone rang. Molly was calling collect from the road. She and two dorm buddies were driving home after finals.

"Do you know what I'm looking forward to?" she said.

"Sleeping for seventy-two straight hours?" I asked.

"No." She sounded a little deflated. "Coming home from Christmas Eve services and seeing all those presents piled up under the tree. It's been years since I've cared what was in them or how many were for me—I just like seeing them there. How weird is that?"

Not weird at all, my love, I thought. I sighed, took a piece of paper, and penciled in a few gift ideas for Ross; Molly; Patrick; his wife, Amy; my grandson, Shane.

And then I snapped the pencil down on the counter. A part of me understood that the kids were in denial. Tom's sudden death eleven months earlier had left them bewildered and scared. And now at Christmas, their shock was translated into exaggerated enthusiasm. The Cobb family Christmas traditions provided a sense of normalcy for them. Patrick had even asked me last week if I still had the old John Denver Christmas album.

But as far as I was concerned, there just wasn't that much to deck the halls about. Tom was gone. I was empty and unmotivated. At worst, I wished they'd all just open the presents and carve the turkey without me.

When the oven dinged, I piled two dozen brown cookies on a plate and left a note for Ross: *I don't want to hear any more complaining! Gone shopping. I love you. Mom.*

The complaining, however, went on in my head as I elbowed my way through the mob at the mall.

Tom was right, I thought. *This is all a joke.*

It really was everything he hated—canned music droning its false merriment, garish signs luring me to buy, tired-looking families dragging themselves around, worrying about their credit card limits as they snapped at their children.

Funny, I thought while gazing at a display of earrings I knew Molly wouldn't wear. *All the time Tom was here pointing this out to me, it never bothered me. Now it's all I can see.*

I abandoned the earring idea and took to wandering the mall, hoping for inspiration so Molly would have something to look at under the tree. It wasn't going to be like years past—I should have told her that. She wasn't going to see a knee-deep collection of exquisitely wrapped treasures about which Tom always shook his head.

"You've gone hog-wild again," he always told me—before adding one more contribution. Instead of buying me a gift, he'd write a check in my name to Compassion International or a local food pantry, place it in a red envelope and tuck it onto a branch of our Christmas tree.

"This is a true *Christ*-mas gift," he'd tell me. "It's a small demonstration that Christ is real in our lives."

I stopped in mid-mall, letting the crowds swirl past me.

Tom wasn't there, a fact that the rest of the family didn't want to face or discuss. But he could still be with us, maybe just a little.

I left the mall and quickly found a Christmas tree lot. The man looked happy to unload one very dry tree for half price. He even tied it to my roof rack.

Then it was off to Safeway, where I bought a twenty-four-pound Butterball and all the trimmings. Back home, the decoration boxes weren't buried too deeply in the garage. I'd barely gotten them put away last year when Tom had his heart attack.

I was still sorting boxes when Ross emerged from the kitchen, munching the last of the two dozen cookies.

"Oh, I thought we weren't going to have a tree this year," he said between mouthfuls.

"Well, we are. Can you give me a hand getting it up?"

Two hours later, Ross and I stood back and admired our Christmas tree. The lights winked softly as I straightened a misshapen glittery angel Molly had made in second grade and Ross's first-birthday Christmas ball.

I wanted to cry.

The house sprang to life when everyone arrived Christmas Eve. In the middle of our church service, however, my spirits sagged. There was no lonelier feeling than standing in the midst of one's family singing "Silent Night"—surrounded by a vivacious college daughter; a sweet, gentle daughter-in-law; a handsome, successful twenty-five-year-old son; a wide-eyed, mile-a-minute three-year-old grandson and an awkward teenager whose hugs were like wet shoelaces—and being keenly aware that someone was missing.

Back at home, everyone continued to avoid the subject.

"The tree is *gorgeous,* Mom," Molly said. She knelt down and began hauling gifts out of a shopping bag to add to my pile.

"I love what you did with the wrappings, Pam," Amy said. "You're always so creative."

"I forgot to buy wrapping paper," I told her. "I *had* to use newspaper."

It was Christmas as usual—easier to pretend everything was normal than to deal with harsh reality. Ross and Patrick sparred over whose stocking was whose, and Shane parked himself in front of a bowl of M&Ms. They all were allowed to open the customary one present on

Christmas Eve, and after doing so, they went off to bed.

But there was one more thing that had to be done. I went over to Tom's desk, found a red envelope in the top drawer, and stuck into it a check made out to the American Heart Association. It seemed appropriate.

"I know the kids—and even I—have to go on with our lives, Tom," I whispered. "But I wish you were here."

It occurred to me as I tucked the red envelope midway up the tree that one of the kids would say, "Oh, yeah—I remember he always did that," and then there would be an awkward silence and perhaps sheepish looks.

I hoped so.

Morning—or at least dawn—came way too soon. Shane was up before the paper carrier arrived. I dragged myself into the kitchen and found it already smelling like a Seattle coffeehouse.

"This is what we drink at school," Molly told me and handed me a cup.

"Is anyone else awake?" I asked.

She nodded her head, and for the first time I noticed a twinkle in her eye that was unprecedented for this hour of the morning.

"What are you up to?" I said.

"Mom!" Patrick yelled from the living room. "You've got to see this!"

"At this hour of the . . ."

What I saw was my family perched on the couch like a row of deliciously guilty canaries. What I saw next was our Christmas tree, dotted with bright red envelopes.

"Man, it got crowded in here last night," Ross said. "I came down here about two o'clock and freaked Amy out."

"I almost called 911 when I came down," Patrick said. "Till I saw it was Molly and not some burglar."

I had never heard a thing. I walked over to the tree and touched each one of the five envelopes I hadn't put there.

"Open them, Mom," Molly said. "This was always the best part of Christmas."

From Patrick, there was a check to Youth for Christ, to help kids go on mission trips like the one Dad supported him on to Haiti five years earlier. From Amy, a check to our church for sheet music, because some of her best memories of her father-in-law were of him helping the children's choir. From Molly, several twenty-dollar bills for the local crisis pregnancy center, "because many of the women who go there have probably never experienced the love of a husband like Daddy," she said. From Ross, a twenty-dollar bill for a local drug program for kids, "since Dad was all freaked out about me staying clean."

The last envelope was lumpy. When I opened it, a handful of change spilled out.

"Mine, Gamma," Shane said, his little bow-mouth pursed importantly. Amy finished his thought. "He wants this to go to the animal shelter—you know, for lost dogs, like the one he visited with Dad just before he died."

I pulled all the envelopes against my chest and hugged them.

"You know what's weird?" Molly said. "I feel like Daddy's right here with us."

"Yeah, that's pretty weird," Ross said.

"But true," Patrick said. "I feel like he's been here this whole time. I thought I'd be all bummed out this Christmas—but I don't need to be."

"No, you don't, my love," I said. To myself, I added, *Neither do I. I have my family, and I have my faith.*

Nancy Rue

Sidelined

I was a postmodern, feminist brand of single mother, so certain I could be both father and mother to my son. Plunging into my dual role, I became the kind of mom who knew the name of every truck, who played catch in the backyard, who wasn't afraid of a vigorous sock war.

But faced with the permission slip my fifth-grader now thrust in my face, I was baffled. This was something I hadn't counted on, somewhere I didn't want to go.

"Football! Honey, you don't want to play football."

Silence. I proceeded with my case.

"Sweetie, football is an excuse for men to celebrate testosterone, legally hit each other and yell inappropriate things at the television set."

My son was unimpressed with my arguments.

"Football was created so that the socially challenged among the male sex could have a topic of conversation. People get hurt playing football," I concluded my summation sounding a little shrill.

My son was stolidly unmoved. "Mom, I want to play football."

Then it occurred to me. Look at this kid, this adorable, round-cheeked, ample-bottomed youth who wanted us to live in an apartment with an elevator so he wouldn't have to walk stairs twice a day . . . whose best subjects are still snack and recess . . . who yells from three rooms away, "Mom, would you hand me that glass of milk!" This child wouldn't survive the rigors of a single football practice.

I signed the Pop Warner football permission slip.

He dragged home from his first practice, heaving, sweating, dirty. I attempted neutrality. "So?"

"Mom," he could barely articulate. "We were . . . *gasp* . . . running laps, and I couldn't do it, and the coach . . . *gasp* . . . screamed at me, 'Kid, I don't care if you walk, I don't care if you crawl, but you finish that lap.'"

"Honey, did that hurt your feelings?"

My son indignantly pulled himself together. "Feelings? Mom, this is football!"

Dutifully, I went to the games. My son played eleven seconds in the first game. One learns quickly to stand well back from the action. Even on "Wild Kingdom" they don't let you hear the cougar cracking the antelope bones.

Coach Reggie performed a kind of choreography during games. When a play went badly, he'd throw his cap to the ground and, Rumpelstiltskin-like, jump up and down as if to crack open the earth. If he didn't like the ref's call, he'd charge the field like a fierce bull terrier. The kids of the Pop Warner fifth- and sixth-grade B Team would beam, feeling protected, fought for, coveted.

The season marched to its end. The team was 3–4. I had learned how to wash uniforms, call out appropriate cheers and appreciate the joys of a "solid hit." My son had completed the season as starting offensive lineman.

At the Pop Warner Football Awards Banquet, the kids hawked down pizza that tasted like the boxes they were delivered in. The three teams in the VFW Hall sounded like the Indianapolis 500 in an echo chamber. Suddenly, all was hushed. Three lads, not a single one with a discernible neck, stood to face the crowd. They were the high school football captains.

Finally, I would be privy to this secret brotherhood, the dreams and promises that pass from almost-man to boy. A captain cleared his throat, looked out over the assemblage and said, "Keep working out in the weight room." He sat down.

Now it was time for the awards. Coach Reggie took the floor.

"It's been quite a year, and there's plenty to talk about. But I want to tell you about this one kid," he began. " He's not getting an award, but I want to talk about him anyway.

"At the first practice, this kid couldn't make it around the field. I told him he could walk or crawl, but he had to finish that lap. He did. And he kept finishing laps and coming to practice and trying, really trying. He started the season with eleven seconds of play, and now he's a starting offensive lineman for me.

"The other day, we had a race. I had the two slowest kids race the lap. This kid is neck-and-neck with the other, and he sees me at the end. He pushes, pushes hard. And knocks me over—right over—the little so-and-so."

Coach Reggie laughed deeply. "He might not be the best player on that field, but I'd trade any other kid for a Solomon Black, who just keeps trying."

My son shot me a don't-you-dare-cry-in-public look.

We never talked about that awards banquet. We didn't have to.

Next year, my son was the first to join the team roster. When no sportscaster-type could be found to call the home games, I took over the mike:

"Well, it looks like Reading is trying a double-reverse in

the back infield, but their runner is brought down by Number 73, Sol Black."

I could swear my kid glanced up at the press box and winked through that insect mask. And I silently thanked him for at least letting me stand on the sideline and watch as he went places a mom just can't take you.

Judith Black

One Man and a Baby

"I have to go potty!" Four-year-old Andrea announces this to everyone in line with us at the bookstore.

"Can you hold it? Please?" I ask.

"No, Daddy," she says, clutching herself. So we head to the bathroom—the *mall* bathroom. The one that says *Women*.

Andrea looks up at me expectantly. "C'mon, Daddy."

"I can't go in there. It's for girls. Can you be a big girl and go in by yourself?" I ask her.

She squints at me for a moment. "Okay!" she says, and marches over to the door, which is too heavy for her to open.

I push the door open for her. "You'll be okay," I say. "If anything happens, just scream. I'll be right here."

Two minutes pass. Three minutes. *Four* minutes . . .

Andrea's mother and I met and fell in love at band camp when I was fourteen and she was thirteen. We were together all through high school.

When I was a senior and Michelle was a junior, she became pregnant with our daughter Andrea. We got married the day after my graduation from high school, when Andrea was two months old. For the next two years, we lived in a government-subsidized housing complex. I worked nearly every night delivering pizzas, and Michelle stayed home with Andrea.

I don't remember when the arguing started. I don't know when our house drained of color and even Andrea's face turned sour. Michelle was sick of me, the apartment, her life. I told her I wanted Andrea to live with me. The next day Michelle was gone.

When Andrea realized that her mom wasn't coming back, she started crying. I tried to console her, but she pushed me away. For hours, she huddled near her dresser, whimpering like a frightened animal.

Within a few weeks, we'd started adjusting to life without Michelle. We fell into a routine. While Andrea stayed home with a baby-sitter, I delivered pizzas until after midnight, came home and passed out. As soon as the sun hit her window, Andrea faithfully waddled in and woke me up. Then we'd stumble downstairs, and I'd dump out some dry cereal and fall back asleep on the couch with the TV blaring. At four o'clock, the baby-sitter would arrive again and I'd leave. I'd tell people I was a single father and make myself sound like a martyr. But really, it surprised me how easy it all was. Just put on *Sesame Street,* heat up some canned pasta and away you go.

Andrea was almost four when the truth hit me. We were brushing our teeth together—toothpaste foam was dribbling off my toothbrush, onto my hand and down my arm. I saw Andrea in the mirror, gawking at me. "You're messy!" she said, and her words shook my heart.

"You're right," I said, reaching for a towel. "Daddy needs to clean himself up." I realized then that she would be learning everything from me—how to brush her teeth, how to dress, how to treat other people.

The next day, after a night of self-examination, I woke Andrea up, and we helped each other make the beds.

Then I took a shower, got dressed and washed all the dishes. I flung the drapes apart and sunlight poured in.

That morning was a year ago. Andrea and I have moved into a house, and I've got a nine-to-five sales job. At last, I feel as if I'm on the right track—as a father *and* as a person.

Andrea's been in the bathroom five minutes when the door wobbles, pulls open an inch, and then falls shut. I step over and swing it open. Smiling proudly, she marches out. I gather her into my arms. "Daddy," she says. "We did it!"

"Yeah," I say, patting her back. "We did."

Paul Breon
Submitted by Bryan Aubrey

"You'll have joint custody of the children. They'll live with their mother and you'll get them whenever they're tired and cranky."

Marty's Friends

When Marty was three, he commuted to work with me for a whole year, to company day care and home again in a carpool of my colleagues. We grew pretty attached.

When Marty was four, his mom and I hired a babysitter in the cul-de-sac where we lived—long days with the quiet and gentle Mrs. Olson.

At Mrs. Olson's, Marty created his two imaginary friends, Shawn and Kawn. He told us that Shawn and Kawn were homeless children and that he had decided to adopt them.

The little guys were forever at Marty's side—giggling, joking, whispering. Marty assigned each of them a place at the table, a shared upper bunk, and seats in the car. Their one-liners, translated by Marty, would have us all in stitches. Of course, Shawn and Kawn were invisible. Only Marty could see them.

Marty's seven-year-old brother, Jimmy, would roll his eyes in head-shaking, shoulder-shrugging acceptance of Shawn and Kawn and all their secret capers. Occasionally, of course, they were scapegoats for Jimmy's own mishaps.

Marty was almost five when his mom and I separated. A short time later, we were divorced. After a weekend together at my small city apartment, I was packing up for the drive home to Mom's. Coming in for one more load, I heard Marty in the bathroom, crying. I opened the door. There sat Marty on the commode, his lower lip laden with sadness.

I had one anguished thought—he wants to move in. He looked at me and said, "Daddy, I'm going to miss Shawn and Kawn." Then he glanced at the bathtub, which was filled with sudsy water and floating toys.

"But they're in the car with Jimmy," I said, "ready to go with you."

Marty shook his head slowly, then sucked a breath. "No Daddy, they're in the tub. We've been doing a lot of talking this weekend. Shawn and Kawn decided that they were going to live with you from now on. We didn't want you to be lonely anymore."

Later that night, I walked in the park, Shawn and Kawn in tow. It was hard holding back the tears, knowing that the most loving thing I had felt in a long time had been the gift of his friends from my four-year-old son.

James M. Jertson
Submitted by Elizabeth Peterson

Outside the Circle of Possibility

Start by doing what's necessary, then what's possible and suddenly you are doing the impossible.

St. Francis of Assisi

"Hey Mom! I'm going to apply to this student exchange program to study art in a foreign country this summer."

I nearly dropped the plates I was carrying to the dining-room table. "Oh sure," I quipped, "and I think I'll apply to be a belly dancer in Nepal for the summer."

"Mom, this is serious. My friend Heather went to Germany last summer. Think of the experience!"

"Jeanne, you're sixteen years old. Besides, foreign exchange programs are for rich kids. They cost thousands of dollars. Have you forgotten that I'm a single parent with three other children to worry about besides you, and that I'm already working three part-time jobs? Please, Honey, be reasonable."

The next day Jeanne sent in her application to Open Door Student Exchange in New York. An enthusiastic art student at the Milwaukee High School of the Arts, she let nothing—

not even a negative mother—dampen her spirits.

I just shook my head and whispered a prayer that she would not be too disappointed when she discovered we really couldn't afford to let her go to Europe for the summer.

A few weeks later when the Open Door people sent her another, longer application to fill out, I read the paragraph that said, "Comprehensive fee of $2,750 covers international airfare, orientation, room and board, insurance, activities, materials, excursions, counseling, and administrative support for the six-week summer program."

Three thousand dollars, including airfare to New York and back. *Impossible!* I thought. *How can she be so bold as to even think that I could consider this?* I tossed the application on the counter and went back to the kitchen sink to peel potatoes.

A few days later Jeanne told me she'd filled out the second application and mailed it.

My heart ached for her and I started to hate my single-parent status even more.

"Jeanne, you know we can't afford it. Besides, you don't know anything about traveling in a foreign country. You don't even speak a foreign language. At least wait until you're in college to dream something this big."

"Mom, I *have* to apply. I'll never know if I can go if I don't try."

Something rang true in her words. Was it the unfaltering optimism I'd always had myself until single parenthood shook me into a sense of gloom and doom?

A few weeks later I received a phone call from Open Door in New York. "Mrs. Lorenz, we received Jeanne's application for the summer program abroad, but she didn't send the application fee."

I politely told the young woman that I couldn't afford the application fee and that spending the summer in a foreign country was out of the question financially for my daughter. I explained that I had recently become a single parent and that paying my bills and getting by day to day was my main concern. "Even with a thousand-dollar scholarship, I still couldn't afford to let her go," I told the woman.

Two months later the vice-president of the student exchange program called me at work. "Mrs. Lorenz, we were so impressed with Jeanne's application that we've called some of her teachers to find out more about her. She would certainly benefit from our fine art workshop in Cologne, West Germany, this summer. The deadline for final applications is past, and we have some scholarship money left. Can you tell me exactly what you *could* afford?"

I sighed, wondering if these people would ever get off my back. Almost facetiously I mentioned a paltry sum that I'd saved for emergencies, something in the neighborhood of three hundred dollars.

"We'll make up the difference with scholarship and grant money," Mr. Lurie responded. "Start the preparations for getting Jeanne a passport."

Was it *possible?* I wondered in a daze. I worried. I prayed. How could such a dream come true? I remembered a Bible quote: *For if you had faith even as small as a tiny mustard seed you could say to this mountain, "Move!" and it would go far away. Nothing would be impossible* (Matthew 17:20).

I wondered where my daughter had acquired such a sense of bulldozing faith.

I called Jeanne's art teachers and asked what they thought about sending her to Cologne for the summer.

"What an opportunity!" one shouted into the phone. "Cologne is one of the art centers of the world! Let her go!"

That afternoon I made a huge sign that said "Bon Voyage, Jeanne" and taped it to the front door. When she arrived home from school she screamed, danced around the kitchen, smeared away her happy tears, then hugged me hard.

When I met my daughter at the airport at the end of the summer after her adventure abroad, I saw a young woman who was different from the daughter I'd kissed good-bye six weeks earlier.

She'd had the most incredible experience of her life. The first three weeks, during the intensive art history/sketching course, she'd lived in a youth hostel. Then she stayed with an architect, his wife and their two children. Mr. Schweizer loved art passionately and was delighted to have a house guest who shared his enthusiasm.

The Schweizers showered Jeanne with trips to museums, cathedrals and travels to other German cities to see examples of Gothic, Romanesque and Baroque art and architecture. She soaked up the culture of Germany, the homeland of our Kobbeman and Lorenz ancestors. She returned to America with a new sense of pride in her own country with its diverse cultures. Most of all, she returned with a sense of confidence in dreaming big dreams.

After she came home Jeanne spent the next few months applying to various colleges and universities. Even though she received an art scholarship to the University of Wisconsin, she also applied to spend a year in Yugoslavia through the Open Door Student Exchange. She was accepted for the program after learning that the U.S. Information Agency was giving each of the fifteen American students going to Yugoslavia a two-thousand-dollar grant—which again brought the program into our reach financially. Without hesitation Jeanne decided to postpone college for a year.

So once again, an incredible foreign experience opened up for the child of a single parent, a parent who never in a million years believed that overseas education opportunities were within her child's reach.

Today, as I look at my daughter—who has since graduated from college and is a successful artist and teacher—I remember her faith in the impossible when, as a sixteen-year-old high school student, she wanted more than anything to visit a foreign country. I see how much she matured and learned from her experiences in Germany and Yugoslavia, and I know that for the rest of her life, the same faith will pull her through.

That Bible verse about moving mountains, taped over my kitchen sink, is a daily reminder to keep my heart open and to believe that, no matter h[illegible] many obstacles there are, I can still reach for [illegible] se when I do there's a very good cha[illegible] whole galaxy in the process.

[illegible]icia Lorenz

mall
, what's this
out of the envelope and
down her cheeks.
r mom a big hug as the card fell
words:
200 million years old. That's
give up on you."
Rob Gilbert and Karen Wydra

For Forever

After the divorce, her teenage daughter became increasingly rebellious.

It culminated late one night when the police called to tell her that she had to come to the police station to pick up her daughter, who was arrested for drunk driving.

They didn't speak until the next afternoon.

Mom broke the tension by giving her daughter a small wrapped box.

daughter nonchalantly opened it and found a rock.

her eyes and said, "Cute, Mom

Mom said.

the card

trickl

Where the Heart Is

No more words. Hear only the voice within.

Rumi

Emma tucked the blue envelope containing her paycheck into her pocket. Another week's groceries, she thought. The mortgage payment, the electric bill.

"Better have a look at that, Em," said Mary, her boss. "I think you'll be pleased."

A quizzical look crossed Emma's face, and she tore open the envelope. Ah, another pay increase, the second since she'd started her job at the defense plant some months before. Shoes for Betsy was her immediate thought.

"That is good news, Mary," she said, with a small smile.

"You've earned it, Em, and more. You're one of the best workers this section has ever had."

Emma smiled again. The truth was that she hadn't wanted to go to work in the first place. Emma's home and family were everything to her; having babies and making a home for Frank and their children were all she'd ever wanted. But now Frank was gone, his lungs destroyed by the tuberculosis that had kept him sick for so long. The small widow's pension Emma received from his company had kept their heads barely above water, but the needs of her children far exceeded the meager amount. The town offered assistance, but the very thought brought a flush to Emma's face. Emma was a proud woman; welfare was unthinkable. No. Emma would have to take over and somehow make ends meet. It wouldn't be easy. It was 1944, and the country was at war.

They tried hard, all of them. Neighbors were quick to buy the loaves of bread that came from Emma's oven, and her expert sewing skills were always in demand, so some money trickled in. Frankie willingly handed over all he earned from his paper route, and Louise helped out at the variety store on Worthington Street, but their small earnings didn't go far—and Emma hated taking their money.

She worried about the children, too: Fourteen-year-old Frankie was up early on bitter cold mornings, steadying a bike loaded down with papers on hilly, sometimes icy roads, and was then faced with a long trek to school. Louise, at sixteen, helped Emma with housework and the laundry when she wasn't in school or at the store, and kept an eye on six-year-old Betsy, but she needed free time, too.

Even Jake tried to help. Three years younger than Frankie, and not very big, his job was to keep wood cut for the stove. He wanted to cut wood for the neighbors, too, but here Emma drew the line.

So they pinched and scrimped and did their best, but regardless of how they tried, there just wasn't enough. Emma would have to go to work.

Jobs at the industrial plant by the river were plentiful; with the men away at war, women now wielded tools, ran machines and turned out motors and engine parts for defense. Getting hired was as easy as showing up. The only shift available, however, was three in the afternoon to eleven at night. Emma wondered how she would

There, in the middle of the kitchen in the middle of the night, stood her children in their nightclothes, radiant smiles lighting their faces. A banner, strung across the kitchen and painted in huge, brightly colored letters, blazoned, WELCOME HOME, MAMA! Hot chocolate simmered in a battered pan on the stove. A slightly lop-sided cake baked lovingly by Louise waited on the kitchen table.

Betsy danced with excitement, her eyes sparkling. "Are you surprised, Mama? I helped with the cake." Jake's face shone with joy. A happy smile passed between Frankie and Louise.

Momentarily overcome, Emma caught her breath and looked into the beaming faces of her beloved children. Tears welled in her eyes and spilled over as she opened her arms and gathered her family to her. Her heart was full. They would make it somehow. She was home to stay.

Brenda Nichols Ainley

For the Record

Less than a year after my wife's funeral I was confronted with the most terrible realities of being a widower with five children.

Notes from school.

Field-trip permission slips, PTA election ballots, Troll Book order forms, sports sign-ups, medical forms and innumerable academic progress reports—an onslaught of paperwork courtesy of the educational bureaucracy.

This "literature" has to be read and signed, or placed at the bottom of the birdcage. Regardless of its destination it must be dealt with on a daily basis.

One day, eight-year-old Rachel was helping me complete five (count 'em, five) emergency treatment forms for school. She would fill in the generic information (name, address, phone number), and I would add the rest (insurance numbers, doctor's name, date, signature). After signing the forms, I checked them for accuracy. It was then that I noticed on each card, in the slot beside Mother's Business Phone, Rachel had written "1-800-HEAVEN."

Rob Loughran

A Wish Seed

Nothing lasts forever—not even your troubles.

Arnold Glasow

Everything was going wrong.

The very day I got off crutches from a knee injury, my teenage son arrived home from camp, on crutches, with a knee injury. He was in agony and needed surgery. We had no insurance.

The previous week our desperately needed new car had proved a lemon, so I had returned it and reluctantly financed a larger model. On the drive home from the dealership, a rock thrown up by the wheels shattered the windshield.

That day's mail held a cheerful letter from the IRS telling me I owed almost twenty thousand dollars in capital gains taxes from a house my ex-husband and I sold two years back. At that time, I was home-schooling the four youngest children, barely surviving on my freelance writing income and wading through the district attorney's paperwork to collect child support.

My world was eroding from under me in a series of

small avalanches. It didn't take long before I was envisioning the IRS seizing our current home, leaving five children and me homeless. That car would be pretty small for all of us to live in! Maybe we could buy a little trailer. What about the four cats and two dogs? Would I have to tell the children to find homes for their pets?

Immediately we put the house on the market. Maybe it would sell quickly. In desperation, I began running ads for everything we had of value. Our furniture, freezer, greenhouse and my wedding ring sold quickly. Then we began regular runs to the local Goodwill truck to drop off anything and everything we could live without and to hunt for boxes.

In between, we made trips to the offices of orthopedic surgeons and pharmacies, and watched Robin grimace with every movement.

Our lives became a grim sequence of sorting, boxing and cleaning. We spent time praying that the real estate agent would produce a miracle quickly.

As the proverbial straws piled up, I noted guiltily that I grew more snappy, stressed and curt toward my children. Unfortunately, the guilt only added to my frustrations, and I spent longer periods hiding in the shower, crying.

One day, during a brief break at the park, the littlest child, Larkin, bounced over to bring me a wish seed, the downy thistle seed that children wish upon and blow away. According to the myth, if the seed travels far enough (the exact distance being unknown), the wish will come true. Half-heartedly, I took the seed and prayed silently to God for serenity, patience and guidance and to be a better parent and handle things more calmly. Smiling at Larkin's eager face, I sent it on its way.

The next few days we spent labeling, boxing and discarding the remainder of our physical lives. Gloom hovered over the house, threatening to swallow what was left of us.

So far, there was no buyer in sight, and the IRS sent a more serious demand. My son needed surgery and was devastated at his inability to help with the physical demands of moving. He was on painkillers and slept most of the day. Meanwhile, the doctor's office fought with the camp's insurance company to authorize surgery.

One afternoon, I took the youngest four to the roller rink to let off steam and keep a semblance of normalcy in our lives. As I skated round and round, the usual routine failed to soothe me. Details of everything that needed handling circled mercilessly in my head. To my embarrassment, tears burned behind my eyes, threatening to spill. Fear, fatigue, being overwhelmed and the unrelenting summer heat chewed at me.

The rink's air conditioner was broken that day and the owner skated past me, throwing open the back doors to allow the breeze inside before we all melted. A wave of warm air rushed past me, and then I saw it. Floating straight toward me was a wish seed. It settled, trembling, into the hand I reached out.

The most amazing sense of absurdity washed over me. What was this? God was rejecting my wish, too? Had he finally grown sick of all my griping and complaining? I began to giggle. Waves of giggles pushed out past the tears and sent them spilling down my cheeks. I skated on, clutching the wish seed between two fingers, tears running down my face and laughing. From my children's expressions, it was quite clear how strange I looked. Mom had finally gone around the bend.

Eventually, the giggling stopped and was replaced by a sense of complete calm. That serene feeling remained when we left the rink, and lingered for days. For the first time since life had begun unraveling, I was able to handle things without a constant undercurrent of panic.

Of course, none of the problems magically disappeared.

However, things began to fall smoothly into place.

My son's surgery was, after all, covered by the camp's insurance, and went off successfully.

The district attorney recovered the year's back support owed by the children's father, allowing me to pay the mortgage and send the IRS the first of many payments.

My sister paid back an old loan.

Two checks arrived for articles that I had sold months back. And so it went. The more I stopped obsessing, the more smoothly events transpired.

On my desk today, I have a framed piece of white paper, on which is affixed a single wish seed. For those who ask, I just say it was the first time that God sent me a return receipt for a prayer.

Lizanne Southgate

Message in a Mug

You have within you right now, everything you need to deal with whatever the world can throw at you.

Brian Tracy

My cries must have woken him. My son, P. J., stands before me, his blue eyes filled with concern.

"What's the matter, Mommy? Why are you crying?"

What can I say to him that won't sound like I'm scared? I'm all my children have, and I need to be strong for them.

"I just find it hard sometimes to take care of you guys and go to college at the same time," I say finally. "Exams are next week, and I'm just . . ." my voice broke, "just tired, I guess."

Just so tired.

Going back to college full-time as a single parent of two children had been a difficult choice. But I didn't want to be a welfare mom. I wanted more for my children—for them to value education, for them to be proud of their mother. Yet without emotional and family support, I had found this to be a journey of being alone, feeling alone and doing it alone.

Tonight it had hit me all at once. It was too difficult to pay all the bills, take care of the children, study for exams, clean the house. Life was piling up around me, and I suddenly wanted out.

"I can't go on, Lord," I cried. "I can't do this! It's too tough. I thought I had the strength, but I don't."

Just then my son interrupted my panicked thoughts for a second time. Holding his Buddy doll tighter, he came closer and said very quietly, "God made the whole world, Mom. And he's a single parent."

I knelt down next to him. "What did you say?"

P. J. repeated tentatively, "God is a single parent, too."

His words washed away my loneliness, my feelings of self-pity, of being angry at the world and God.

"P. J., that's wonderful! I'm going to put that saying on posters, cards, T-shirts—just everything."

I took his little hands, and P. J. and I danced around the living room laughing and singing. Then I carried him back to bed.

My spirit renewed, I studied most of the night.

After exams were over, I made good on my promise to P. J. With the help of a friend, I ordered one thousand coffee mugs; I had them printed with the words, "God Is a Single Parent, Too!" Then I went door to door in my building, giving a mug to all the single parents I knew—my version of a message in a bottle.

Some just thanked me, with tears in their eyes. Others invited me in for a cup of coffee and told me their own experiences and feelings about being a single parent. Trading stories showed me that my struggle was not a unique one, that mine was not a journey taken alone. Many others trudged daily beside me; I'd just been too focused on myself to notice my fellow travelers.

I still have some mugs left. Once in a while I become newly acquainted with single parents who need encouragement. I tell them my story. I give them a mug.

I leave them with more than a parenting slogan. I give them a message from the mouth of a babe, the message that God is there for all of his children, all of the time.

Tina French

"My mom has a lot in common with God. They're both single parents."

Reprinted by permission of Martin Bucella.

Dr. Mom

The only way of discovering the limits of the possible is to venture a little way past them into the impossible.

Arthur Clarke

I knew that I wanted to become a doctor for a long time. However, at the beginning of my senior year in high school, I became pregnant. I was still determined to become a physician, but I knew that it was going to be very difficult to do so. Many teenage mothers did not even complete high school. I was thinking about enduring college, medical school and residency on top of that!

I began attending a high school for teenage mothers. On my first day I asked a teacher, "How do I apply for college? I want to be a doctor." With a puzzled look on her face, she replied, "This is a reading, writing and arithmetic school. We just want to see you graduate, dear."

I walked out of the office and decided that I would apply to college anyway. I was happy to receive an acceptance letter a few months later. At that time, Jonathan was just three weeks old, and I was excited about pursuing my dreams.

When I needed to choose a major, my mom told me, "Melanie, it is going to be really difficult for you to be in school for such a long time. You need to find a way to support Jonathan and yourself. Why not become a nurse and then when you are older, you can return to school to become a doctor?" But I told her, "Nursing is not my dream. Becoming a doctor is. I will apply for financial aid to support us for now. This is what I really want to do." And with that, she didn't bring up the idea of changing majors again.

The first two years of college were rough. I can remember waiting for the bus in the snow while carrying my son, my backpack, my baby-bag and a stroller. I would repeat this four times a day—to get my son to day care, get myself to school, pick him up and head back home. I was determined to follow my dream. My junior year of college, I took the medical college admissions test (MCAT). When my scores came back, I asked a professor's advice on which schools to apply to. "Well, I don't think your scores are competitive. I wouldn't spend much time and money applying to many top schools." But I decided to apply anyway. How would I ever know if I could have gotten in to one of those "top schools"?

Little did the professor know that I would attend Stanford University Medical School.

What a great feeling it is to be pursuing my dream! I am now in my first year of medical school. My classmates think that it must be difficult to balance medical school with my responsibilities as a single mom. Difficult, but not as difficult as one may think!

At the end of my day, looking a bit disheveled and haggard and dressed in scrubs, I pick Jonathan up from his school. He runs to me with open arms even though I smell like formaldehyde and says, "Hi, Mom!" and immediately, my spirits are lifted. When volunteering at his preschool, sometimes I overhear him proudly exclaim, "You know, my mommy goes to medical school. She is going to be a doctor!"

He asks to bring my bones for show and tell. He wants to be a skeleton for Halloween. He tells me, "Mom, I have to study really hard to be a doctor, too," and he draws pictures at the table while I am studying. And at night, when I don't have the energy to read Dr. Seuss to him sometimes, he says, "That's okay, Mom. I am going to read a story for you."

Jonathan and I have grown up together. We have made it through high school, teething, tantrums, first words, first steps and college. Undoubtedly, we will make it through medical school, elementary school and residency, too. I am often asked, "What keeps you going?" I reply, "Words of inspiration from my son."

Melanie M. Watkins

A Real Family Christmas

Few words strike more terror into the heart of a single mother than a merrily delivered "So, what are you and the kids doing for the holidays?"

In those first, terrifying years of single motherhood, I would bite my tongue so I wouldn't respond with the first thought that came to my mind: *Oh no! It can't be Christmas again already! I haven't gotten remarried and given my kids that perfect stepfather they've been wanting! I don't even have a relationship! Hey, maybe I can meet the man of my dreams, fall instantly in love and get married on Christmas Eve. Yeah, sure, I can lose thirty pounds this week, get a fab new haircut, and then and then. . . . Oh God, please don't let it be Christmas again so soon!*

One of the worst Christmases was the year when every other adult in my large, extended family was newly married and euphorically happy, while I was newly divorced and pretending I liked it that way. That was the same year my son asked the Santa at Marshall Fields for a brand new daddy. I spent that Christmas with the shades drawn and the cable disconnected with only Fannie Mae chocolates for company. Well, Fannie Mae and the kids.

But the kids were small, and it was easy enough to

distract them with gifts and goodies. They were more interested in toys than in whether we were a real family. As they grew older, however, it was harder and harder to ignore the fact that we were different. I judged our family to be faulty, defective. Missing some important parts. Missing the father part. My son never helped his dad put together a new bike, or an elaborate race track. The guy at Wal-Mart did it for an extra fifteen dollars. My daughter never modeled her new velvet dress for an adoring father. Instead, she twirled and smiled for me, and later, her own mirror.

Then, one year when my daughter was in junior high, and I was alternately sweating and crying over an oven full of homemade gingerbread men, I heard her talking to a girlfriend.

"Sure, if your folks are giving you flack, you can just come over here on Christmas Eve," my Rachel said. "It'll be cool. The only rule is we have to eat up everything in the fridge to make room for the Christmas leftovers."

"Everything?" her friend asked. "What's everything?"

Rachel shrugged. "Whatever's in there. Bologna, hot dogs, spaghetti, cheesecake. Everything's got to go!" Then she laughed out loud. "Just tell my mom you love her gingerbread, and feed it to my brother's dog when she's not looking. My mother is soooo clueless." She laughed again, and the girls left. I worked extra hard on my gingerbread that year, and gave Wolfie plenty of Pepto-Bismol.

The year my son turned sixteen, he was invited to a holiday ski trip with some of his best buddies. He turned them down without even talking to me about it. "Rick," I told him when I found out, "You can go. It'll be fun. You always wanted to learn to ski!"

Rick rolled his eyes. "They're leaving on Christmas Eve. What kind of idiots want to be away from home on Christmas? And who would pop our popcorn for *It's a*

Wonderful Life? Rachel always burns it. You hate that. Besides, Wolfie wouldn't survive four days without me—you barely remember to walk him."

"I don't think he should be allowed to go skiing," Rachel chimed in. "If I have to be in the church Christmas pageant, he should too." Rick ignored his sister. He put his Walkman back on, whistled to the dog and strolled out into the snow.

In his first year of college, Rick brought his roommate home for the holidays. "They don't do anything at his house for Christmas," he confided to me later. "His dad just drinks too much and yells at everybody. I thought he might like to have a good Christmas for a change." We kept our yelling confined to football games that year, and I made lots of nonalcoholic punch.

My kids aren't so little anymore. Rachel now organizes the church pageants, and Rick starts his ski trips on New Year's Day. My gingerbread remains a work-in-progress. It's Wolfie's son that I occasionally forget to walk. I still don't have that cute new haircut or that perfect stepfather I've been wanting for the kids. God only knows what we'll be eating on Christmas Eve. But anyone can ask me what we're doing for the holidays, and I won't even blink. We're going to have a real family Christmas, just like always.

Kay Bolden

No Time for Dreams

Today, for once, I am *not* late.

For my effort, my thirty-two-year-old son needles me affectionately as he opens the door to his home. "Yo, Mom, fourteen minutes early!"

I smile, try to seem calm, but I'm antsy. I've been playing catch-up since my life began itself over, this time as a single mom. Today, I'm determined to get things right from the start.

Spying Mike's car keys, jacket and the wrapped gifts sitting on the counter, I think we're ready to leave. But no, my bachelor son is making small talk. I shift my weight, put my present on the counter and try to look attentive, but finally blurt out, "Honey, let's go! They're expecting us soon. We can chat in the car."

This is important. Christmas dinner at Sarah's house. First meeting with the girlfriend's parents.

"All right," Mike says, catching on to my mood. "Just let me do something upstairs." Over his shoulder he says, "Relax, Mom, it's going to be a great day."

Somewhat calmed by his good humor, I unbutton my coat and wait, fidgeting with the clippings and photos Mike has tacked to his refrigerator. Photos of his friends . . . his latest interests . . .

My firstborn has turned into a loving, well-adjusted man, I realize—marveling that he even survived his adolescence, with a crumbling marriage as a backdrop and a controlling father for an antagonist. I remember that critical night (was he just sixteen?!) when he cornered me in the kitchen and lectured me: "Mom, you deserve better than this."

At the time, I wasn't sure if it was a plea for my liberation or his.

Did I do right by him? I think so, but did he come through unscathed? After the divorce it was a struggle to raise Mike's teen brothers and try to help him heal, too, into a whole adult. We are close now, maybe because he admired my courage. Or perhaps he respects the life I've carved for myself that makes no demands on his.

Mike's step on the stairs interrupts my reverie. He plants a kiss on my cheek and presents me with an unwrapped box. I'm confused; we already exchanged presents on Chanukah.

The box is filled with travel brochures for the Hawaiian Islands, and I finger them enviously. I almost made it to the islands three years ago, but my mother became ill at the eleventh hour, and I had to cancel my flight.

Here's my son looking out for me again. Still trying to renew my dreams.

"These are great, Honey," I say, but inside I know I have no room for dreams. With my parents to care for, so many expenses, I can't even think about a vacation right now. And right now it's time to meet our dinner obligations.

"I can't wait to read these at my leisure," I hint, none too subtly, and slip the cover back on the box. Mike stops me.

"Have a look *now,*" he insists.

"We're going to be late, Mike," I almost plead.

"I'm not going anywhere until you look these over," he says quietly.

I work through the brochures and find an envelope at the bottom of the stack.

"What's this?"

My son just shrugs.

I gasp as I open the envelope to find a gift certificate for an open-ended, pre-paid, round-trip airline ticket to Oahu.

"I don't believe this!" I breathe out. "You're *giving* me this? Honey, I can't accept this from you."

Mike beams. "What do you mean, you can't accept this from me?" he laughs.

"Mike," my voice down to a whisper, "you work too hard for your money."

He's whispering now, too. "Mom, who deserves it more than you?"

Suddenly, I know: He really is okay.

Suddenly, I don't feel so lost for time.

Barbara Feder Mindel

A Faded Card

It's a quintessential Snoopy card: chipper message, bright colors, though a little yellow and faded now. Its simple message was never intended for someone like me, and though I've received fancier, more expensive cards over the years, this is the only one I've saved. One summer, it spoke volumes to me.

I received it during the first June I faced as a single mother, divorced after nineteen years of marriage and raising two teenage daughters alone. In all the emotional chaos of this sudden single parenthood, I was overwhelmed with, of all things, the simplest chores: leaky faucets, crabgrass, oil changes, even barbeques. Those had always been my husband's jobs, areas in which I was a total write-off. The girls were great cheerleaders, yet I stung with embarrassment every time I hit my thumb with a hammer or couldn't get the lawnmower started. My faltering attempts only fueled my underlying fear: How could I be both a father and mother to my girls? Clearly, I lacked the tools and skills.

On this particular morning, my girls propelled me into the living room to see something. (I prayed it wasn't another repair job.) The "something" turned out to be an envelope and several wrapped, misshapen bundles, clustered on the carpet. My bewilderment must have been plain as I gazed from the colorful packages to my daughters' bright faces.

"Go ahead! Open them!" they urged. As I unwrapped the packages, I discovered a small barbecue grill and all the necessary utensils, including a green kitchen mitt with a frog pattern on it.

"But why?" I asked.

"Happy Father's Day!" they chorused.

"Moms don't get presents on Father's Day," I protested.

"You forgot to open the card," Dawn reminded. I pulled it from the envelope. There sat Snoopy, on top of his doghouse, merrily wishing me a Happy Father's Day. "Because," the girls said, "you've been a father and mother to us. Why shouldn't you be remembered on Father's Day?"

As I fought back tears, I realized they were right. I wanted to be a "professional" dad, a Bob Vila who had the latest tools and knew all the tricks of the trade. The girls, though, were asking for a Tim Allen, a parent who wasn't afraid to make mistakes, who could laugh at herself and get up and try again. They only wanted a parent they could count on to be there, day after day, performing the repetitive, maintenance tasks of basic care and love.

The girls are grown now, and they still send me Father's Day cards, but none of those cards means as much to me as that first one. Its simple message told me being a great parent didn't require any special tools at all—just a willing worker.

Louise Lenahan Wallace

"Mom, you've been a real father to me."

Reprinted by permission of Andrew Toos.

What I Did on My Son's Summer Vacation

Example is not the main thing in influencing others. It is the only thing.

Albert Schweitzer

When I was a young boy, I keenly missed doing things with my father. He was always just too busy, too unavailable. As young as I was, I vowed I would never be like my father when I grew up.

As a grown-up, I found myself a single father to my son Kelly. A working freelance writer, the only thing scarcer for me than money was time—time to play with Kelly. But remembering my childhood promise, I made the time.

In the summer of 1984, when Kelly was ten, we decided to enter the Auburn Funk Soapbox Derby, held in Auburn, California, just northeast of Sacramento, where we lived. It's a historic gold-rush town, with steep and scenic streets, and the derby attracts dozens of entries and thousands of spectators.

The unique requirement of this race is that your soapbox racer be as "funky" or outlandish as possible. Almost anything goes. That stumped me, but Kelly decided he wanted a go-cart with an enormous Groucho Marx nose and glasses on the front.

Operating on a tight budget, we began the search for materials, and in the next few days Kelly and I scavenged for anything that might work, including a piece of plywood that we found along the highway, old newspapers for papier-maché, chicken wire, garbage bags and much more.

With enthusiasm, my son molded the nose from chicken wire. I covered the wire shape with dozens of wet strips of newspaper, creating a papier-maché skin.

When the racer was almost done, Kelly added a special touch that only a boy would think of: drag chutes to stop the racer, made of garbage bags.

I looked at our racer with the huge nose and glasses. Kelly pulled the lever that wiggled the eyebrows, and I thought, *You can't get much more outlandish than this!*

The day of the race Kelly and I could hardly contain our excitement as we watched the activity of Sacramento Street where the derby was in preparation.

But when we wheeled him to the starting line, Kelly took one look down the steep and winding hill, lined with thousands of spectators, and paled.

I thought he might chicken out, so I promised to run alongside him, and he decided to give it a try.

He was stiff when I helped him into the car, and when the starting gun sounded he was slow to go. Still nervous, Kelly rode the brakes too much, but he faithfully wiggled the eyebrows, delighting the onlookers. When he neared the finish line, he deployed his drag chutes, and the crowd roared with cheers and applause.

But riding the brakes had taken its toll. His momentum spent, he stopped just a few yards short of the finish line.

It cost us points, but I pushed him the rest of the way,

feeling sick inside. *All the work we put into this contraption, and now Kelly is going to be so disappointed,* I thought.

I was wrong.

Hopping out of the car, he yelled, "Can I do it again?"

Kelly won second prize in his age category, which led to interviews by a local TV station and *Westways* magazine. Elated by his success, a "funky" Kelly wore his Groucho glasses throughout the interviews.

Going home, Kelly turned to me and said, "This is the best day of my life!"

And that, of course, made it one of the best days of my life as well.

When Kelly grew up, he entered the United States Military Academy at West Point. It was while he was stationed in Korea that I came upon the mouse-eaten remains of that derby soapbox nose and glasses, as I was cleaning out the garage.

I e-mailed Kelly and mentioned my find. In his reply, he reminisced about that day at the derby. "You know, building that crazy nose cart was something that factored into my decision to major in engineering at West Point."

I laughed to myself.

"Even though that derby was fourteen years ago, I remember it like it was yesterday, and I appreciate it more now that I realize how lucky I was to have a good father who took the time to do such a project. It wasn't just a half-hour game of catch or a two-hour movie. We did a major project together—and it was a scary event. It helped me confront my fears early in life."

My face sobered as I thought about him jumping out of airplanes in the middle of the night and other scary adventures that happen in the military.

It was the last two lines of Kelly's message that brought tears to my eyes: "A kid who does things like that with his dad will want to do them with his own children. To be that kind of a dad is an important goal of mine."

I knew then that every minute I had set aside for Kelly had been worth it. I had kept my vow, achieved my goal and passed on a loving legacy to my son.

Tom Durkin

Making the Grade

Suddenly, there I was: a single mother of four half-grown children. At first I was so overwhelmed by grief, I didn't know the difficulty of the task that lay ahead. But as the days turned into weeks and months, I felt increasingly inadequate.

My job was temporary, so when it ended we had to move. The next two jobs didn't work out. We ended up living in four small towns in three states over a period of only five years. This was so different from my own experience as a child, in which I had lived in the same house from age seven to twenty-one. How could I provide that same stability for my children, who had to adjust to a new home, a new school and new friends every two years?

My teaching job allowed me to see my children at school every day, but the high school activities I sponsored kept me away from home too many evenings and Saturdays. While I was gone, things happened that weren't good. Heavy rains flooded the basement, and while my children soaked up the water with layers of newspaper, the woman I'd hired to stay with them watched TV; my thirteen-year-old son took up smoking in the garage; and my ten-year-old daughter was befriended by a little girl who hung around with teenagers on street corners late into the night.

"Broken home!" I had heard the term whispered in my childhood. Whereas kids in stable two-parent homes like mine grew up to be well-adjusted, productive citizens, children from broken homes, everyone knew, were sure to fail in school, become juvenile delinquents and wind up in jail.

I tried. Oh, how I tried! I enrolled my sons in scouting, baseball and hunter safety programs so they could have male role models. But for the father-son events, they had to choose neighbors.

I tried to help them catch, throw and hit, but I was a terrible ballplayer.

We hiked and camped in national parks. When they were teenagers, we went on a pre-dawn duck-hunting foray in which I struggled to keep the pace but became hopelessly mired in a snowdrift. "We'll take you home, Mom," they offered.

Yes, I was a poor substitute for a father.

As for my daughters, well, I took them to ballets, gave them music lessons, watched them play basketball and do gymnastics. I did my best with curling irons and combs on school picture days. But I wasn't making the grade even as a mother. "Never mind, Mom," they told me as braids sagged, curls flopped.

"We like our hair plain."

I felt especially bad for my oldest daughter. At the tender age of twelve, she became my second-in-command, my lieutenant, my live-in baby-sitter. She nursed me through the emotional traumas of job losses and job hunting. She took her responsibilities as Head Kid seriously, alienating her brother who didn't want to obey her when I was gone. Oh, I taught her to drive, pump gas and check the oil; I sewed her prom dresses and made small talk with her dates while she finished fixing her hair. But secretly, I knew I had stolen her childhood.

When she went on to college, she loved it, as I knew she would. On her first Christmas break, she asked if I would like to read the essay she'd just received back from her freshman comp instructor. I thought it would be an English-teacher thing-we'd discuss split infinitives, semicolons and pronoun agreement, just as I had done with my father, who had been an editor.

"No," she told me. "Just read it. It's about being from a single-parent family."

I couldn't hide my dismay. Our dirty laundry, our hopelessly "broken" home displayed in the public forum of her English class!

"Okay, I'll read it to you," she insisted. "Just listen."

In silence, I listened to my daughter's version of her youth. She'd learned responsibility and independence, she wrote. Through our shared trials, our family had become more closely bonded than the families of her more privileged friends. She could pack a suitcase, a car trunk, a household, a trailer-even a rental moving truck. Our home was a place other kids came to play, a gathering place for preteens, a refuge for teen friends whose own families were in turmoil.

I was stunned. The list of advantages she had derived from being in a single-parent family just went on and on. When she finished reading, I didn't know what to say. Where I had seen only misfortune, she had discovered blessings.

That incident took place over fifteen years ago. Today my daughter is a happily married mother of two sons. I don't know that I have ever told her how much I admire her. All those years I'd labored under the guilt of my inadequacies, she had found opportunity. Where I had seen the proverbial glass as half-empty, she had found it not just half-full but overflowing.

There had been nothing broken about our home after all.

Perhaps I did make the grade as a mom.

6

SINGLE AGAIN

There will come a time when you believe everything is finished. That will be the beginning.

Louis L'Amour

Love Is Just Like a Broken Arm

Storms make trees take deeper roots.

Claude McDonald

"But what if I break my arm again?" my five-year-old daughter asked, her lower lip trembling.

I knelt, holding on to her bike, and looked her right in the eyes. I knew how much she wanted to learn to ride, how she often felt left out when her friends pedaled by our house. Yet ever since she'd fallen off her bike and broken her arm, she'd been afraid.

"Oh, honey," I said. "I don't think you'll break another arm."

"But I could. Couldn't I?"

"Yes," I admitted and found myself struggling for the right thing to say. At times like this I wished I had a partner to turn to, someone who might help find the right words to make my little girl's problems disappear. But after a disastrous marriage, and a painful divorce, I'd welcomed the hardships of being a single parent and had been adamant in telling anyone who tried to fix me up that I was terminally single.

"I don't think I want to ride," she said and got off her bike.

We walked away and sat down beside a tree. "Don't you want to ride with your friends?" I asked.

"Yes," she admitted.

"And I thought you were hoping to start riding your bike to school next year," I added.

"I was," she said, her voice almost a quiver.

"You know, Hon," I said. "Most everything you do comes with risks. You could get a broken arm in a car wreck and then be afraid to ever ride in a car again. You could break your arm jumping rope. You could break your arm at gymnastics. Do you want to stop going to gymnastics?"

"No," she said, and with a determined spirit she stood up and agreed to try again.

I held onto the back of her bike until she found the courage to say, "Let go."

I spent the rest of the afternoon at the park, watching a very brave little girl overcome a fear, and congratulating myself for being a self-sufficient, single parent.

As we walked home, pushing the bike as we made our way along the sidewalk, she asked me about a conversation she'd overheard me having with my mother the night before.

"Why were you and Grandma arguing last night?"

My mother was one of the many people who constantly tried to fix me up. How many times had I told her "no" to meeting the Mr. Perfect she'd picked out for me? She just knew Steve was the man for me.

"It's nothing," I told her.

She shrugged. "Grandma said she just wanted you to find someone to love."

"What Grandma wants is for some guy to break my heart again," I snapped, angry that my mother had said anything about this to my daughter.

"But Mom—"

"You're too young to understand," I told her.

She was quiet for the next few minutes, then she looked up and in a small voice gave me something to think about. "So I guess love isn't like a broken arm."

Unable to answer, we walked the rest of the way in silence. When I got home I called my mother and scolded her for talking about this to my daughter. Then I did what I'd seen my brave little girl do that very afternoon. I let go and agreed to meet Steve.

Steve *was* the man for me. We married less than a year later. It turned out Mother—and my daughter—were right.

Christie Craig

"I think your dad should take my mom out to dinner. They both look like they could use a good meal."

Reprinted by permission of Martha Campbell.

LET the MAGIC BEGIN

Your vision will become clear only when you look into your heart . . . . Who looks outside, dreams. Who looks inside, awakens.

Carl Jung

About six years ago, it seemed as if I had achieved everything I could ever have imagined. I had international fame as an actress, producer, writer and star of a top-ten television series, *That's Incredible!* In addition, as a former international tennis champion, I was an all-around athlete in top physical condition. I was also involved in an extraordinary, loving relationship with someone I believed was the man of my dreams. To top it all off, I enjoyed the comfort of a seemingly tight-knit family, I had become a multimillionaire and I had even started my own charitable foundation! Everything I had ever dreamed of was coming true—fame, success, wealth, happiness.

Then, in a matter of months, I lost it all! I lost everything [illegible] orked my entire life to achieve, everything I [illegible] ered. My fall was as meteoric and dramatic

of self-esteem I might have had. I'd gone bankrupt all right. Not only that, the insidious disease had also found its way into the center of my psyche.

I am nothing!?

I sat in that courtroom for nearly eight hours, enduring all manner of humiliation. Once outside, I made a beeline for my car, and the minute I got inside, tears began streaming down my face. Within seconds, the tears had become sobs—deep, hysterical sobs, the likes of which I had never experienced before. The dam had finally burst.

When I got home, I collapsed on the living-room floor. Time passed in a blur. Then suddenly, I heard a phone ringing on the table beside me. It was my sister, Linda Lou, in Washington, D.C.

"Hi," she said. "How are you doing?"

I couldn't utter a word. My entire body was racked with sobs.

"What's wrong?" she asked. "Tell me. I can't hear you. Talk to me."

No words came. Only more sobs.

"Talk to me, please."

Nothing.

In the inimitable Crosby family fashion, my sister immediately called our aunt, Gene, for help. My aunt assured Linda Lou that she would take over and drive straight to my house. Because she and my uncle live in Pasadena, which is a forty-five-minute drive away, she decided to call first. Interestingly, when I later sat down to write my book, *LET the MAGIC BEGIN,* I would have sworn that she had made that drive and had stayed with me the whole time. But the truth is, she didn't. She stayed on the telephone for almost five hours, because once she had me on the line, she was afraid to hang up and lose the connection.

"Nothing can kill your spirit, Cathy Lee, nothin
Gene kept repeating. "Even when you coul

you were always ready for life. You wanted to try everything now. You would even wake up laughing, raring to go, raring to explore. Remember? You were this free spirit always ready to climb the highest mountain. Even though so much has been taken from you, you're still Cathy Lee. You're still you. Now is not the time to give up. The sun will come up tomorrow, I promise."

And on it went, hour after hour, aunt to niece, friend to friend, soul to soul. Finally, at about two o'clock in the morning, I began to fall asleep.

My aunt whispered, "Sweet dreams, Li'l Kitten," and we both sleepily hung up the phone.

I slept for only about three hours, but what actually happened during that time I wouldn't fully understand for quite a while. Maybe Mr. Haberbush, in an odd twist of fate, had been right. Maybe I did become "nothing" that night. Whatever the case, those three hours of sleep would turn out to be a gift so magical that it would change my life forever.

When I awoke in the morning, I felt as if I had landed in a whole new world. It seemed as if every ounce of the scar tissue I had acquired during the last five years had been miraculously ripped away. The "me" I had known no longer existed. I felt strangely peaceful. Interestingly, I had "nothing"—no viewpoint, no opinions, no judgments. I had no desire for anything and no need for anything. There was "nothing" to win, and likewise, there was "nothing" to lose. All that remained was a clear, calm connection to Everything.

I couldn't believe that someone like myself, who had experienced such a life of activity, energy and passion, was actually enjoying the feeling of *nothingness!* The magnificence of the feeling astonished me.

Even more remarkable, perhaps, was the total absence of fear. For the first time in my life, I felt that there was *nothing* to be afraid of. Nothing could ever stop me, or hurt me, or betray me or do anything to me again—because I realized that my "experience" of life and who I was were actually one and the same. More precisely, how I experienced the events in my life had very little to do with the "facts" of those events—yet everything to do with my "interpretation" of those facts.

My slate had been wiped clean. It was as if each moment of my experience was a mirror, and in that mirror I was looking straight at myself and my connection to Everything.

In my journey through "nothingness," and back onto my destined path, I reconnected with the magical realm of pure possibility we all knew as children, a place I call the Bliss Zone™, I became aware that a distinct, Divine "energy" was moving through me at every moment, a "life force" alive with joy and wonder and unlimited potential.

I realized that being aware of and connecting with this flow in each and every moment allows us to join in the "dance of the Universe," always open to the "coincidences" and infinite possibilities within.

Stepping into the "Dance" allows us to bring the full potential of our *essential nature* into physical form. This is the key to our journey back into the "Magic" of life in all its passion and wonder.

Of course, God had been trying to tell me this for a very long time. It's just that I finally learned how to listen.

Cathy Lee Crosby

The Drawer Wouldn't Close

Though no one can go back and make a brand new start, anyone can start from now and make a brand new ending.

Anonymous

"I'm sorry, Ma'am. There must be a mistake. We have your husband scheduled as being on vacation."

The voice on the other end of the line spoke in carefully arranged words.

"Vacation! No, no. He's supposed to be on a business trip."

"I'm sorry." Pause. The voice began to falter a little as we both realized what was happening. "We have no information about a business trip."

And so it was that a life that began in bliss ended in betrayal.

It's not a cliché when it's your life.

My husband had kissed me tenderly before he left for the airport that day. "You've never looked more beautiful," he said. "Don't forget Wednesday is our date night. I love you."

I had noted how handsome he was, as always, with tall frame, salt-and-pepper hair, and a sharp busi

After thirty years of marriage, three children and three grandchildren, I could honestly say my heart still flip-flopped every time he walked in the door.

After he left, though, I spent the day fighting off an unusual feeling of loneliness. Blaming it on the dreary weather, I spent the day by the fire with a book until I finally retired, still uneasy. At 6:00 A.M. I awoke feeling that something was very wrong. Thinking I'd had a bad dream, I waited for the panic to pass, but it didn't. Finally I decided to do something I almost never did: phone my husband at his hotel. Every night when he was away on business he would phone me. I had never felt the need to call myself. This time I did.

It was after the hotel call, the one where a desk clerk found "no one registered under that name," that I called the office hoping for a hotel mix-up.

A few months later, my husband filed for divorce.

A few years later, still working through the pain, I began leading divorce-recovery workshop groups at my local church. I had endured personal loss, defeat and rejection. I had dealt with the pain my family had to bear on my behalf. My deepest wounds, though, had been self-inflicted, brought on by my anger at being an unwilling participant in a divorce.

While doing housework one day, I was thinking about how much pain I could have avoided—and others could, too—when I suddenly turned off the vacuum and sat down with a notepad and pen. I began writing. Page after page. Spilling out words of healing, a few lines at a time.

When I ran out of thoughts, I looked at the pages and shrugged, wondering what it was all about. Then I stuck them in a desk drawer.

Yet I kept feeling the urge to get those notes out and read [illegible]em again. After a while, I did, and was surprised to find [illegible]y read like greeting-card verses. Where was I going with this? I had no funds to hire an artist or pay a printer.

I put the notes back in the drawer.

The nudgings continued. Then it occurred to me that I did know one artist. Without giving myself a chance to back out, I called my former husband and, in a rush of words, preluded with "This is strictly business," I told him my idea.

He asked me to read some of the verses, then after hearing a few said he'd love to design original watercolor art for them. He would provide funds for printing costs, as well.

A week later, my former husband delivered to my door a bouquet of eight beautiful watercolors, all perfectly matching the emotion of my verses.

I named the cards "Ex's & Oh's."

A front-page article about my venture and my unique partnership with my ex-husband appeared in the business section of the Colorado Springs newspaper. The story was picked up by the Associated Press, generating phone calls from across the country. I did radio, television and newspaper interviews, and even got a call inviting me to be a guest on the *Today* show.

Thanks to all this publicity, "Ex's & Oh's" have been sent to spouses, children, parents, in-laws and friends going through divorce. And the calls that have meant the most to me by far haven't been from media. They've been from individuals who have told me how they've used the greeting cards to work through the "I'll-get-you-back" kind of pain that can be the most debilitating in a divorce.

One woman who ordered the greeting cards wrote me saying, "Thank you for being a light in the darkness."

That's what astonishes me the most about all this. God had plans for me. He somehow squeezed light from the darkest moments of my life.

I had a drawer that wouldn't close. So I looked inside it. And I found the plans for a new life.

Jan Nations

"I've finally gotten over Michael. It took three weeks just to get him out of my computer system."

The Ten-Dollar Bill

All the art of living lies in a fine mingling of letting go and holding on.

Havelock Ellis

After years of tolerating marriage to an alcoholic husband, I finally reached the painful decision that the only way for my two young children and me to survive was to get a divorce. It wasn't something I wanted to do, but it had to be done.

However, even after the divorce, problems with my ex-husband continued, and I realized I had no choice but to leave town. Once again, I didn't really want to, because I liked my house and the neighborhood, but I had to do what was necessary.

I found a real estate agent, listed my house for sale and made arrangements to transfer my insurance sales job to Seattle, fourteen hundred miles away. Then I sat back and waited for something to happen. And waited. And waited. Nothing happened for months on end. I changed real estate agents twice, but still there were no serious buyers in sight. And I couldn't afford to leave town until I sold my house.

The stress of the divorce and the subsequent living in limbo was almost too much for me. I had difficulty sleeping. In fact, the only place I could sleep turned out to be church. I'd go there every week and sink wearily into the third or fourth pew. I was all right through the early part of the service when we sang hymns, passed the collection plate and listened to the sermon for the children. But by the time the main sermon started, I would nod off and not wake up until it was over.

I guessed that Reverend McKinley, the minister, had noticed my somnolence because one day he announced that the title of his sermon was "On Sleeping in Church." I don't have any idea what was actually in that sermon because, as usual, I slept soundly through the whole thing. I apologized to the minister that day after church. He took my hand and shook it warmly. "Don't worry about it," he said. "Obviously this is where you're supposed to be."

Spring came. More than six months had passed and still my house was not sold. If my prayer to be shown whether I was right to move to Seattle was being answered, the answer was obviously a resounding no.

One Sunday, Reverend McKinley called the children to come up for their sermon. Once they were seated in front of him, he told them all to hold out a single hand. Reaching into the pocket of his robe, he pulled out a roll of one-dollar bills and placed one in each outstretched hand. Then he reached into another pocket and pulled out a ten-dollar bill.

"You can have this," he told the children, who were sitting attentively, clutching their one-dollar bills. "But in order to take this, you have to let go of what you already have." He held the ten-dollar bill out at arm's length.

It was an amusing sight. Not one of those little children was willing to let go of his one-dollar bill. Yet they were all old enough to know that ten dollars is better than one.

Eventually, Reverend McKinley put his ten dollars back into his pocket.

At least that little demonstration kept me awake for a while, before I resumed my customary slumbers. I didn't even hear what the minister said to the children after that.

But that night in bed, as I tried to go to sleep, suddenly, the penny dropped. My eyes opened, and as I stared up in the darkness, I knew exactly what I had been doing wrong—I was clinging on with my little fist to a puny, tattered one-dollar bill! Of course my house hadn't sold. I was still so attached to it. I was so accustomed to moving in the same groove, day in, day out, through each room, attached to the placement of everything like a prisoner who has come to love the familiarity of his own jail cell. In short, I had loved my house too much. And I also realized in the same moment that I wasn't confident enough that a "ten-dollar bill" was out there for me in Seattle. I couldn't see it, I couldn't taste it, I couldn't touch it. As far as I was concerned, moving out there was a leap in the dark, and I was scared of it.

As the lesson of the sermon continued to percolate into my suddenly alert midnight brain, I knew I just had to let go. Strip off the habits of many years. Make the big leap. Know that I had a parachute and that I would land safely.

And that was exactly what I did. My attitude underwent a 180-degree turn. I was ready to cast off the old, and I was eager for the new challenge. I wanted that ten-dollar bill, and I released my one dollar to the four winds.

Soon after this my house sold, and the children and I moved to our new lives in Seattle.

Letting go of my "one" set me on a path that allowed me to follow a long-postponed dream of becoming a writer. It also led to a new husband, three more children and eventually three grandchildren. My "ten" includes countless blessings that I never could have imagined in my old life, but before I could have any of them, I had to open my hand and release everything I was holding on to.

And yes, my "ten" also includes staying awake during sermons.

J. A. Jance

Looking Toward the Light

If a man happens to find himself, he has a mansion which he can inhabit with dignity all the days of his life.

James A. Michener

I hadn't planned on finding myself alone in an underwater cavern beneath the jungle floor near Akumal, Mexico. Truth is, I'd expected to be with my wife. But two weeks before this long-anticipated vacation, she ended our fifteen-year marriage and turned my life upside down.

The trip had been planned for months. Tickets had been purchased. Friends had been told. And, after making careful arrangements for the care of our children, my wife and I eagerly awaited departure.

Then our lives fell apart.

Of course, it had been a long time coming and both of us had seen the signs. Yet when the final breakup occurred, it took me by surprise—the hand of life had seized me by the throat and given me a good shake.

The final scene of our marriage remains etched in my memory as if it happened this morning: me standing in the front yard, already feeling the heavy weight of fear and loss and panic closing in as her car screeched off.

That awful feeling stayed with me in the weeks and months that followed—a certainty in the pit of my stomach that the bottom of my world had dropped out and that nothing would ever be the same.

But in the midst of my depression, I decided to make the Mexico diving trip anyway, believing, I suppose, that the diversion would do me some good. I had been diving since I was sixteen and, over the years, felt as if I'd seen it all. I had glided through the dancing kelp forests off Southern California, spotted the dim vision of a shipwreck in Florida waters, plunged ecstatically into an underwater canyon in the Cayman Islands and encountered a shark in Hawaii.

Something I hadn't experienced, though, was a cenote—one of those dark, mystical ponds in the jungle, the mirage-of-a-swimming-hole that shouldn't be there. I'd heard that some cenotes open into awesomely beautiful underwater caverns, and I intended to see one with my own eyes.

The sense of foreboding was still with me as I stepped off the plane and shuffled, alone, into the airport in Mexico. As divers, we are taught to stay out of the water when in emotional turmoil, that panic is the number-one enemy of survival underwater. Nonetheless, I told myself, the experience would help me leave the past behind and move on to the future.

I turned out to be right, but in ways I never imagined.

It was cold the day I arrived at the cenote in the Yucatan jungle. Our group of divers—none of whom I had met before—was accompanied by a local guide. I remember struggling to pull on my wet suit, shivering with excitement tinged with the subtle anticipation of doom to which I had grown accustomed. Slowly, tentatively, we swam out to the middle of the pool and descended.

At the bottom, thirty feet down, we paused for a

moment, gazing at the otherworldly mineral formations on the walls. The first thing that struck me was the quality of the light. It was weird, eerie—somehow ethereal.

In front of us lay a wide cavern. Entering the mouth, we swam toward the back wall, where the cavern narrowed into a small, dark tunnel, snaking deep into the earth. The tunnel entrance was marked by rusty metal signs in Spanish. *Peligro,* they warned—Danger—and *No Pase Adelante*—Do Not Proceed.

Legend has it that the ancient Mayans used cenotes to make human sacrifices. Staring at those ominous signs illuminated in the beam of my light, I thought about what might lie in the tunnel beyond. Not that I would find out: None of us in the group were certified cave divers, nor had we brought any lines. Right then and there, sucking hard on my regulator, I decided to keep the cavern exit in sight.

We swam up to the ceiling of the cavern. There, cut into the rock as if honed by some ancient hand, a small indentation thrusted upward. One of the other divers, a young man who'd been here before, stuck his head into the hole and motioned me to follow. I did, and was shocked to find my face above water—a dank air pocket with room for just two heads. Grinning, the man spit out his regulator and looked me in the eye: "Is this cool, or what?"

His voice, bouncing off the pressing walls, was disembodied and muffled, like it was coming from inside a coffin. I pulled out my regulator and responded, "Very cool!"

But the voice was not mine. It was the small, distant sound of a man in a bottle. A man caught in a place he shouldn't be, struggling to control the rising wave of dread that, until now, had been willfully kept at bay.

I stuffed the regulator back in my mouth and slid out of the hole to the bottom of the cavern. Then it happened. My fins must have stirred up the silt on the cenote floor because suddenly I was enveloped in a blinding cloud.

Frantically I tried to keep my bearings, tried to keep the light of the cavern opening in view. But as silt billowed all around me, it became increasingly difficult. For what seemed like an eternity, I peered into nothingness, determined not to move my eyes from the spot where the exit had been. Then, with a sinking feeling, I realized I no longer knew the way out.

Panic. It growled at me, bared its gnarly teeth. Every pore of me wanted to bolt, to escape, to swim frantically in the direction I had last seen the light. The only thing that stopped me was the knowledge that I could just as easily be rushing toward my death in the dark.

They tell you about panic in dive class. Don't give in to it, they say. The solution is simple, really. Stop. Breathe. Think. Act. And so began the voice of reason, more a whimper than a shout.

"Don't move," the voice told me, and I froze. "Think," it said, and I tried to figure my way out. Silt rises and so it also must fall. For what seemed like forever, I hung there, totally alone, with my guts churning. Then, as quickly as the cloud enveloped me, it disappeared, and once again I could see my way clear.

After that, the lesson of that dive—indeed, of all dives—became a mantra for me, a metaphor for what was happening in my life: Stay calm, don't bolt. Keep your eye in the direction of the light, even if you can't see it. Have faith that one day you will see it again.

It's been six years since my wife left me and I encountered darkness in a cenote. During that time I often felt like bolting. I frequently thought I would lose my sanity altogether. But I didn't. As in the cenote, I hung there in silence, staring toward the invisible light. My patience was rewarded with the eventual settling of the silt that was obscuring my vision. It returned slowly to the bottom of the cavern that was my life until, at last, I saw my way clear.

Boy, what a view.

David Haldane

Lightning's Gift

The morning began like the others before it, with no warning or premonition of what was coming. I lay in bed and watched the red ball of sun creep over the horizon as depression drained away all anticipation of the day ahead. During the past months despair had convinced me there was nothing beyond this dismal, dark moment in my life; it would go on forever, unlighted, unchanged.

With twenty years of marriage ended, I was now one of the single parents I had only read about before. Taking my two daughters "home" to be with family hadn't helped. Housing in a town with four colleges was impossible, staying with relatives was difficult and I'd become obsessed with finding a job and a place for the three of us to live. Today was my younger daughter's birthday, and I had done nothing in preparation for it.

Overwhelmed by these circumstances as I watched daybreak's orange streaks spread across the sky, I whispered a prayer. "God, I can't do this alone. It's too hard being a parent all by myself—help me, please. Help me to give Katy a special birthday today and help me find the will to live so I can be the parent my girls need."

I spent the morning checking apartments and job

openings before taking birthday cupcakes to Katy's class. I wasted two hours looking for the perfect gift within my budget—an impossibility—so it was late afternoon before I headed to my cousin's home in the country.

A radio weather bulletin warning of rapidly approaching thunderstorms, hail and high winds caught my attention. I drove faster. I needed to do my running before the storm hit. Since my daily two-mile jog temporarily lifted my spirits, I didn't want to miss it. I parked at the driveway's edge, changed to sneakers and began to run.

The sky to the west was darkening as I left the driveway for the road, and I saw faint streaks of lightning in the distance, accompanied by low rumbles of thunder. The storm was so far away as I turned toward the east that I quit worrying and enjoyed the quiet countryside while I ran.

It was still a typically warm autumn afternoon when I entered the large grove of trees that marked my usual turnaround point, but as I emerged from the leafy tunnel's darkness for the run home, I saw massive black clouds boiling up from the west, their edges hanging in shreds. Sharp, jagged streaks of lightning snaked down from them. The incredible fireworks would have been beautiful to watch if I hadn't been so far from home. The growls of thunder grew louder and more insistent as I started the second mile; fear increased with every step, making it difficult to breathe, but I ran faster, adrenaline spurring me on. I told myself the storm was still a long way off.

The air was suddenly, impossibly, still. The sun cast a strange, greenish light over the landscape. No birds sang. The trees, even the meadow grasses, stopped their swaying. The breath had been sucked from everything, leaving me running in a vacuum. I had to keep going, but every step was agony.

Now only one long, steep hill lay between me and the safety of home. I pushed down my rising panic and concentrated on breathing and running. As I neared the crest of the hill, the hair on my body lifted in a strange, crawling way. Confused and disoriented, I stopped. Suddenly, a hard thrust like a large hand across my back shoved me to my knees. The whole world exploded. A brilliant flash of light blinded me. The ground shook underneath me. A terrible roar filled my ears.

I felt another hard thrust; its impact knocked me flat to the ground. I lay there—my hands ground into the gravel, my face pressed hard into the pavement—and hung on while the world shook and trembled. Gradually my vision cleared and the violent shaking eased. My only thought was to get home. I tried to stand. Every muscle in my body cramped. I crawled on hands and knees, moving crab-like toward the top of the hill. A screaming wind whipped dirt into my mouth and eyes while I gasped for breath. I turned my head to clear my vision and saw a bolt of lightning strike a tall metal fence post at the edge of the field. A ball of fire rolled across the ditch, blinding me with its glare. I flattened out on the pavement again, beyond caring where the ball of fire had gone.

The earth vibrated with violent thunder. On both sides of the road, trees bent double in the wind. Lightning cracked the sky open, and thunder roared all around me. I knew terror in a way I never imagined possible—I was trapped. As surely as if I had stumbled into a field of land mines, there was no way out. I screamed in terror, my cries to God rivaling the storm's fury. Fear became frenzy and then subsided into something else; it was strangely exhilarating to have life simplified to this wild struggle for survival, and for the first time in months I felt alive. I lifted myself on all fours, ready to take my chances against the storm. Bent double, I moved slowly up the hill while the elements battered me. I made it to the driveway and fell into my car.

When the girls got home and the storm clouds cleared, we drove back along the road. Less than ten feet from where I fell the first time, the metal fence post was melted into a blackened, grotesque sculpture. We saw the path the fireball burned across the meadow, stopping within inches of where I had flattened against the road. I looked in the rearview mirror at my red, swollen face and black eyes and laughed for the first time in weeks. I was alive!

Nothing would ever be the same again. Confronting death made me realize the preciousness of life; I intended to live it to the fullest. I might be single, but I was not alone. God brought me through the storm, and my daughters were waiting for me. Katy put her arms around me, "Mom, right now the best birthday present I could have is for you to be alive to celebrate with me." A lightning storm had been the unlikely means to answer my prayer—it gave Katy a gift and me the will to live.

Maggie Baxter

Starting Over

I try to avoid looking forward or backward, and try to keep looking upward.

Charlotte Brontë

Four years ago, on a rainy January night, I picked my mom up from the San Diego, California, airport. Her flight from Seattle had been relatively short, but nonetheless she looked drained and frail. Just hours before, her best friend in Washington had helped her pack some belongings, and had somehow maneuvered her onto that plane. After being in an abusive relationship for many years, my mom had finally decided she was ready to take control of her life, so we had agreed she would leave her home and come live with me.

That first night I held her as she cried herself to sleep. The ache in my heart called out to the deep sadness in hers. I had always loved my mom but was shortsighted, as children often are, when it came to seeing her as an individual. But now as we lay together I felt how wounded she was. This wasn't the mom whom I, as a child, had always expected to be strong and all-knowing. Nor was she the uncool, boring old-timer I saw through the lens of my rebellious teenage years. No, this was a flesh-and-blood woman in her own right, with a heart and a soul, with her own hopes, dreams and disappointments—and her own pain.

In those first few weeks at my house, the only thing that held my mother together was her faith that God would help her find her way, somehow. I often heard her pray for guidance and strength, and I always added my silent "Amen" to her petition.

In February, the local Christian university advertised a degree completion program. "Earn a bachelor's degree in just two years," the announcement read. I immediately thought of Mom, who never had the opportunity to complete her education. I showed the ad to her, and she agreed it looked interesting, so I made an appointment with a guidance counselor at the college. Mom and I walked in thinking that we would just be gathering information that day. An hour later, my mom walked out a newly enrolled university student.

Over the next twenty-four months, every Tuesday night, my mom packed up her school bag, kissed me good-bye and drove herself to class. At first, she was apprehensive about being a fifty-three-year-old college student. However, she soon found herself in a tightly knit group of people from all stages and walks of life, and her spirit took flight.

Each month that passed brought her battered heart a renewed sense of hope, strength and independence. I watched with joy as she began to view herself differently. No longer was she timid about her own capabilities and achievements. No longer was she reticent about expressing her own opinions. She was realizing once more that she was a person who mattered. A person whose hopes and desires could still float on the updraft of dreams. A person who had courage and stamina. A person who was valuable, not because she was or had been a wife or a mother or a friend, but because of who she essentially was, in herself. My mom discovered her own worth.

Just over two years later, on a warm May afternoon, I helped my mom gather together the things she needed. I tied the sash on her dress and assisted her into the long, black satin gown. I took pictures as we headed down the stairs, into the car and across town. I laughed as she climbed the steps of the university and ran to join her classmates, who were joyfully hugging and congratulating each other.

I cried tears of happiness as my mom crossed the stage and received her diploma. She was beaming. And for a moment I thought back to the broken-hearted woman who had arrived at the San Diego airport two years before. But that woman was nowhere to be seen now. There was only this confident, firm-stepping lady—my honored and beloved mother—descending from the stage, her black gown swirling, her face radiating delight, ready for the next adventure that life would bring. She had left the only life she knew and found herself as a result.

Jennifer Harris

My Sailor Man

The naked truth is always better than the best-dressed lie.

Ann Landers

Both of us between husbands and feeling carefree, a friend and I ventured to a dance club playing sixties rock 'n' roll music one night in the early eighties.

We stood in the back, watching the theatrics of both dancers and band. Absorbed in the atmosphere, I hadn't noticed the young man standing next to me until he asked for a dance.

His name was Terry, and he served as a first mate on a dredge ship currently in dry dock on the banks of the Columbia River. A merchant marine, he enjoyed the luxury of working one week on and one week off. As we talked, I recognized a spiritual kinship. On his reading list were *The Road Less Traveled* by M. Scott Peck and *Illusions* by Richard Bach. All evening we discussed the power of positive thought, the creative potential everyone possesses, the oneness of humanity—not the usual bar conversation. But we both communicated that neither of us wanted a committed relationship, just companionship. We both lied.

I admired his appearance—six-foot-three, great physique, dark, thick hair, dark-brown almond-shaped eyes and an exotic aura, the result of his Indonesian and Dutch heritage. I imagined him posing for the pages of some studly magazine, instead of holding me in his arms on the dance floor. That evening, I left the club enamored.

The following day he met my three children. I warmed at his instant rapport with them. His potential as a partner increased moment by moment. Already I'd formed a list of positive attributes beyond the obvious physical ones—like the mutual fondness between him and my children, and his embrace of a similar spiritual philosophy.

Over the years, I came to discover a deeply compassionate soul, an attentive listener, a wise human being. The measure of his thoughtfulness and kindness caught me off-guard. When my children's birthdays came around, he offered gifts to both them and me. "It's a big day for you, too," Terry said. "This is the anniversary of the day you labored them into life." I thrived on his unconditional love of me.

In the four years we dated, I kept watching for the emergence of his dark side. The only annoying thing I ever came up with was that he held his face too close to his plate when he ate—a ship-borne habit. Without a good handle on his "grub," his plate might end up in his shipmate's lap, especially on the open seas. It wasn't much of a defect, but it was all that surfaced.

We had, however, one irreconcilable difference, which we both ignored. Terry was eleven years younger than I. At his age, I'd married, borne three children, owned a home and struggled through a divorce. I'd already lived a life he had yet to experience. Terry never kept his love of children a secret, or his desire for parenthood. He became a volunteer in the Children's Celebration at our church, joined a Big Brother program and visited his home in North Carolina, as much to play with his nieces and nephews as to see the rest of his family. I'd made it perfectly clear that there'd be no more babies for me. The years of raising three children alone had convinced me.

Neither of us wanted to address the issue, so we tiptoed around it. After all, we fit together, were comfortable, happy and in love. But always, in the back of my mind, I couldn't bear the thought of his relinquishing parenthood to remain with me. On St. Patrick's Day, 1985, while both of us sat crying into green beers at Paddy's Bar, I said good-bye. We agreed to continue supporting each other emotionally until we discovered our perfect mates. His arrived sooner than mine. Within a year, he met Rita, a young Irish student majoring in early childhood education. A suitable match. Too distraught to attend the wedding, I sent my love and then hopped on a plane for San Francisco to visit my daughter.

After he married, I stumbled in and out of meaningless relationships. Occasionally, I'd see him and Rita at church, but I tried to avoid them. One look at my face, and Rita would know that I still loved her husband. I'd spare them that. *True relationships are eternal,* I told myself. *I'll keep his memory close to my heart. Maybe we'll meet again in the afterlife.*

Sundays, it was my job at church to attempt to regulate the noise during the minister's meditation time by bouncing noisy children with their parents into the family room. One Sunday, hearing a whimpering child in front of me, I placed my hand on the father's shoulder. Terry's eyes looked up. Neither of us spoke. Slowly he rose to face me, then he held out his arms, offering me his baby girl. Except for her blonde hair, she epitomized Terry. I held her close to my heart, cradling and comforting her. "You could have been mine," I whispered in her ear. "You could have been mine." Tears streamed from my eyes, dampening her blanket. When Terry and Rita rose for the group song, I returned their child. In the darkened church, I felt certain my tear-smudged makeup wouldn't give me away. Terry's soft eyes held mine for a long moment. We remained silent. Then he turned his attention back to his family and to the service. Quietly I slipped out of the room to weep over this final chapter in our love story.

Within a few more years, I'd meet and marry my life partner. But that day, the radiance in Terry's face as he offered me his child assured me that I'd made the right choice. I could only thank God for teaching me the truth about unconditional love. Sometimes it's best to love from a distance. . . . Other times, it means letting go.

Linda Ross Swanson

Paid in Full

Change your thoughts and you change your world.

Rev. Norman Vincent Peale

Dorothy was a devoted mother of four young children who desperately needed the court-ordered child support from her ex-husband, already a year in arrears. The fall school term had arrived, along with the usual expenses. There was no money for gym clothes and tennis shoes. There was no money to buy longer pants for the two boys who had grown several inches taller over the summer. Dorothy could barely contain the rage she felt toward her former husband when she saw her children, especially the youngest, go without things they needed.

She contacted the children's father, only to find him uncooperative. He had no job, he claimed. No extra money. Dorothy was furious. All she could think of was "that man" and his faults. Her thoughts were hateful, vengeful and constant.

In the mornings, she gritted her teeth in anger as she

helped the children dress for school. At work she found herself talking badly about her ex-husband, keeping her anger on the front burner. At the grocery store she shopped resentfully, choosing food she could stretch the longest for the least money. Whenever the children asked for something she couldn't afford, Dorothy would angrily point out that they couldn't even buy the basics because their father didn't send his child-support payments.

Every time she slipped into her old, beat-up car, Dorothy reminded herself how much she hated it. And him. Even in bed at night, Dorothy's stomach churned as bitter thoughts kept her from sleep.

Finally, though she knew it would do no good, Dorothy went to the district attorney's office and swore out a complaint against her ex-husband.

"That way, if he ever does get any money, I will get it," she told a friend. "And besides, this way the sheriff's department will make his life difficult. At least I can make him pay in some way."

But Dorothy never received any money from her action, nor any personal peace, not even satisfaction. The uppermost thought in Dorothy's mind continued to be her lack of money and her anger.

One morning, Dorothy woke with a strange sense that she should close out the complaint against her ex-husband. Startled, she shook away the thought as crazy. That man owed her the money so she could care for his children. Without the complaint there would be no pressure to pay support.

"But he isn't paying now," said her inner voice. "You are!"

Even as she comprehended the high emotional price she was paying for her anger, Dorothy refused to consider forgiving the debt and releasing herself from bitterness.

The thought persisted, however, throughout the day. Dorothy resisted. But by five o'clock, she made a sudden decision. She would go to the district attorney's office and if there was anyone there to help, she would cancel the complaint. Not quite believing what she was doing, Dorothy found someone on duty at the office and withdrew her complaint.

Outside the building, Dorothy felt sudden relief, as if a heavy burden had been lifted. She walked with a lighter step, an unexpected smile flooded her face and a strange peace settled over her.

"I still don't know how we're going to get along," she told her friend later. "But I did the right thing. I can't understand why, but I'm almost happy. My ex still owes us money and still ought to support his children, but I'm not going to be the one to make him. That's someone else's job now."

The next day, Dorothy's boss called her into the office and gave her an unexpected promotion. The net increase in salary was one hundred dollars a month more than the amount the court had ordered her ex-husband to pay in child-support payments.

Like many other fathers, Dorothy's ex-husband never did pay the child support. Like many other mothers, Dorothy made do with what she had. Sometimes it was tough, sometimes easier, but she never regretted letting go of her vengeful spirit. She had set herself free from a focus of resentment and, as result, got her life back. That was payment enough.

Bobbie Reed

7

LOSING A PARTNER

To live in hearts we leave behind is not to die.

Thomas Campbell

Rudy's Angel

I walked into the grocery store not particularly interested in buying groceries. I wasn't hungry. The pain of losing my husband of thirty-seven years was still too raw. And this grocery store held so many sweet memories.

Rudy often came with me, and most every time he'd pretend to go off and look for something special. I knew what he was up to. I'd always spot him walking down the aisle with three yellow roses in his hands. Rudy knew I loved yellow roses.

With a heart filled with grief, I only wanted to buy my few items and leave, but even grocery shopping was different since Rudy had passed on. Shopping for one took time, a little more thought than it had for two.

Standing by the meat, I searched for the perfect small steak and remembered how Rudy had loved his steak. Suddenly a woman came beside me. She was blond, slim and lovely in a soft green pantsuit. I watched as she picked up a large pack of T-bones, dropped them in her shopping cart, hesitated, and then put them back. She turned to go and once again reached for the pack of steaks. She saw me watching her, and she smiled.

"My husband loves T-bones, but honestly, at these prices, I don't know."

I swallowed the emotion down my throat and met her pale blue eyes. "My husband passed away eight days ago," I told her. Glancing at the package in her hands, I fought to control the tremble in my voice. "Buy him the steaks. And cherish every moment you have together."

She shook her head, and I saw the emotion in her eyes as she placed the package in her basket and wheeled away.

I turned and pushed my cart across the store to the dairy products. There I stood, trying to decide which size milk I should buy. A quart I finally decided, and moved on to the ice cream section near the front of the store. If nothing else, I could always fix myself an ice cream cone.

I placed the ice cream in my cart and looked down the aisle toward the front. I saw first the green suit, then recognized the pretty lady coming toward me. In her arms she carried a package. On her face was the brightest smile I had ever seen. I would swear a soft halo encircled her blond hair as she kept walking toward me, her eyes holding mine.

As she came closer, I saw what she held and tears began misting in my eyes.

"These are for you," she said and placed three beautiful, long-stemmed yellow roses in my arms. "When you go through the line, they will know these are paid for." She leaned over and placed a gentle kiss on my cheek.

I wanted to tell her what she'd done, what the roses meant, but still unable to speak, I watched her walk away as tears clouded my vision. I looked down at the beautiful roses nestled in the green tissue wrapping and found it almost unreal. How did she know?

Suddenly the answer seemed so clear. I wasn't alone. "Oh, Rudy, you haven't forgotten me, have you?" I whispered, with tears in my eyes. He was still with me, and she was his angel.

Wilma Hankins Hlawiczka

He Has Not Left Me

There is no end. There is no beginning. There is only the infinite passion of life.

Federico Fellini

My husband was tall, trim and handsome. He played squash three times a week and rode his bike for miles. Weekends he gardened, cut brush, sanded floors, put up shelves. Milt was a supremely healthy man.

Then in his early fifties, he developed hypertension. His internist put him on medication and advised him to stop smoking. A few years later, he developed a heart flutter. His doctor prescribed more medication and again asked him to stop smoking.

Milt was a physician. He knew that tobacco causes cancer. Yet he smoked like a furnace. Now he told me he wasn't going to smoke anymore. But he didn't really stop—he just wouldn't smoke when I was around, and I knew there was nothing I, Joyce Brothers, world-renowned psychologist, could do about it.

One morning in July 1987, Milt noticed blood in his urine. He checked into New York's Mount Sinai Hospital, where the surgeon found a malignant polyp inside his bladder. He cut it out and told us he thought he had gotten it all. The prognosis was good.

By late summer Milt resumed his practice. At times his clothes smelled of smoke when he came home at night. I think he tried, but even knowing he was putting his life at risk, he found it impossible to stop. Still, he was feeling stronger, and we picked up the threads of our life. It was a time of closeness for us.

In October, Milt went into the hospital for a checkup. "Everything appears fine," his surgeon told us. "But we won't know for sure until we get the biopsy results on Monday."

Monday dragged on and on. It was after 5 P.M. when the call came. Milt listened intently. Finally, he said, "Well, thank you," and hung up. The cancer had reappeared. I threw my arms around him. "You're strong," I told him. "You can beat it."

He ran his finger around my face and summoned a half smile. "I'll do my damnedest," he promised. "I've got a lot to live for."

Milt underwent a successful operation to have his bladder removed, and he never smoked again after the surgery—it took a scare of this magnitude to make him stop. As soon as he quit, his heart flutter went away. I could not help thinking, *If you had only stopped twenty years ago, none of this would have happened. How could he have been so stupid!* I was angry.

Milt's recovery seemed to go well, and he began seeing patients again. But in January 1988, another exam showed that the cancer had spread.

Milt's oncologist started him on chemotherapy. The side effects were horrendous: his hair began to fall out, he got exhausting hiccups and he was in constant pain. I was able to stop his hiccups with gentle massages. I would also brush his hair. He grumbled that I was babying him, but he loved it. I loved doing it. These were peaceful hours, and I felt overwhelmed by my love for him.

By spring, Milt had to close his office. He got hundreds of letters and calls, which cheered him immensely. I don't think he had realized quite how much his patients liked him and how important he was to them.

Milt was now in and out of the hospital so often that my visits to him there seem like a blur. We never talked about death. Instead we would say, "When I get back on my feet . . ." or "As soon as you regain your strength. . . ."

He seemed to be feeling stronger one sunny October morning, so I drove him up to our farm in the country. We stopped to buy eggs so we could have our ritual weekend breakfast. Fried eggs were his culinary specialty. He had a frying pan dedicated to eggs. I was not allowed to use it for anything. I made the toast and squeezed the orange juice. He ate everything. I was thrilled—he had not eaten that much for weeks.

After breakfast, he went outside alone. I watched him stand looking at the meadow where our daughter, Lisa, had been married. I watched as he walked down to the brook where he and our grandson Micah used to fish.

When it was time to leave, the last thing he said as he locked the door behind us was, "It's so beautiful here." There was a wistful note in his voice. We both knew he would probably never see the farm again.

That fall and winter, Milt's health went steadily downhill. The cancer spread to his bones.

He grew weaker, thinner—and angrier. I understood. After all, life is sweet; who wants it to end?

When Lisa's fourth child, a girl, was born, I flew to Iowa to see the baby. "Give her a kiss from me," Milt told me from his hospital bed.

The next day, I held little Ariel in my arms. I kissed her,

and kissed her again for her grandfather. But I stayed only an hour. I felt uneasy being away from Milt.

Once home, I was tired and thought I'd wait to see Milt in the morning. Something made me change my mind. I went to the hospital and up to his room. When I took his hand, he opened his eyes.

"Oh, Joyce," he said. "Sit down."

He closed his eyes again, and I sat beside him, holding his hand.

I talked for hours, telling him about Lisa's baby and reminiscing about everything in our life together. Then I told him over and over how much I loved him and how happy he had always made me. I do not know if he heard me. Finally, well after midnight, the nurses told me I had to go. My telephone woke me before 6 A.M. Milt had just died.

When I walked into his hospital room, Milt was still lying in the bed. He looked peaceful; the cruel lines of pain had left his face. I kissed him good-bye.

There was no time for grief. There were only details: people to notify, flowers to order, the funeral to arrange. I was too busy and numb to feel anything, which was a blessing.

It was not until a few days later that I really grasped that Milt was gone. Then it hit me: He would never walk through the door. Never hold me again. I made coffee and contemplated the rest of my life, with tears streaming down my face.

As a psychologist, I had lectured about grief and loneliness hundreds of times. But suddenly I was facing them myself, a new, unknown territory, and the pain was horrendous. I'd cry when I reached out in the night and Milt was not there. I'd pass a restaurant he and I used to like, and tears would start anew.

When someone asked me if I felt angry at Milt, I was shocked. Angry with my husband? Never!

But I was. Whenever I thought about his having smoked all those years, I was enraged. There were so many things we had looked forward to doing together. Now all of it had been snatched away by those lousy cigarettes.

It was nearly a year before I was able to think of Milt without crying. The turning point came when I remembered how he used to call me the Cabinet Lady. I tend to leave cabinet doors open when I'm cooking. Milt would say, "I see the Cabinet Lady is here. You're going to hurt yourself one of these days." And I'd reply, "I'm too short to hit my head."

One day I ran head-on into an open cabinet door and raised a huge bump on my forehead. After the "ouch!" I thought about Milt's millions of warnings. Despite the pain, I smiled.

But my greatest weapon for recovery was something Milt had told me after my father passed away. "He has not left you," Milt said. "Children always carry with them a part of their parents' souls. Husbands and wives remain part of each other."

I knew he was right. Milt *was* part of me. From that time on, life gradually began to brighten again. I still cried, but less and less. It had been a terrible year. I had felt that loneliness would eat me alive. But I had survived.

Today I am more accepting of the changes I've faced. I have started looking beyond my own horizon. My grief has also, I think, made me more sympathetic and sensitive to people. I have learned how comforting a few understanding words—and shared tears—can be.

I will always have a pocket of sorrow in my heart, but that will not keep me from plunging into life again. It will make me value every minute. And I will speak out against smoking whenever I can.

The second spring after Milt died, I had a dream. We were at the farm, just the two of us. It was snowing, but the house was warm, with a fire blazing on the hearth.

Then, suddenly, Milt and I were outdoors in bright sunlight. We were holding hands and laughing, slipping on the snow as we made our way down the hill. But when we got to the brook, a miracle: daffodils were blooming on low, woody bushes. The trees blossomed with roses and daisies. And Milt was no longer bone-thin and drawn, no longer angry, no longer ravaged by cancer. We went back to the house together, our arms full of flowers.

Joyce Brothers

Love, Leo

It wasn't fair! Leo, my devoted husband who was seldom sick, was diagnosed with acute leukemia in 1991, at the age of fifty-nine. Twenty-three days later, just before our thirty-fifth anniversary, he died. We were counting on so many more years together! We didn't have enough warning!

The daughter of a pastor, I couldn't remember a time when I didn't feel close to God. But I never felt further from him than now. I wanted to cling to him, but I was so bitter that he would allow somebody as strong as Leo to die, and leave someone as emotionally fragile as I. Well-meaning friends gave me a print of Jesus welcoming a man into heaven with open arms. Sometimes I put it out of sight and ranted at God, "You've had Leo long enough! I need him more than you do!"

Leo and I had truly been one—I felt ripped apart. Another widow told me it would be three years before I began to feel whole. "Lord, will the pain always be this intense?" I anguished. "I need to feel your love! I need to feel Leo's!"

I lived on automatic pilot, going to my nursing job, coming home to my Leoless house. Every problem seemed overwhelming. One morning I saw ants in the kitchen; Leo used to get rid of any ants. I grabbed a broom and jabbed at them futilely, growing angrier and angrier, screaming, "Leo, where are you? You belong here!" I flung open the back door and wailed into my suburban backyard. A neighbor rushed over, asking, "Is anything wrong?"

"No, I just have to scream," I answered, crumpling at the enormity of my loss.

Leo and I had grown to love each other deeply, but we weren't really in love on our wedding day in 1956; we hardly even knew each other! Poor, dear Leo. We married unaware that we were opposites. He was immaculate—almost perfect!—and assumed his nurse wife was also; cobwebs didn't faze me. He loved classical music; I fell asleep at the first concert he took me to. He was a gourmet cook; I rotated the ten recipes I used as a bride. He was reserved; I hugged spontaneously.

Our first years of marriage, Leo was not demonstrative. I desperately needed to hear him say "I love you," but he couldn't bring himself to say it. He'd say, "I like you—isn't that enough?"

After we'd been married about twenty years, we attended a marriage renewal retreat. The leaders encouraged us to write each other a love letter, mail the two letters in about a month, read them, and hide them to rediscover later. Leo wrote a beautiful letter full of words he found difficult to say in person. From that time on, he had no trouble telling me he loved me.

But now he was gone.

I couldn't bear to part with Leo's belongings. Any scrap with his handwriting—even doodling—was precious to me. A graphic arts professor, he was a man of many interests. I spotted, on his desk, the conductor's baton our three children and I had given him because he loved to conduct the invisible orchestras of his Bach and other tapes. I cried at that and mementos of his love of sailing and photography. A new wave of grief assaulted me with each reminder.

I went to our room and splashed some of Leo's cologne on me so our bed would smell like him. I glanced down wistfully at our pillows. Leo and I used to clip out cartoons and leave them on each other's pillows. One of my last ones to him was a woman kneeling by a bed praying, "Dear God, make Mr. Perfect do just one thing wrong!"

We had lots to tease each other about. Because my purse had been stolen twice, I was obsessive about keeping it nearby. Leo and the kids said they were going to have "Where's my purse?" engraved on my tombstone.

Two years went by, and I screamed less and less. One day I opened a cookbook and found a valentine from Leo I had used as a bookmark. Another day while shopping I saw a sailboat-shaped picture frame that reminded me of my beloved sailor and shutterbug. I bought the frame, put it on the TV and inserted one of Leo's spectacular sunsets. I gazed fondly, not weeping.

Another day I was going through the pockets of Leo's blazer, finally able to give it away, when I found in the breast pocket a cartoon of archaeologists unearthing a mummy with a purse and exclaiming, "It is! It is! It's the mummy's purse!" I laughed out loud, knowing Leo intended to put this on my pillow.

A realization startled me: A reminder of Leo had brought not tears, but a chuckle.

Shortly afterward, I was cleaning out a cardboard-lined dresser drawer where I keep scarves. I glimpsed a long envelope under the cardboard and felt a surge of warmth at the familiar curve of Leo's handwriting. I shivered. It took my breath away. This was the letter Leo had written after the couples retreat fourteen years before! I eagerly dug out the sheet of paper and my eyes hungrily devoured "Dearest Doris—."

Leo quoted the poet Shelley's "One word is too often profaned/For me to profane it" and went on to say, "I truly do love you in all of the true meaning of the word—even if I am negligent or hesitant to say it—I love you—We are as one and I must put forth the effort to make this a more complete oneness. . . . We were united in Christ's name and together we will grow in Christ's Love. Amen—Let it be so.

"With Everlasting Love—

Leo (Just me)"

I was ecstatic! I needed this affirmation so badly. I clutched the letter to me and carried it from room to room, stopping every now and then to reread its words. Words I don't think I could have handled right after Leo's death, but ones that brought healing now. I folded the letter carefully and tucked it into my ever-present purse to open often. Just reading it makes me smile.

I still feel incomplete. But I feel surrounded by God's and Leo's love. When something reminds me of Leo, there's a little less grief and a little more gratitude for what we had. My eyes get watery, but I can control it better now.

And sometimes I even laugh.

Doris Delventhal
As told to B. J. Connor

Cultivating My Garden

It was a summer's evening when my husband Tim's minivan spun out of control on a rain-slicked road, leaving me a young widow with a little daughter to raise.

On a fall day three months later, as I struggled to work through the grief, the pain and even the anger, I stood on the back steps of my house, surveying the large vegetable garden that Tim had put so much of himself into. From the yard, my eyes wandered over to the wooded slope beyond it and to the cemetery where Tim was buried, and then back to the garden.

The garden was a mess. I couldn't possibly keep up with it all. I didn't even know where to begin. The bright, green-bean wall Tim had constructed was covered with rotting beans, and every other green growing thing had been choked out by the ornamental gourds we had mistakenly planted last spring. What was I to do with it all? I certainly didn't want to turn it back into the sort of manicured greenery that both Tim and I had always loathed.

After much pondering, I decided to make an herb garden out of it. Something that I could lose myself in.

The bean wall came down and was hauled to the town dump. I closed my heart to the memory of the warm late-spring morning when Tim had been up early, painting it gaudy green, and threw myself into ripping down the ragged sunflowers and sadly faded cosmos he had planted all along the edges.

Then came the herbs. Lamb's ears, rosemary, angelica and costmary. Lavender, speedwell, lemon balm and valerian. Spearmint, apple mint and—would you believe?—chocolate mint.

In the strawberry bed that Tim had made for me the second Mother's Day after our daughter Marissa was born, I planted a white birch. Well, it was gray just then, but Eric, one of my garden wizards, told me that it would turn white some day. It became the Tim Tree.

In the spring, with the help of my friend Cel, I put down wood chips. Another friend, Jan, went on an herb shopping trip and came over with plants I'd never seen or even heard of, with names like woad, soapwort, felicity, amaranth and woundwort.

The garden was taking shape all right. But I still felt lost and unhappy in my own skin. I toyed with the idea of selling the house and moving with Marissa into my grandmother's old farmhouse. There would be no memories of Tim to gnaw at me there.

But I still kept puttering with that garden. I moved the white marble birdbath that Tim had given me on our last anniversary into the center. I bought a stone angel, her eyes downcast and her face filled with Renaissance piety, and placed her next to the birdbath.

Still, it seemed that something was missing. Then it occurred to me that my garden had no central theme. I had always been fascinated by "theme gardens"—Shakespearean gardens, moonlight gardens, witches' gardens and the like. But mine was simply a hodgepodge of herbs, flowers, trees and shrubs.

Late that summer, Marissa and I traveled to New York

state. We stopped at an herb farm, and I came across some new herbs with bewitching names, such as boneset and all-heal. Boneset leaves, I learned, were originally used in setting broken bones and in tonics. All-heal, or self-heal, was a remedy for a variety of internal and external wounds. It was then that I decided that my garden would be a healing garden. Not only in the literal sense, but perhaps in the spiritual sense as well.

One afternoon not long afterwards, I stumbled right smack into my epiphany. I had fallen in love with my garden. My bane had turned out to be my blessing. I gazed around me, just as I had the previous fall, but with such different eyes. The garden had made me remember what I had tried so hard to forget: that I loved this place where Tim and I had started our journey as husband and wife and as parents of a vivacious daughter. That part of the journey was over, but the journey continued. Marissa and I still had miles to go and promises to keep—to each other, to Tim and to the garden. We'd make good where we were.

Over a year later, I'm still working at my garden. I've moved the trees out and put a tiny iris garden in one corner. And I've been putting down flat bricks, fieldstone, and anything else I can lay my hands on, to make little wayward paths that branch out, then circle back on themselves. Sometimes I just sit on the marble bench that I put in, and at other times I hunt around for the four- and five-leaved clovers that often crop up, good-luck signs that assure me nature is working for me.

I don't go down to the cemetery much now. If I want to find Tim, I feel him in this garden he gave me. The pain has gone from my memories now, leaving them full of laughter and warmth. The healing garden has lived up to its name.

T. J. Banks

A Widow's Workshop

Life couldn't have been any better.

My husband Charlie and I were retired, so we sold our big house and the extra car and moved into a cottage, with an office in back for me and a workshop for Charlie.

Side by side, Charlie and I puttered at our work in blissful contentment.

Nineteen months later Charlie died of a massive heart attack.

I was completely unprepared for singleness. *Why, Lord, why?* I half-prayed, half-cursed. *This happens to other people. It isn't supposed to happen to me.*

Suddenly I felt totally unloved, unprotected, unwanted. "It's a couples' world," I muttered, angrily. "I'm like a fifth wheel." I raged with jealousy when I saw couples in the mall holding hands. I wore my anger like chicken pox.

I took in a stranger who needed temporary housing. We cried together, prayed together, and when she finally left, we were lasting friends.

And the loneliness returned with a rage.

Work was always good for what ails me, but working around Charlie's shop only stimulated painful memories—every nook and cranny held his ghost.

The Journey

If I try to be like him, who will be like me?

Yiddish Proverb

I stood in the small kitchen as the Florida sunshine streamed through the curtains, giving the room a golden glow. It should have been a lovely morning, but grief hung thick in the air. I watched my grandmother as she scurried back and forth from stove to sink, wiping, straightening . . . busy work. Any minute now I expected her to break down again, to lean against the counter and give in to tears. Two days before, her life, as she had known it, had come to an abrupt halt. My grandfather, B. B., her husband and the love of her life for fifty-eight years, had died.

Suddenly my grandmother's quick movements slowed. I watched as she clutched the dishtowel in both hands, then stood completely still. A knot formed in my throat, and I prepared myself to go to her at the first sign of tears. But she didn't cry. She just stood there staring at the counter as if noticing something for the first time.

I followed her gaze to see what had caught her interest. Was it the toaster? Perhaps she was just staring at nothing.

But then she reached behind the toaster and picked up a small vase of cheap plastic flowers.

She wiped them off with her towel, then turned and placed the faded arrangement on the tiny table. When her eyes met mine, I saw in them grief mingled with self-awareness. "I can put my flowers anywhere I want now," she said. Then she shook her head as if surprised she'd said these words aloud.

Her brow creased. Then she quickly turned around and continued wiping the already-clean counters. My heart swelled with emotion, not for my grandmother's loss but for the painful yet awakening truth I'd seen briefly in her eyes as she stared at the simple vase of flowers.

Only days away from her eightieth birthday, she was about to embark on a journey. It was a journey that would be painfully lonely for a while, but which would eventually lead her to discover the woman she'd left at the altar fifty-eight years ago when she'd become my grandfather's wife. No, my grandfather had not been some evil, selfish man, but he had been a man of his times. More importantly, my grandmother had been a woman of hers.

She had dressed to please her husband; she had supported his strong views on life and politics; she had lived to be the wife he wanted. It was not that he had robbed her of her identity—she had freely given it, along with her heart and soul. But now he was gone, and she was left to discover who she was without him.

It has been four years since my grandfather passed away and since then I've watched and am amazed at the woman my grandmother has become. Oh, she is still kind, giving to a fault, but this journey has changed her. Her muted shades and small-print clothing have become bright and busy. Her house is now filled with colorful tablecloths, flowers and feminine knickknacks. She still watches the evening news but is quick to switch to a

game show or a sentimental show that my
would have scoffed at. She laughs a lot, ev
jokes. She has friends over, goes out t
romantic comedies are her favorite—an
word puzzles over the phone with gir
to a pinochle group and has started
She walks three miles a day with

She still misses my grandfath
was the love of her life. Recen
a dream.

"I was at the bottom of
there was a lot of mud
looking back and tell
us a new house on
me seeing it. I was
denly I saw a li
she was lost. I
Then I told
I'm going

After
wonder w

I placed my
That little girl is

She blinked away
take care of him," she sa

"I know," I told her. "You di
did. Now you're just doing wha

She hugged me and pulled away.
got a pinochle game to attend."

As I watched her walk away, a lovely visi
ple pants and flower-printed shirt, I realized h
was to have met this woman, and I'm glad she's st
around to take care of the little girl inside her. That litt
girl has waited a long time.

Christie Craig

"Go ahead without me," he said. "I want to sit down for a moment." When Anne looked back, he had fallen on the ground, and before the ambulance reached the hospital, he had passed away.

Aunt Anne was left there alone, without her traveling companion. I fretted for her. How would she handle this turn of events? Would she finally take down her sails and cast out her anchor? It seemed so. She moved to Wisconsin to be near her son and grandchildren. *So she's finally settled in for a life of quiet resignation,* I thought. *She has come to shore for good.*

I received word from her not long ago, confirmation that I was completely mistaken. "I'm so excited about the sculpting classes I'm teaching in Madison," she exclaimed. The art community was thriving there, and of course Aunt Anne was in the thick of it. "Isn't it wonderful?" she said. *Yes, it is,* I thought as I read one of her poems:

There is always tomorrow, a brand new beginning,
Time for another home run before the last inning.
There is always a sunrise after the sun has gone down,
God's hand reaching out, holding you up when you feel down.
Rest while you can, but don't give up living, Thankful for what you receive—and blessed for what you are giving.

Aunt Anne knows that life isn't where you're going: It's how you're getting there.

Anne Marion
As told to Eileen Lawrence

Unk's Fiddle

Unk played the violin—called it a "fiddle"—but never played when anyone was around. Except Eleanor. He'd play for her. They'd been friends seventy years. Neither married. Eleanor was Perryville's old maid. And Unk—well, everybody jokingly called him Perryville's most eligible bachelor—ironic because Unk was short, with liver spots. One eye was dried up from a metal shaving he caught as a teenager, and he had a pock-marked face. His knee had been crushed when logs broke loose off a railroad flatcar he was unloading, leaving him with a draggy limp.

Eleanor ran the general store after her folks died, but sold it when it became too much trouble. Church seemed the extent of her social life, except for Unk coming by Saturday nights with his fiddle. She sang in choir, served at suppers, sewed for the Ladies Aid. It was rumored she played harmonica, but not in public. She taught Sunday School children for years, then an adult Bible class. That's when Unk, who mysteriously dropped out of church when he was ten years old, started attending.

Unk lived with Grampa and Grandma most of his life, working the farm. When they died and left him the place, he surprised everyone by selling it and moving in with us. We fixed him a room in the shed attached to our house, so Unk's room shared a common wall with my bedroom. Despite the wall's thickness, once in bed I could hear Unk play that fiddle every night except Saturday when he was at Eleanor's. The music was faint, but on a good night it would work its sweet and mournful way through the wall.

One day, when I was eleven, Unk and I fished Thatcher Pond. As I fumbled to get a worm on my hook, Unk mumbled, "Eleanor baits a hook faster'n that."

At first I thought he was jibing me, but then I realized he hadn't said it to put me down. In fact, he wasn't talking to me at all, he was talking to himself, simply stating an observation: Eleanor, the old maid who played a harmonica when nobody was around, a woman nobody ever saw fish, could bait a hook fast. Unk knew.

We spent all day in companionable silence. As we packed up, Unk put his arm around my shoulder and told me selling the farm was the best thing he ever did, because it gave him time to do the things he loved. He didn't tell me what it was he loved, but if he could have mouthed the words, I expect they'd have ushered forth in a holy whisper—fishing, fiddling and Eleanor. I tried to imagine Unk and Eleanor after Saturday dinner, sitting in her parlor, tapping their toes and conversing through fiddle and harmonica.

One afternoon I was pulling carrots, handing them to Unk. I asked why he only played his fiddle in private. He said, "When I was ten, I was learning Dad's fiddle. He played barn dances. I mentioned to Reverend Hotchkiss, who's dead now, that I hoped to be good enough to play in church some day. He shook his head no, told me a fiddle ain't suitable for church and giving glory to God."

When I looked up, Unk's face was like granite. I guessed that was the year Unk stopped going to church.

Unk was seventy-nine when Eleanor died. She simply didn't wake up one Tuesday morning.

Her viewing hours were Friday night. Mom, Dad and I went. Unk refused. He stayed in his room, preferring to remember her the way he'd last seen her. I thought she looked fine, in a pretty black dress with pink and purple flowers. Her hands were folded on her stomach as if praying, and her knuckles didn't look gnarly or arthritic. I tried to imagine those fingers baiting a hook.

Next day, church was full for the funeral. Unk didn't come along when we left the house by car. He said he'd catch up, but I doubted he'd show. After all, he hadn't been able to face visiting hours.

The pews filled as Mrs. King played familiar hymns. Eleanor's two elderly cousins sat in the front pew. The choir sang "In the Garden" and "Abide with Me," two of Eleanor's favorites.

Reverend Winters read scripture, offered a eulogy and invited folks to share memories and thanksgivings about Eleanor.

Roberta Gerrity spoke for the choir, saying, "Eleanor was a faithful and committed choir member." A man spoke of the inspiring Sunday school teacher that Eleanor had been. A long silence followed. I wanted to fill the void myself, but I didn't know what to say and my body felt heavy as a stone.

That's when Unk limped down the aisle, fiddle in his left hand, bow in his right. He walked slowly, reverently, toward the pulpit. His head was bent and he trudged, like a man climbing a gallows. When he reached the golden oak communion table, he looked out over the congregation. He wanted to speak, but his lips only trembled. Tears mixed with streams of sweat. The saltiness stung his eyes, and he blinked and blinked. I wanted to run up and comfort him.

Unk raised the fiddle to his shoulder, cradled it under his chin and drew the bow across the strings. He began with "Amazing Grace," slipped seamlessly into "Greensleeves," then wove strains from both into a sound more mournful and sweeter than any I've ever heard. We cried, the whole church and I, watching and hearing Unk honor and weep for Eleanor through his fiddle. When he stopped, we sat stunned. Unk walked out, fiddle and bow in hand, and trudged home.

No music seeped through my wall for months. Then one morning Unk came down to breakfast, smiled, and said, "Want to fish Thatcher's?"

By mid-morning we had a beautiful brown trout.

That night I lay in bed, thinking about the trout, the warm sun, how good it felt to have Unk back. Then I heard it—Unk's fiddle, singing.

He played in his room every night after that, until his dying day. And many a night, I swear I don't know how, Unk made that fiddle wail and cry, just like a harmonica.

Steven Burt

A Single Long-Stemmed Rose

"Every day since my husband, Jack Benny, has been gone, the florist has delivered one long-stemmed red rose to my home . . ." Mary began. "For the first few weeks, I was in a state of deep mourning. It never occurred to me to ask who the roses were coming from.

"I can't begin to express the grief I felt. Jack's loss . . . Our separation after forty-eight years of complete togetherness . . . My feelings of utter loneliness, even though I was surrounded by relatives and dear, dear friends who tried to cheer me up.

"Jack died the day after Christmas. The New Year of 1975 came and went without my noticing it. I heard of people 'being numb with grief,' but I had never *fully* understood what those words meant—not until I went through it myself.

"It must have been seven or eight weeks before I finally asked the maid who the daily flower was from. To my surprise, she had no idea. I called our florist and asked him . . .

"He told me that quite a while before Jack passed away, he stopped in to send a bouquet of flowers to a friend. As Jack was leaving, he suddenly turned back and said,

'David, if anything should happen to me, I want you to send my doll a red rose every day . . .'

"When the florist finished, I was silent for a moment, and tears started running down my face. I thanked him and said good-bye."

Subsequently, Mary learned that Jack had actually included a provision for the flowers in his will. One perfect red rose was to be delivered to her every day . . . *for the rest of her life.*

Mary Livingstone Benny and Hilliard Marks
with Marcie Borie

8

WE ARE NOT ALONE

Remember, we all stumble, every one of us. That's why it's a comfort to go hand in hand.

Emily Kimbrough

Angels, Once in a While

In September 1960, I woke up one morning with six hungry babies and just seventy-five cents in my pocket. Their father was gone.

The boys ranged from three months to seven years; their sister was two. Their dad had never been much more than a presence they feared. Whenever they heard his tires crunch on the gravel driveway, they scrambled to hide under their beds. He did manage to leave fifteen dollars a week to buy groceries. Now that he had decided to leave, there would be no more beatings, but no food either. If there was a welfare system in effect in southern Indiana at that time, I certainly knew nothing about it.

I scrubbed the kids until they looked brand new and then put on my best homemade dress. I loaded them into the rusty old '51 Chevy and drove off to find a job. The seven of us went to every factory, store and restaurant in our small town. No luck. The kids stayed crammed into the car and tried to be quiet while I tried to convince whomever would listen that I was willing to learn or do anything. I had to have a job. Still no luck.

The last place we went, just a few miles out of town, was an old Root Beer Barrel drive-in that had been converted to a truck stop. It was called the Big Wheel. An old lady named Granny owned the place, and she peeked out of the window from time to time at all those kids. She needed someone on the graveyard shift, eleven at night until seven in the morning. She paid sixty-five cents an hour, and I could start that night.

I raced home and called the teenaged baby-sitter down the street. I bargained with her to come and sleep on my sofa for a dollar a night. She could arrive with her pajamas on, and the kids would already be asleep. This seemed like a good arrangement to her, so we made a deal.

That night when the little ones and I knelt to say our prayers we all thanked God for finding Mommy a job.

And so I started at the Big Wheel. When I got home in the mornings I woke the baby-sitter up and sent her home with one dollar of my tip money—fully half of what I averaged every night.

As the weeks went by, heating bills added another strain to my meager wage. The tires on the old Chevy had the consistency of penny balloons and began to leak. I had to fill them with air on the way to work and again every morning before I could go home.

One bleak fall morning, I dragged myself to the car to go home and found four tires in the backseat. New tires. There was no note, no nothing, just those beautiful brand-new tires. *Have angels taken up residence in Indiana?* I wondered.

I made a deal with the owner of the local service station. In exchange for his mounting the new tires, I would clean up his office. I remember it took me a lot longer to scrub his floor than it did for him to do the tires.

I was now working six nights instead of five, and it still wasn't enough. Christmas was coming, and I knew there would be no money for toys for the kids. I found a can of red paint and started repairing and painting some old toys. Then I hid them in the basement so there would be something for Santa to deliver on Christmas morning. Clothes were a worry, too. I was sewing patches on top of patches on the boys' pants, and soon they would be too far gone to repair.

On Christmas Eve the usual customers were drinking coffee in the Big Wheel. These were the truckers, Les, Frank and Jim, and a state trooper named Joe. A few musicians were hanging around after a gig at the Legion and were dropping nickels in the pinball machine.

The regulars all just sat around and talked through the wee hours of the morning and then left to get home before the sun came up. When it was time for me to go home at seven o'clock on Christmas morning I hurried to the car. I was hoping the kids wouldn't wake up before I managed to get home and get the presents from the basement and place them under the tree. (We had cut down a small cedar tree by the side of the road down by the dump.)

When I approached the car I suddenly grew apprehensive. It was still dark and I couldn't see much, but there appeared to be some dark shadows in the car—or was that just a trick of the night? Something certainly looked different, but it was hard to tell what.

When I reached the car I peered warily into one of the side windows. Then my jaw dropped in amazement. My old battered Chevy was full—full to the top with boxes of all shapes and sizes.

I quickly opened the driver's side door, scrambled inside and kneeled in the front facing the backseat. Reaching back, I pulled off the lid of the top box. Inside was a whole case of little blue jeans, sizes two to ten! I looked inside another box: It was full of shirts to go with the jeans. Then I peeked inside some of the other boxes: There were candy and nuts and bananas and bags of groceries. There was an enormous ham for baking, and canned vegetables and potatoes. There was pudding and

Jell-O and cookies, pie filling and flour. There was a whole bag of laundry supplies and cleaning items.

And there were five toy trucks and one beautiful little doll. As I drove back through empty streets as the sun slowly rose on the most amazing Christmas Day of my life, I was sobbing with gratitude. And I will never forget the joy on the faces of my little ones that precious morning.

Yes, there were angels in Indiana that long-ago December. And they all hung out at the Big Wheel truck stop.

Barb Irwin
Submitted by Lauren Andrews

Flowers from Our Garden

Some say that the world is a vale of tears, I say it is a place of soul making.

John Keats

I am in my late forties and have two teenage daughters. My life has been difficult but, by the grace of God, I am a survivor.

My girls and I spent much of their childhood in shelters and living on the street. Though we were together six years, I never married the girls' father. He couldn't hold a job and although I am a hard worker, without a college education, the money just wasn't enough to support us. He spent most of my money on hard liquor, and he didn't come home for days at a time.

One day, after he had threatened to kill me (he was a violent drunk), I packed up my babies and our belongings and headed for a better part of town. I figured I would give my girls a good education, even if we had to live on the street.

I managed to find a job as a waitress at a local coffee shop, and I enrolled my girls in a good public school. My job didn't pay enough for rent, so we moved from shelter to shelter. I was nervous about the address, so I got a post office box and used the address for the school paperwork.

No one suspected we were homeless. My girls went to school every day. If the shelter was nearby, we walked. If we had to, we took a bus.

My girls were always very presentable. I let them go to friends' houses as much as possible, and I often tried to buy them special gifts. But, mostly, the little money we had was put away for their future.

We had made a pact that we would not tell anyone we were homeless because I was sure this fine school wouldn't allow my daughters to remain if they knew about our situation.

One day, several years later, one of the girls came back to the shelter and told me her friend's mother had invited all three of us over for supper the next evening. I managed to talk the director of the shelter into allowing me to use the kitchen to bake cookies.

We knocked on the door of a beautiful two-story home. It was spotless and comfortable. Mary, the mother, was so appreciative of the cookies. We had a wonderful evening, and I knew I had found a friend.

A few days later, Leticia, my youngest, came home and said that Mary had asked for our phone number. She wanted to call me to get together. Leticia told her we were having trouble with the phones, and she would have *me* call *her.* I hated that my girls had to lie.

I called Mary and again we got together at her house. She and I became good friends. I constantly told her that I wanted to have her over to our place, but then I would lie and say we were having trouble with the landlord of our apartment building or that something wasn't working, like the stove, the air conditioning, etc.

Mary came into the coffee shop one day and asked if I could spend my break with her. We took a walk, and then she stopped at a vacant house a few blocks down the road. It had a For Rent sign out front and was the most adorable little home.

Mary said, "Do you like this place?"

"Oh, very much!" I exclaimed. "But it's way out of my league."

"Why don't we call and find out?" Mary said.

This upset me. I told her that the most I could afford was $350 a month. No one would rent a house for that little—especially this house.

The next day, Mary came into the coffee shop with a big grin on her face and a For Rent sign in her hands. She was so excited that she couldn't hold back the news. "I spoke with the owner of that house and guess what? They're renting the place for $350 a month! It couldn't be more perfect for you and the girls."

I told her, "That's impossible. Houses rent for three times that much in this neighborhood."

She explained that the owners didn't really need the money. They just needed someone who would appreciate living there and would take special care of it.

A few weeks later, we moved in. We managed to get some furniture from the Salvation Army. Shari, my oldest, took wood shop in school and made us a fine coffee table. We fixed the place up, and I even planted some flowers, which made me feel like I was planting my roots. I hoped to stay here a long time, raise my girls, and always have a place for them to come home to.

But secrets, I've found, don't usually stay secrets. One month, I had to mail my rent check, but it was during the holidays, and I didn't want it to be late, so I decided to drop it off at the appropriate post office box. I was standing in line at the post office when I heard a familiar voice ask for a package from the box where I sent my rent. I peeked around the line and was shocked to see Mary!

She was thumbing through her mail when I touched her arm. Tears were starting to form in my eyes, and I could barely speak. "Mary, is it *your* house we're living in? Did you do this for us?"

She put her arm around my shoulder and walked me outside. By the time we reached the sidewalk, I was sobbing. I am a very strong woman and tears don't come easily. I have been through a lot in my life, but no one had ever been so kind.

Mary told me that Leticia had slipped and told her daughter we were homeless. She said she never would have guessed. The girls were always so clean and well-dressed. She said it was her and her husband's first home, and it was very special to them, that they had owned the house for a long time, and it was paid for. She and her husband had talked about it and wanted to rent the house to us. She hadn't wanted me to know because she was afraid I would think it was charity.

Shari is graduating from high school this year, and because we were able to save enough money, she is going to college.

Mary is my Earth Angel, and I want her to know that I appreciate her kindness and generosity, and that I love her.

I bring Mary fresh flowers every week from our garden.

Jerry and Lorin Biederman

A Small Miracle in Nashville

Dawn Weiss awoke suddenly in a cold sweat. In that early January morning of 1994 the secure world Dawn knew was literally crumbling around her. Her bed shook and the walls started to crack open. For a moment, her mind flashed back to the days when she was an active alcoholic. But she was sober now; this was not a hangover and she knew it. The noise was deafening. What Dawn could not know was that Northridge, California, was being rocked by an enormous earthquake.

Dawn sat bolt upright in bed. Her first thought was for her beloved Harley, a gray angora cat. "Harley!" she screamed. But the floor was literally swaying beneath her. She had no time to waste as she sprang from her bed. Plaster was falling in large chunks from the ceiling. Her instincts told her that she had no time to save Harley and only seconds to save her own life.

She suddenly realized that her second-floor apartment afforded an escape. She ran immediately to the open window. Within her reach was a large tree branch, which she immediately grabbed.

As the building continued to shake, she lurched for the branch with both hands. Cautiously, she groped her way down through the branches to the firm ground below. As she ran to her car, her apartment building came crashing to the ground like a pile of toy bricks. Neighbors who had managed to escape stood huddled together, comforting one another yet in shock themselves. Amidst the pandemonium, Dawn spotted Harley. She ran to him and held him tight.

Through rubble and fallen power lines, Dawn walked in the darkness, holding Harley, for more than a mile to a friend's apartment. Desperately the two of them searched the area for loved ones. Within two days Dawn had accounted for all her friends, parents and other relatives—all, incredibly, alive and uninjured.

For the next two weeks the earthquake's aftershocks made it difficult to trust the earth underfoot. Dawn's nerves were worn thin, leaving her uneasy and anxious.

She decided she couldn't go on living like that. She had to move to a place where she would feel secure again, and she decided on Nashville, Tennessee. Her parents tried to persuade her to stay.

"Dawn," her father implored. "You sound just like you did when you were drinking. You don't know anyone in Nashville! This is irrational. You have your network of Alcoholics Anonymous buddies here in California. Are you relapsing into old behavior?"

"I'm not relapsing, Dad," said Dawn. "I've just got to get out of this maddening place."

So with a mixture of sorrow and excitement, Dawn said good-bye to her family and friends, took Harley and embarked on her journey.

Starting her new life in Nashville, Dawn grabbed the first job that was offered to her, as a waitress in a country-style restaurant and bar. She worked the evening shift so that she could enroll in Middle Tennessee State University and work toward a degree in mass communications.

For a couple of weeks everything seemed fine. But then the excitement of her new life began to wear off. She was in a strange new place with new people. Everything that was comfortable and familiar was gone. Dawn felt a tremendous sense of loss.

In painful self-recognition she turned to God. "I have been sober for three years! Haven't touched a drink in all that time. Is this the reward for all my hard work?"

Dawn felt the old familiar urge to drink, and hated it. She was overcome with grief and pain. Having been a member of Alcoholics Anonymous for several years, she knew what she was supposed to do—pick up the phone and call someone for help. She also knew that if she reached out to the Alcoholics Anonymous community, she would find someone with a compassionate ear—someone who would understand and lend as much support as was needed.

Dawn knew all that, but at this moment all she wanted was a bottle to drown her feelings.

Every night, when she should have been focusing on her job, Dawn's thoughts turned more and more to drinking. Alcohol, she felt, would help her blot out a life that was too hard to bear. She watched, almost with envy, the chattering, happy patrons at the bar. It only intensified her desire for a drink.

"That's it," she declared one Friday night on the way to work. "I'm going to have a drink." Dawn figured that there would be more customers than usual at the bar that evening. She could easily blend in unnoticed.

She entered the restaurant through the back door and proceeded directly to the ladies' room. There she broke down and cried. She was tired of reaching out to new people. She resisted anyone who might understand her plight. Instead, she turned once again to God.

"How can you do this?" she found herself repeating. "I sponsored three people who have themselves sponsored others. I volunteered in a women's prison, reaching out to pregnant women and their babies. I went into the program with so much. I was an upstanding, cultured girl. I went to the best schools, had loving parents. I had a good job. I'm not supposed to be afflicted with this disease! I feel so abandoned! I want a drink and now!"

The door to the ladies' room opened and Kim, one of the waitresses, came in. Dawn quickly wiped away her tears and muffled her sniffles. Being new at her job, she didn't want to expose herself to anyone.

"Dawn," Kim inquired, "who's Bill W.?" Dawn's heart seemed to stop. She was thrown completely off guard. It was the first time she had heard that name since coming to Nashville.

"Bill W.?" Dawn repeated. "He was the founder of Alcoholics Anonymous. Now why would you be asking me that?"

"Haven't you noticed?" Kim replied with some exasperation. "Everyone out there in the restaurant is wearing a pin saying, 'I AM A FRIEND OF BILL W.'"

"What?" Dawn blurted out in total astonishment. She opened the door and surveyed the fifty tables, each filled with an average of five to six people—there must have been close to three hundred people in the restaurant. Sure enough, everyone was wearing a pin declaring his or her allegiance to Alcoholics Anonymous. Then Dawn looked over at the bar, where she had been planning to have her first drink in three years. It was now completely dark, shut down for the night.

"Oh, my God!" Dawn declared. She approached the first table. "Uh . . . what's going on?"

"Why?" came a voice from the table.

Dawn guessed that no one wanted to break the anonymity of an alcoholic in recovery. "I, too, am a friend of Bill W.," she said, her voice quivering.

They all sensed her despair. They knew her immediate need. Together they applauded. Then one person spoke up. "We're all here to attend the Alcoholics Anonymous convention. It's our biggest convention ever. Thousands of people from around the world have come to this."

Dawn could hardly believe her ears. Another patron caught her glance. "Yes, we rented out the restaurant for the night, and as for the bartender, we told him that he might as well go home. He was sure to be bored with us."

Dawn sat down at the table. Her fellow AA members intuitively understood it all. Intently they listened to her painful story and showered her with love. When she was through, another member spoke up: "What time do you finish work?" she inquired.

"Midnight," answered Dawn.

"What are you doing after work?" the woman asked.

"Well, I was going to drink," said Dawn, "but now. . . ."

"All six of us were going to the movies after dinner," said another member at the table. "But instead we'll all sit right here until midnight. When you complete your shift we'll all go over to the convention together. There will be Twelve-Step meetings through the night."

"Imagine this," said Dawn with gratitude and awe. "Here I was just praying for one person to talk to . . . but God must have thought I was in really rough shape, so he sent me three hundred."

Yitta Halberstam and Judith Leventhal
Excerpted from Small Miracles II: Heartwarming Gifts of Extraordinary Coincidences *by Yitta Halberstam and Judith Leventhal*

The Best Seat in the House

The doctors said they found a grapefruit-sized tumor in his lungs. I guess I shouldn't have been surprised. My dad, John Mathew Morris, had been a two-pack-a-day guy for the better part of forty years. He loved his "cancer sticks," and maybe now he was paying the price.

It was April of the 1987 baseball season when I received the bad news. Instantly, I wanted to be transported home, but I was one thousand miles away, and there was little I could do for him. So I continued doing what I could: I played baseball to the best of my ability so Dad could feel proud of his son.

Since I was single and totally devoted to my baseball career, my teammates and coach were my support system. I spent almost all of my time with them.

Our team, the St. Louis Cardinals, was serving notice to the rest of the National League that we were legitimate pennant contenders. As the season progressed, we built a ten-game lead heading into the All-Star break. Following the break, we came to New York to play the Mets. Before each game, I drove the Long Island Expressway to visit Dad at the Suffolk County hospice facility.

While Dad and I were together, our conversations centered

on baseball and the Cardinals. Dad loved baseball. It was his one true passion in life. As a matter of fact, he had been quite a player himself back in the 1920s, when he played first base for a semi-pro team.

The series gave Dad and me some quality time together. I felt good knowing I was bringing some joy into a life that was now full of pain and struggle. He was a proud father who, given the fact that his youngest son was playing major league baseball, liked to show me off to all the nurses and doctors when I visited. He loved telling them that his son was a major leaguer. As embarrassed as it made me, I played along, letting him enjoy the attention, all the while hiding my own pain. My whole life away from Dad was playing baseball with my teammates. How could baseball ease my grief?

Two months later, in September, my team returned to Shea Stadium to play the Mets again. Our lead over the Mets had been reduced to one game. During the series, there was a great deal going on in my head—Dad's failing health, the pressure of the pennant race and our lead slipping away. For the first time in my life, I began to use baseball to bring some sense of joy to a sad situation. I played each day with the hope that it would allow Dad to think of something other than his illness.

I visited with Dad all three days while we were in New York playing. Dad was in a helpless state. He weighed about one hundred pounds and was unable to walk or talk. Seeing him in that condition was almost too much to handle. Every day before I left the hospital to go to the stadium, Dad would communicate one thing to me. Scribbling on a note pad, he'd write that he'd be watching our game on TV. My fellow players knew about Dad's faithful support, but they couldn't know my pain.

The series proved to be a battle between two longstanding rivals. Fortunately, we won two of the three games. Meanwhile, back on Long Island, Dad was watching. He spent whatever energy he had left in his shrunken body watching our games. But they were to be his last games. Three days later, we were in Pittsburgh to play the Pirates when manager Whitey Herzog knocked at my hotel door in the early morning hours. Right then, I knew Dad was gone.

I flew home that Wednesday afternoon for Dad's wake and burial. I'd known this day was coming for some time, but the knowledge in no way eased the hurt.

The Sunday morning after the funeral began with a scheduled 6:30 flight to St. Louis, but the flight was canceled, and I was left unsure if I could make it to St. Louis for the start of the afternoon game against the Chicago Cubs. But somebody was on my side that day. A seat opened up on a later flight, allowing me to arrive in St. Louis at 11:30.

Entering the clubhouse, I was greeted warmly by my teammates. Their genuine concern touched and calmed me. Then Dave Ricketts, our bullpen coach, walked over to me. "Johnny, Whitey wants to see you." I walked into the skipper's office, not knowing what to expect. I noticed that the lineup card was missing from its usual spot on the wall adjacent to his office.

When I turned the corner, Whitey rose from behind his desk. "Hey, kid! It's nice to have ya back." He paused for a moment, as if he was trying to gather his thoughts.

"Look, I know there's nothing more trying than a funeral and that you've been through a lot the past few days," Whitey continued. He grabbed two cards from the top of his desk. "Johnny, I'm gonna leave it up to you. I've made out two lineup cards. One has you starting, and the other has you on the bench in case you're not ready yet. Whatever you decide is fine with me."

A string of questions exploded in my head. *Was Whitey actually waiting for me before he was going to post the lineup?*

Was I dreaming? Managers just didn't do this; was he serious with this unusual offer? It dawned on me that Whitey was offering me more than a choice: He was offering a challenge.

I responded: "I just flew one thousand miles to get here. I'd love to play today." Whitey smiled with approval. "Great! You're in there," he said. His face softened. "Now, go get a few hits for your dad."

In the first inning I came to bat with the bases loaded. Greg Maddux hung me a slider, and I drove in the first two runs with a single to center field. In the third inning, my grounder to the shortstop scored another run. In the eighth inning I drove in another run with a single up the middle. Our lead was now seven to two.

Though I could have no idea that these four RBIs were a career high, I did know I had just done something special. The fans knew about my loss, and the crowd of 46,681 stood to acknowledge my performance and to lend their support in my time of grief. While I stood on first base and listened to their applause, the ovation seemed to last forever. A lump formed in my throat as a mixture of joy and sorrow swelled inside me. I realized I had just paid Dad the greatest tribute I could have given him, and I realized that I had never been alone in my pain. With both feet planted on top of first base, my eyes glistened as tears ran freely down my cheeks. I glanced upward, and seeing the gorgeous blue skies, I suddenly had an image of Dad smiling down on me with approval and pride, content in the fact that his youngest son was winning the game he loved. Dad was indeed watching over me that day, and his vantage point provided him with the best seat in the house.

Days later, the Cardinals clinched the division title, and a week later, we became National League champions. We were off to the World Series to play the Minnesota Twins. The season was complete, and so was my relationship with Dad—all because Whitey Herzog and my enormous extended baseball family gave me the chance to say a special farewell to my biggest fan.

John Morris

Santa Redeemed

Typically, young kids start out believing in Santa Claus, then learn later that Santa was just their grandpa dressed in a red suit. Me, I was onto the truth pretty quickly. As a savvy seven-year-old, I knew that Santa Claus was just another adult scam. Anyone could see that. The problem was that as the two oldest grandchildren, my sister and I were expected to help convince the younger grandchildren that Santa was real. I went along with this farce reluctantly. "You ask for what you want, and Santa brings it to you," I would say, dutifully.

But how could I, or anyone else for that matter—young or old—be expected to believe it? Life just wasn't like that. You didn't get what you wanted. You got what you didn't want. Look at us. We had recently lost our dad, and now, after thirteen years of staying at home, Mom had to go out and look for a job. This was tough. Mom had few qualifications for the world of work. She had been raised during the Great Depression, and had dropped out of school at an early age to help support the family. Not only had she little education, she had limited experience and no special training.

For months she searched unsuccessfully for work as we

sank further and further into poverty. Mom was unable to hold on to the home that Dad had built, and a relative in another town allowed us to live in a back room of her home for a while. The family car disappeared into the night as the repo man performed his duties. Thus Mother's options were further limited to jobs that were within walking distance.

In our new town, there were a number of bars that could be reached on foot, but Mother believed that her working in a bar would not be good for her children. So she continued the search.

As Christmas approached, Mother planned to take my sister and me to the school festival. Admission was free, and we could walk there. After we had spent some time looking around, Mother asked us to get in line to talk to Santa, which was the only activity you could do for nothing. I got in line, just to please her.

After Santa lifted me onto his lap, he asked what my Christmas wish was. It didn't really matter what I told him, because I knew Santa was just somebody's grandpa dressed in a red suit. Naming a toy would only sadden my mother because she couldn't afford any toys. I decided to tell the truth. "My wish is that my mother would get a job so we can buy groceries," I said in a bold voice.

"And where is your mother?" Santa asked. I pointed her out. "Ho, ho, ho," said Santa, "I'll see what I can do."

Why do they always say ho, ho, ho? I thought.

A few days after Christmas, the phone rang and Mother picked it up. There was a brief conversation. "Yes . . . yes . . . oh, I would love to, yes. . . . All right . . . Good-bye."

She turned to my sister and me with a smile that I hadn't seen in a while.

"I've been offered a job in the school," she said, her voice rising with excitement. "In the lunch room. Now we're going to be all right." She hugged us both. Then she added, "I wonder how they knew I needed a job?"

Later I found out that Santa Claus, whether he is your grandpa in a red suit or the school superintendent doing his bit at the Christmas festival, is not such a scam after all.

And the following Christmas I told the younger kids that if they didn't believe in him they were really missing out.

Jean Bronaugh

A Bunch of Violets

Just out of college, I began working at an upscale gift gallery near San Francisco's Union Square. After several months, my hurried morning walk to work, past a small flower stand, became routine. Then one morning, passing that stand, I felt an overwhelming desire to buy flowers for someone. I found myself looking intently at different bouquets. On the bottom shelf there was a nosegay of violets. Mrs. Cairns, a grey-haired widow who worked at the gallery, came to mind. I could just see that nosegay on the lavender tweed suit she often wore to work.

We weren't close friends. To me she seemed interested only in her job. I was even a little envious because she always helped the wealthy San Francisco dowagers who came to shop and usually rang up four or five times my sales. But, I followed my instinct.

A few minutes later, I saw her standing inside the gallery doors, dressed in her lavender tweed suit.

Hesitantly, I handed her the nosegay. "These are for you, Mrs. Cairns."

There was a second or two of silence before she said, "I've never told anyone here. How did you know?"

"Know what?"

Her faded brown eyes teared. "Today is my wedding anniversary. My husband passed away years ago, so now I'm the only one who remembers."

As she pinned on the nosegay, I told her how pleased I was that my impulse purchase happened on her anniversary.

She took both of my hands. "But, my dear . . . I must tell you that I married forty years ago in a small town in Oregon. It was a cold, winter day and there were no flowers in town, so my wedding bouquet was a nosegay of violets."

Carol Fannin Rohwedder

Everything He Had

Thanksgiving Day had arrived in New England. Our old blue Rambler whizzed past snowy fields, picturesque farmhouses, bare trees and bright red barns. My twelve-year-old twins and I had been invited to spend the holiday with a deacon's family from our church. We had recently moved to a Boston suburb while adjusting to a painful divorce.

At the deacon's house, we ate a delicious turkey dinner, sang songs, played games and laughed a lot. We enjoyed the day along with another guest named Tinker who was unusually quiet. Our host excused himself after pumpkin pie and coffee to give Tinker a ride home. Soon after, we left too.

The twins' excitement built as Christmas drew near. Late one night, I sat alone at the kitchen table sorting through mail. Underneath the pile lay the children's simple Christmas gift list.

"Lord, they ask for so little," I prayed. "How will I buy these gifts and a Christmas tree and food for dinner?"

A few days later, a friend helped us cut a small, spindly Christmas tree. We strung popcorn, cranberries and handmade paper loops for decoration. I had saved a chicken in the freezer for Christmas dinner.

"Mommy, gifts don't matter so much," my son said after I explained we had no money.

"I don't *need* that jacket. I just wanted it," his sister chimed in.

Then they knelt next to the little tree and in childlike faith asked God to meet our needs.

Four days later, I pulled a bundle of letters from the mailbox. A small envelope with no return address caught my eye. When I opened the card, four hundred-dollar bills fluttered to the ground. I knelt to scoop up the money and read the message scrawled on a scrap of paper: "Merry Christmas, and God bless you." No signature. No hint of the sender's identity.

The children grew up and left home. I remarried and moved out to California. Eventually my husband and I flew back East to attend my son's graduation from Army basic training. While we were in the area, we visited the deacon who had welcomed us that Thanksgiving long ago.

As we reminisced, I told the story of the children's trusting prayer and our anonymous Christmas blessing. His eyes filled with tears. He took a moment to regain his composure, then he spoke. "Do you remember the young man at the Thanksgiving table with us that day? Tinker was his name. He is a convicted murderer serving a life sentence. Because I was deacon in the prison ministry, officials released Tinker on a six-hour pass into my custody. When I drove him back that night, he told me he had never heard people show such a strong faith in God the way your family did. He asked me to come by the prison later and pick up some Christmas money for you and the children. He gave you all he had."

I sat in silence as I realized how human kindness and compassion can be alive and working through anyone.

Judith Gillis

Nine Years and Nine Days

When my husband died in 1989, the lights went out. After nearly a decade of marriage, I was suddenly alone. I pulled the shades, turned out the lights and settled into a world of shaded seclusion.

For the next nine years our house slowly ran down, like a clock someone forgot to wind.

Normally the houses on our Mission Viejo street were abuzz with happy children playing in the daytime, and street parties in session at night. But our house was now dark, like my spirits. My will was as worn as our carpets, and any happy thoughts leaked away like the roof and the plumbing.

Trash began to accumulate around our house and anxieties accumulated in my heart. Our furniture sagged, the paint was peeling off the walls, even our dinnerware was chipped and darkened. My two daughters, ages twelve and fourteen, were hesitant to invite their friends over to visit.

They say that the longest year of a woman's life is her thirty-ninth year. It was proving true for me. My heart, like our street, was a cul-de-sac.

Just when I thought the world couldn't get any darker, there was a knock at the door. Reluctantly I opened it and recognized two neighbors, Shelly and Cindy. I knew I looked a fright, but they didn't seem to notice.

"We've been concerned about you, Teresa," Shelly explained.

This was the first time anyone had said that to me in a long time, and I felt like I was going to cry.

Shelly went on. "We know that you can't afford to keep up the place the way you would like, so. . . ."

"Some of us would like to put down new carpets for you," Cindy chimed in.

"Right," Shelly added. "It's not much, but it's something we can do for you, to help you get back on your feet. Please let us do this for you."

I was somewhat bewildered by all this attention.

Shelly went on. "The catch is, you'll have to move out for a few days, so the workers can be free to work. Is that possible?"

I nodded, unable to speak.

When our station wagon headed off to my parents' home in Santa Barbara, my heart was beating with a melody of hope for the first time in years.

When I returned home nine days later, I arrived late in the evening. My usually dark house glowed radiantly on a dark street. Every light in the house was on! I had to remove a large, white bow from the front door. When I stepped inside, it was like walking out of death and into life!

During our absence, teams of neighbors and professional volunteers had completely renovated every room of our house.

"Oh, my," was all I could say, as I ran from room to room like a child in a candy store.

The air was fragrant with newness, as I plopped into chair after chair of new furniture and squished my toes in thick new carpeting. I studied the walls that throbbed with color and light, and watched my daughters dance around like two-year-olds.

Nothing had escaped the sharp and loving eyes of my neighbors. The plumbing was healed, the ceilings were dry and clean. Our new dining-room table was set with crisp new dinnerware and flatware. Even the closets had been cleaned, with new shelf liners in place. New pictures hung on the walls, illuminated by new lamps.

Needless to say, I did not sleep that night. I couldn't stop crying! For the next two weeks I was busy giving tours to my neighbors and hugs of thanks to all the volunteers who had given me a part of their lives and hearts.

I never dreamed that nine years of darkness could be brushed away by just nine days of kindness, but it's true. Now, every night I leave some lights on in the house just to remind them of my gratitude for their gift of light.

Bonnie Harris
Submitted by Lauren Andrews

Rescued by a Drowning Dog

"Bubba, this is the last time," I bellow as the big brown dog jumps to the table, grabs the script I am working on and bolts away. He skitters across the kitchen floor as I give chase.

"No!" I shriek in anticipation of the disaster. A large clay pot crashes, its dirt-and-flower contents emptied all over the floor.

"Darn you," I say. I slide to the floor and begin sobbing.

I don't want to be here. I don't want to be alone. Hurting this much. And I don't want to be dealing with this demon dog.

Why does anyone think animals are good companions? I wonder bitterly. *They're no substitute for people and certainly no solace for loneliness.*

But my husband Arnie had been a believer. Two years ago, Arnie proudly lugged home a large carton. "A surprise for you," he announced, as a filthy dog sprang from the box onto our new white sofa and leaped onto the end table, scattering my prized collection of miniature glass figures.

"How could you?" I asked Arnie in disbelief. "Get that mangy animal out of this house!" With that, the dog put his teeth into my new sweater.

It was hate at first sight for Bubba and me.

Arnie liked to say Bubba had a touch of German shepherd in his mutt mix. More like a touch of the devil. When Bubba and I were alone, he destroyed my clothes, broke cherished possessions and hid whatever project I was working on. When Arnie was around, he was Mr. Nice Dog.

"I don't see why you're always so angry with this guy," Arnie would say, stroking the big, coffee-colored head. "He's such a gentle dog." On cue, Bubba would settle at Arnie's feet, wag his tail leisurely and smirk. At me.

I tolerated Bubba because Arnie loved him. As he grew to almost one hundred pounds, the dog became part of our household but not of my heart. He was 100 percent Arnie's dog. Each evening as the clock chimed seven, Bubba plopped down on the area rug in the front hall, blocking the door, to await Arnie's homecoming.

One evening, Bubba waited and waited. The clock chimed eight, then nine. I joined Bubba in his anxiousness, pacing beside him. Finally, the bell rang. A policeman stood in my doorway twisting his hat. There had been an accident. Arnie was dead.

Friends and family came and went. I sat in my chair rocking. I think someone told me they were taking Bubba home. I don't remember much about the next few weeks. Until one day, the doorbell rang again, and Bubba was back.

He growled at me and dashed past, flying through the house, in and out of rooms. After a while, he quieted somewhat, his pace slowing. He took up vigil in the front hall, getting up only occasionally to search for Arnie, eat or ask to be let out.

When he needed out, I opened the back door to the fenced-in yard I shared with my neighbor. I tried a couple of times to walk him, but he snarled whenever I came near.

I only kept the ungrateful mutt because Arnie had loved him.

One day, two hours passed and darkness came before I noticed Bubba hadn't scratched at the door to be let back in. I called. No Bubba. I tried to switch on the back light only to be reminded that the outside electric had been disconnected because lights were being installed around my neighbor's new in-ground pool. It had just been filled, not even heated yet. . . . No, it couldn't be! Bubba hated water!

But the pool had a black liner. . . . I grabbed a flashlight and approached the water, panicking as I heard a whimper. There in the circle of my light aimed at the deep end was the forlorn, sodden dog, hanging by his paws onto the edge of the pool. He'd probably chased a chipmunk and fallen into the unfamiliar landmark, paddling around until his strength gave out.

I hauled Bubba from the cold water, dragged him back into the house and wrapped him in the nearest thing I could find: my favorite afghan. The last present Arnie had given me.

I held the dog close until his shivering subsided, then held him some more. He made no attempt to leave the security of my arms until the clock struck seven. It had been almost a year since Arnie had died, yet each night Bubba faithfully took up the vigil when the bell chimed. Tonight, he left my lap, started toward the front hall, and hesitated. Turning, he looked me in the eye and came back to my chair, settling at my feet.

I don't know which of us had been more oblivious to the other's pain, Bubba or me. But it took a nearly drowned dog to pull me out of my grief-induced isolation.

I imagined Arnie was smiling.

Carren Strock

The Face of Compassion

How a person masters his fate is more important than what his fate is.

Wilhelm Von Humboldt

When I was young, I was very arrogant. I was blessed with good looks and charm, and I was extremely vain: I would often look in the mirror and admire my own face. I was also a good athlete. I dated many girls throughout high school and was rarely without a girlfriend.

But I was impossible to deal with. I was very demanding, and I made it clear to my girlfriends that there was only one way for them to be with me: Do it my way or take the highway!

Until the day I met Teri. Teri was three years younger than I. She had blonde curly hair, dimples that melted my heart and a smile that you couldn't ignore even if you tried. There was such sweetness in her manner. We started to date, and within a few months we had become very close friends. For the first time I actually had a relationship that I was contributing to in a constructive way, and I was really enjoying it.

One day, however, Teri informed me that she had decided to return to a boyfriend who was exactly her age. She thought they had more in common. My heart was broken. For the first time in my life I had been dumped, and it hurt. Of course, I was soon dating other girls, but a hole remained in my heart where Teri had been.

One year passed, and I didn't see Teri at all. Then a group of friends let me know that Teri wanted to see me again. So we fixed something up. I was quite apprehensive before our first meeting, but when I saw that smile and heard that voice I knew I could relax. Once again Teri and I started seeing each other on a regular basis.

I graduated from high school and took a job on a construction site. On Labor Day 1980, I was working with a construction crew. It was warm enough for me to take my shirt off, and I was enjoying the work. Directly above me, a man was working with a bucket of hot tar. Suddenly, without a moment's warning, the bucket toppled over. At the time, I had no idea what hit me. All I could feel was the burning pain and confusion and terrifying fear. The truth was that I was covered in hot tar from head to toe.

An ambulance arrived and I was rushed to the hospital, my life flashing before my eyes. I had no idea what my fate would be.

I do not know how many hours passed as the doctors attended to me. Finally, a surgeon looked down at me and said, "I am going to tell you the truth." He told me that I had burns over 55 percent of my body. But that was not the worst of it. The most devastating effects of the tar were on my face, the same face that in my vanity I used to admire in the mirror. The surgeon told me I would no longer have my nose, bottom lip or chin.

It took a while for this news to sink in. At first I just felt numb. Then I had a feeling of hopelessness that I had never known before. My grip on life seemed to loosen.

Never again would I be the good-looking charmer. What did I have left to live for?

Over the next few hours my face swelled up; I could not see, and I could hardly breathe. In spite of this, however, I was not kept for long in the hospital. Instead, I was moved to my brother's home.

It was hell. I heard the doctor tell my brother not to let me sleep for more than twenty minutes at a time. And I didn't. But I remember waking up to find Teri looking down at me. That sweet smile that I knew so well. I didn't want her to see me in that condition, but she insisted on staying with me. She woke me every twenty minutes and took care of me throughout the night, before going to her job during the day.

I spent the days alone. All I could do was sit up and watch TV. Any movement brought extreme pain. And I still didn't know what I looked like. As the days passed, I began to entertain the stupid notion that maybe what the doctor told me about what had happened to my face hadn't really happened at all. Maybe everything was all right.

One day, I finally gained enough strength to crawl to a mirror. I had to know the truth. I remember that moment to this day. My whole world shattered. All I had been so proud of—my complexion, my bold features—had changed, and my only thought was, who will want me in this condition?

In the following months, I became bitter and hard to deal with. I did everything possible to make Teri go away. I didn't want her to be saddled with me. I was impossible to be nice to. Yet Teri did not go. She stayed and cared for me, refusing to become upset with me. She must have made a deep commitment. She, who was not my wife, loved me as much as any wife could. It didn't matter to her that my face was destroyed, and that many people almost fainted upon seeing me. Many of my other friends couldn't handle it at all.

Time passed, and through the care of a good doctor, I began to make great progress. I knew I was finally beginning to recover from my injuries. Teri remained a faithful help. She cared for me and was my companion, and I realized that true friendship was so much more important to a relationship between a man and a woman than I had formerly thought. It is friendship that makes a relationship grow. For years I had it backwards.

Teri and I developed a mutual understanding that although we were fast friends, we would not marry. We just knew, that's all. But we also knew we had a friendship that would be special forever. I was so thankful to her that she persevered in spite of my disfigurement, my depression and my immaturity. She gave me her gift of compassion.

Some years later, Teri married someone else, and so did I. I love my wife very much, and we have a family. Every day, I try to use the lesson in compassion that Teri taught me. I know now that compassion is to look outward, beyond oneself, and to care for someone else. I have no need of mirrors now.

Michael Clay

9

FRIENDS AND FAMILY

We are here to help one another along life's journey.

William J. Bennett

A Lasagna Kind of Christmas

You don't just luck into things as much as you'd like to think you do. You build step by step, whether it's friendships or opportunities.

Barbara Bush

Looking out the window into the cold, Michigan whiteness, I realized Tim might be late. No matter. I was already packed. I took a quick inventory: the red-and-white striped shopping bag piled high with gifts for Mother . . . the chocolate layer cake that was the only proper finish to the annual turkey dinner . . . the cut-glass decanter filled with cashews . . . and the three packages for Paul, my new eighty-three-year-old stepfather of only two months.

I turned again to watch for my son. Despite the light falling snow, today didn't seem like Christmas. How strange to be going without my father.

"Your first Christmas should be spent at my house," I had suggested to Mom. "It will be easier on everyone."

Easier on me. Just a little less change to get used to. Since my divorce fourteen years ago, Mother and Daddy had spent the Christmas holiday at my house. They lived in a mobile home with a postage-stamp-sized kitchen, and we all agreed it was just easier since I had the most room.

But Daddy was gone now, and Mother gently reminded me that it would be "their" first Christmas together, hers and Paul's. They wanted to spend it at home. "Besides, Paul wants to cook dinner for you and Tim," she added.

I liked my new stepfather; he was a fine man. He and my parents had attended the same church for more than forty-five years. But when only eight months after Daddy died my eighty-year-old mother announced she and Paul were to be married, I didn't care how nice a man he was. "Just too soon" was all I could say.

I was jealous, I realized later. When I had become single again, Mom and Dad helped fill the gap emotionally, providing more support than perhaps I realized. Now Mom's attention would shift, and I would have to share her with Paul and his grown children. I was happy she had someone, but maybe a little resentful that we wouldn't be sharing our aloneness.

Tim was indeed late. To pass the time, I walked into the living room to look at the tree covered with ornaments from Christmases past—silly baubles that meant little to anyone except me. Paper stars Tim had made in first grade. The red, wax Santa Claus boot that Daddy had given me as a child. It had a hole in the toe where it melted from once being placed too close to a light bulb.

I knelt down to plug in the lights. The tiny, clear bulbs seemed to breathe life into the tree's adornments, transforming the valueless trinkets into priceless, individual memories. Pieces of life, pieces of one another. More than ornaments, they were our family story of growth and change.

"Hey, Mom!" Tim's stomping abruptly interrupted my reverie. He poked a snow-covered head through the door. "Ready? Don't forget the chocolate cake!"

I was relieved Tim had volunteered to drive. The swirling white made driving extra serious, so under the circumstances, I thought my silence seemed natural. But Tim looked over at me. "What's wrong, Mom? You're acting weird."

"It's the weather," I stammered. "Just trying to let you concentrate on your driving."

He didn't believe me, but he didn't pry.

As we rounded the corner to Mother's mobile home, I planned my escape route. Though the snow had subsided, I could still use the bad weather as an excuse to leave early. But as we pulled into a freshly shoveled drive to see Mom and Paul waving wildly from the kitchen door, I felt sheepish for my plotting.

Mom held the door wide for us while Paul stood ready to help carry. Inside we hugged and rehugged, then shed our winter wraps. I suddenly smelled something unlike our traditional turkey dinner.

Quick to pick up on my reactions, Mom said brightly, "I know you've always had turkey for Christmas dinner, but Paul wanted to do something special, just for you. So he made lasagna. Took him a whole day, too," she added proudly.

No turkey? My chocolate layer cake with lasagna? It sure didn't take him long to change tradition.

We took our places at the small, kitchen table, Mother at one end, Paul at the other, Tim and I in between. The room was lit by just two white candles Mom had placed on either side of the lasagna pan.

Closing clouded eyes, Paul smiled, then extended his huge, weathered hands to us for prayer. Those same hands that tilled warm, spring earth, that had made the lasagna set before us, trembled as he began. . . .

"Dear God, today is hard for Tim and Linda. But we are so grateful for the love we share and for their acceptance of me. . . ."

I can't remember anything else except trying to choke back the lump in my throat as I fidgeted in my chair.

I had no idea of Paul's sensitivity to the situation. And ashamed, I realized I'd been so consumed with my own losses, past and present, that I failed to understand Paul's own concerns that he be welcomed into my heart.

The soft candlelight seemed to have the same effect on those gathered here as the tree lights had on my time-worn ornaments. I looked at the chocolate cake, the lasagna, Mom's ancient kitchen table, and the loving faces surrounding me. I realized that where love is, all things blend.

Linda LaRocque

Between Two Worlds

At Pillar Point Lighthouse, south of San Francisco, where the ocean gives way to the land, I stood on the edge of two worlds. That day my thoughts were as restless as the relentless sea pummeling the shore below. I was floundering, torn between the deep attachments of the past and the pressing need to let go of them forever. I was almost ready to give up.

Me, single again? I can't do this! Two months earlier, my husband had suddenly walked out of our marriage. The discovery of multiple affairs going back decades left me breathless. Now, as a single working mother of a teenager, I felt overwhelmed. Sometimes I felt I could make it through, but at other times I just wanted to die.

That particular Sunday afternoon, Eleanor, a woman I knew from church, suggested that we go and pick blackberries at the ocean. So we had driven down the coast and stopped at this bluff to stretch our legs and absorb the view.

I didn't know Eleanor well, but she turned out to be good company. As we gazed down at the ocean she turned to me and said, very deliberately, "The kind of men who sneak around and walk out on marriages are not worth crying over."

So began my friendship with Eleanor. I soon discovered that as a divorced woman herself, she had also stood where I was now—and that she had not only survived, but flourished.

In the months that followed, Eleanor taught me how. "Lighten up. Simplify," she said. I began by getting rid of the heavy furniture I couldn't lift on my own.

"Why hold on to all those knickknacks and holiday ornaments, if they have such heavy memories?" she asked. So I held a garage sale to make room for new memories and traditions. I bought a small house across town and redecorated the black vinyl and beige with colorful floral patterns. Instead of bemoaning that my daughter chose to spend that first Christmas with her father, I took the week off work to travel to Israel.

Slowly, I got my feet wet with all this single stuff. Eleanor was always there for me. She let me have the keys to her house so I could have a quiet place to go when she was at work, and she said I could call her anytime, day or night. I thought of her as my "3 A.M. friend." What a gift she gave me!

I found myself wanting what Eleanor had. That wisdom. That twinkle in the eye that said that life is good and we are here to enjoy it. Just watching her move smoothly, creatively through her life helped. I thought, *Maybe one day I'll be where she is.*

Although our paths took different directions in the years that followed, Eleanor and I always managed to pick up our friendship where we left off. To this day, I continue to admire how she carries herself with flair through life's ups and downs. She has a way of putting things into perspective.

It is in part because of Eleanor that I have realized one special dream. While I was going through all my emotional turmoil, I hoped that someday I would be able to write about it and so help other women in the same situation. Inspired by watching Eleanor turn a hobby of oil painting into a home business, I left behind a thirty-year career to become a freelance writer.

One day I was at a writer's conference having an article based on my experience reviewed by an editor. In the middle of our session she suddenly broke down and said, "I'm going through this same thing right now!"

She was obviously in distress. I gave her a hug and told her she would get through it; there was a future out there, even though she might not be able to see it at the moment.

Over the next few months, we stayed in touch, and then it occurred to me that she and I would make a perfect writing team. The combination of my weathered experience and her raw pain would enable us to write a book that would mentor other women in similar situations. When I told her my idea over the telephone she was very enthusiastic, and as we said good-bye she added, "I want my twinkle back—the twinkle that I see in your eyes!"

I closed my eyes for a moment as I realized what had happened: I had become for my new friend what my old friend Eleanor had always been for me. Twelve years had passed since that Sunday afternoon when Eleanor and I stopped at the lighthouse. And now I knew what Eleanor must have known as we stood looking down at the ocean pounding at the shore: There is a place where the turbulent sea gives way to firm, dry land. And when you find that place, you become a beacon of hope for others who are still floundering in the waves.

Kari West

Dad Is There for Me Again —and Always

I was a Daddy's girl, I'll confess it. My father was almost forty when I was born, far older than all my friends' fathers, but this only served to make him gentler with me, more tender. He treated me like a treasure.

Even after I was grown up, with a job and an apartment, Dad still called me "Monkey," the pet name he'd given me as a child. Even after I was married and had children of my own, Dad would slip me money on the sly. "Get yourself a treat," he'd whisper. Even after he was diagnosed with cancer and his physical strength was nearly gone, I thought of him as "my protector."

I have so many memories of Dad. I see him stretched out in his big easy chair, watching the Cubs game. I see us together at the ballpark, Dad patiently teaching an impatient little girl how to keep a box score. The smell of newly mown grass takes me right back to lazy summer Saturdays, when I'd be on the porch reading, and Dad would be behind the lawn mower.

I can count up my Christmases by my memories of Dad, too. There was the very early Christmas when my present to him was a crayon drawing of the two of us side by side. Dad had a big grin, his arms came directly out of his head, and he was on red roller-skates. After Dad's death, Mom and I found that picture still in his dresser drawer, tucked away under his handkerchiefs. There was the year I cried on Christmas morning because the only present I could afford for him was a very ordinary wool scarf, but Dad made such a fuss over it, I felt I'd given him a present beyond price. And then there was the Christmas Eve when I was fifteen and didn't have much time for Dad. He came into my room that night, put his arms around me and whispered, "Don't worry, I know you still love me—and I know you know that I love you, too."

Last Christmas was the hardest one of my life. I was newly divorced, my son was off at college and unable to afford a trip home, and although Mom had been planning to come for the holidays, ill health had canceled her trip. My son had called, and friends had invited me for dinner, but Christmas morning found me feeling more than low.

Always before, from when I was small to when I had small ones of my own, Christmas morning had been the most magical time of the whole year, the time we opened presents and shared love and made memories. Even last year, when my marriage was rocky, my husband and I had managed to make that morning a special one for our son. Even on our first Christmas without Dad, Mom and I had spent part of the morning reminiscing, celebrating his life in spite of our tears.

But this Christmas morning, sitting by a tree I hadn't had the spirit to decorate, I felt more alone than I'd ever been in my life. Worse than that, I felt I would always be alone.

I started shivering, cold almost beyond bearing. I turned up the thermostat, but it didn't help. I was cold from the inside out, numb at the thought of all those bleak

Christmas mornings—all the mornings of my life—that waited for me. And then Mom called. She wanted, of course, to wish me a Merry Christmas, but also to ask how I'd liked the presents she'd sent. "I haven't opened them yet," I told her. "I don't know when I'll ever feel like opening them."

"I can understand that," Mom said, "but why not at least open the one from Dad?"

"You mean the one you wrapped up and said was from Dad," I answered her. "That was very sweet of you, Mom, but. . . . "

"But it is from Dad," she insisted. "Go and get that package—right now!"

I did as I was told. As I sat there holding the package on my lap, Mom told me how "that present was the last thing Dad bought for you before he got sick." He had wrapped it up himself and, sure enough, when I looked at the tag, I saw it was in Dad's handwriting. "He meant it for that last Christmas, of course, before he died, but he was so ill and everything happened so fast, the present just got misplaced. And then in all the confusion after his death, I forgot all about it—until just recently, when I was going through some old boxes and found it."

After Mom and I hung up, I opened the present and found a silver trivet, decorated with a hand-painted Christmas tree. It was elegant and understated, the kind of special gift Dad would have known I'd love, and one that only Dad could have hunted down for me. With one hand I picked it up and held it close, the other hand lovingly tracing its circular shape. *Dad and I were a part of each other's life circles,* I thought. He'd been there at my beginning, and I'd been there at his earthly end.

But circles have no real beginnings or ends, I realized, and suddenly, sitting in the Christmas morning stillness that only moments before had numbed me with loneliness,

As soon as I was released from the hospital, I went to visit Al. I was told that he wouldn't be able to communicate with me. But when I walked into his room, his eyes lit up and he smiled. I had no trouble understanding what his heart was saying to mine.

My husband had cut out a big red wooden apple puzzle, with a long green worm as one of the pieces, for me to give to Al. When I placed the puzzle in his hands, tears fell from his eyes, and he said, "Tu."

This was the only sound that Al could make. But that didn't stop us from talking. I learned to differentiate between a Tu that meant yes, and a Tu that meant no, and we did just fine. Although at this time I did most of the work, we still put an occasional puzzle together, and invariably the final piece would be found in Al's pajama pocket.

Not long after going to the nursing home, Al died at the age of eighty-eight. His life had been full, he had known love and happiness, and I knew he had a great faith in God. I would miss my friend, yet I felt a sense of serenity at his passing.

Because I had never met his family, I was a little uncomfortable going to the funeral home to visit him for the last time. But the minute I walked into the parlor, his son and daughter-in-law came rushing over to hug me and to introduce themselves. When I started to explain who I was, they said, "Oh, we know who you are." They told me that Al had often talked about me, and how much he had loved me. When I asked how they had recognized me, they said they had just sensed it.

I went up to the casket to pay my last respects, to say good-bye to my very special friend. Al's son came up and knelt beside me. Later as we were walking away, he reached into his pocket and handed me a small plastic bag. I could see it contained the pieces of a puzzle. "Dad wanted me to give this to you." Along with the pieces there was a scribbled note.

I stood beside Al's son and read the paper.

> *This is my final gift to you. You will discover that one of the pieces is missing. I know you will never give up until you find it. Good luck, my little friend, for I am taking it with me. Someday, hopefully a long time from now, when you join me in heaven, your final piece will be there. Until then, have a beautiful life, I will love you from afar. . . . Always, Al*

As tears flooded my eyes, Al's son explained that his father had written that note right after he visited me at the hospital the last time. He had given the puzzle and the note to his son, instructing him to give it to me if he passed away first. He had also requested that the one missing piece be placed in the pocket of the vest he was to be buried in, next to his heart.

I truly hope that some day I will meet him again, and both of us will have finally gotten it all together.

Barbara Jeanne Fisher

The Makeover

"So, what are you doing for Thanksgiving?" asked Stacey, my hairdresser, who paused her gentle backcombing and smiled at me in the mirror.

I stared back, dismayed and embarrassed. For several moments, not one coherent thought would form. Then I tried to get around her question: I asked her what she and her family were doing.

"Oh, the whole family is meeting at Mom's," she answered. But she wasn't about to be sidetracked so easily. Again, she asked, "What about you and the kids?"

With no way out, I stammered, "Nothing. We're staying home and will probably play games." Tears stung my tired eyes as I admitted the truth.

Stacey and I stared at each other in the mirror, my haircut and style forgotten. It seemed just a simple answer to a simple question, but in that moment, all of my embarrassment, frustration and fear seemed to erupt into one miserable recognition: I had no feast for my family's Thanksgiving dinner; I had no warm family circle of support, no home, no job, no husband or friends I could rely on.

Stacey had been doing my hair for several years, long

before the divorce. She knew how hard I'd worked to save a long-term marriage to an increasingly unpredictable man. Now she was watching me learn to live as a single parent, with a daughter struggling to stay in college while working part time at a grocery store. She knew my son was disabled and although he provided patient encouragement for me, he also required extra care.

She also knew my unemployment compensation was about to end, and that there was no teaching job in sight. What no one knew was that I staggered through my days, so scared I could hardly breathe.

Even this visit to Stacey had been discussed and carefully evaluated from a financial standpoint: We decided that I simply had to have my shaggy hair coaxed into shape for an upcoming interview. The three of us had agreed to just eat homemade vegetable soup, our everyday staple, for Thanksgiving.

Tears trickled down my cheeks and my voice stuck in my throat, unable to escape. Stacey, giving me a hug, let the subject drop, and I soon regained my composure. When I left the shop, my hair looked great, but I felt awful. I needed more than a new haircut.

Stacey called later that afternoon from a pay phone, casually asking if she could drop by for a second. "I was in the neighborhood, and I was handing out a little gift, nothing big, really, to all my clients for the holidays." I invited her over, expecting a token of appreciation, a little bottle of shampoo or soaps. I was dumbfounded when I opened the door!

There stood Stacey and one of her friends, arms laden with boxes of food: a large turkey, stuffing mix, pumpkin, pie crusts, yams, rolls, Jell-O—even paper towels!

Suddenly, I couldn't pretend anymore. I didn't care how I looked. I needed help, love, concern and compassion. That act of generosity wiped away every last bit of my false pride, and I broke down. I sobbed in front of Stacey and her friend, and I sobbed after they left, for a long time. My nose and eyes were fire-engine red, my face a blotchy mess and my hair a catastrophe.

I looked horrible. I felt great. It was the best makeover Stacey could have given me.

Maggy Rose McLarty

Unbroken Circle

Mom had told Dad to fly all us kids into Scottsdale, Arizona, no matter what the cost. So, in February 1994, we flew from Iowa, Montana, Kansas, Illinois and New York to where Mom was lying in a hospital bed. Three-and-a-half years earlier, she had been diagnosed with congestive heart failure. The prognosis then was that she would live only six months. She had managed to confound those dire predictions, but now the time had come.

Many years before that, as the youngest daughter and the only one of five children who never married, I had left the Midwest for the East Coast. This move had created a wall between my mother and me. She had resented my going so far from home and staying there, and I had resented her trying to clip my wings just when I started to fly as an adult on my own.

It was midnight in New York when I got the call from my Dad in Phoenix. All I felt was dread. Now I would have to face the wall between my mom and me. What if it had become too solid and we were unable to break through it?

I was the last to arrive at the hospital in Scottsdale. The rest of the family stood in a semicircle around Mom, who lay under a sterile white hospital blanket in the intensive care unit. She began to talk to each of her children—two sons and three daughters—as if each of us were in our own private confessional with her.

As the others leaned towards her and tears began to fall onto her laboring chest, I excused myself for a few moments. I went outside to the courtyard where the palm trees were swaying gently in the hot desert breeze. My heart twisted and turned, wrestling with old issues of forgiveness and resentment. I knew I had to go back inside, even though I felt sick to my stomach.

I took the elevator up to Mom's room, where all eyes turned to me as I entered. As I neared her bed I took a deep breath. I felt dizzy and weak, afraid that in our last moments together, the words that needed to be said would not come out.

"Mom, I'm sorry that I hurt you by going to New York City, and just, just . . . staying. Can you forgive me? I didn't mean to hurt you."

My brothers and sisters looked at me, then down at her, and back at me again.

"Mom," said Paula. "Laurie was just trying to live her life. She didn't mean to hurt you."

Mom looked at me out of her once-feisty blue eyes, which were growing misty with pain.

"Yes, I was hurt, but I do forgive you," she said in a low but steady voice.

We had both said the right words, but I still felt as if a stone were pulling my heart downward, and that things had not been fully resolved.

The following evening, which was a Saturday, we all gathered around her bed again. We felt that her passing was imminent. We prayed and joined hands while we sang "Amazing Grace" and "How Great Thou Art."

At that point, Mother looked up past the television attached to the wall in the upper right corner of the room.

She seemed to be gazing heavenward and there was an other-worldly calm about her.

"Do you hear them?" she asked in a raspy voice.

"Do we hear what, Mom?" several of us asked in unison.

"The bells, the bells. They're ringing," she whispered, and leaned forward a bit.

We could feel her spirit leaving us, and Brian said, "Mom, you can go now, we're ready to let you go."

At that moment, she closed her eyes tight, sighed and sank back down into the covers. We knew she was still with us.

I was grateful that she chose to stay a little longer. We both knew we weren't done.

Very early on Sunday morning, Dad and I were at Mom's bedside next to the east window. The sun was streaming in, shining on the freshly laundered white blanket.

I had my Bible, and asked Mom if she would like me to read a passage of scripture.

"No," she said, determined. "I have something I need to say first." And in words that forever echo in my soul, she continued. "Paul, I want to be buried in that charcoal blue dress you like on me so well. And Laurie, I want you to have my mother's and my wedding rings."

My heart started racing. I stared at her lying there so still. Her eyes closed and then opened again. She looked to the other side of the room and then back at me for a brief moment.

"You're the only one not married, and I want you to have these."

I lay my head down on her chest and wept.

Mom had made it right. She was giving me the rings she had possessed for a lifetime, and they would forever be symbols of the unbroken circle of love that exists between mother and daughter—love that can never be broken, not by misunderstanding, resentment, lack of forgiveness or even death.

For the first time in years, the heaviness lifted from my heart. I saw Mom's wedding ring sparkle in the sunlight that now flooded the room. Outside, the palm trees were waving, reaching upwards to the blue sky of heaven.

Laurie L. Oswald

A Shining Thing

At the touch of love, everyone becomes a poet.

Plato

They sat together on the porch steps, so close that their moon shadow was a single wedge of blackness against the weathered wood. Tomorrow was the wedding, with all the excitement and confusion, tears and laughter. There would be no privacy then. But this quiet hour was their own.

She said, "It's peaceful, isn't it?" She was watching the great stately clouds march over their heads and drop from sight into the quicksilver sea. He was watching her and thought he had never seen her so beautiful.

The wind blew; the waves made little hush-hush sounds, sighing against the sand. "You know," she said, "I always wondered how I'd feel the night before my wedding. Scared, or thrilled, or uncertain, or what."

"You're not scared, are you?"

"Oh, no," she said quickly. She hugged his arm and put her face against his shoulder in the impulsive way she had. "Just a little solemn, maybe. Solemn and gay, and young and old, and happy and sad. Do you know what I mean?"

"Yes," he said. "I know."

"It's love that does it, I suppose," she said. "That old thing. We've never talked about it much, have we? About love itself, I mean."

He smiled a little. "We never had to."

"I'd sort of like to—now," she said. "Do you mind? I'd like to try to tell you how I feel, before tomorrow—happens."

"Will it be any different after tomorrow?"

"No, but I may not be able to talk about it then. It may go down somewhere deep inside, below the talking level."

"All right," he said. "Tell me about love."

She watched a cloud ravel itself against the moon. "Well," she said, "to me it's a shining thing, like a golden fire or a silver mist. It comes very quietly; you can't command it, but you can't deny it, either. When it does come, you can't quite see it or touch it, but you can feel it—inside of you and around you and the person you love. It changes you; it changes everything. Colors are brighter, music is sweeter, funny things are funnier. Ordinary speech won't do—you grope for better ways to express how you feel. You read poetry. Maybe you even try to write it. . . ."

She leaned back, clasping her hands around her knees, the moonlight bright and ecstatic on her face.

"Oh, it's so many little things! Waltzing in the dark; waiting for the phone to ring; opening the box of flowers. It's holding hands in a movie; it's humming a sad little tune; it's walking in the rain; it's riding in a convertible with the wind in your hair. It's the quarreling and making up again. It's that first warm, drowsy thought in the morning and the last kiss at night. . . ."

She broke off suddenly and gave him a desolate look. "But it's all been said before, hasn't it?"

"Even if it has," he told her gently, "that doesn't make it any less true."

"Maybe I'm just being silly," she said doubtfully. "Is that the way love seems to you?"

He did not answer for a while. At last he said, "I might add a little to your definition."

"You mean, you wouldn't change it?"

"No. Just add to it."

She put her chin in her hands. "Go ahead. I'm listening."

He took out the pipe she had given him and rubbed the smooth grain along his cheek. "You said it was a lot of little things. You're right. I could mention a few that don't have much glitter. But they have an importance that grows. . . ."

She watched his lean fingers begin to load the pipe. "Give me some examples," she said.

"Oh, coming home to somebody when the day is ended—or waiting for somebody to come home to you. Giving, or getting, a word of praise when none is really deserved. Sharing a joke that nobody else understands. Planting a tree together and watching it grow. Sitting up with a sick child. Remembering anniversaries—do I make it sound terribly dull?"

She did not say anything; she shook her head.

"Everything you mentioned is part of it," he went on, "but it's not all triumphant, you know. It's also sharing disappointment and sorrow. It's going out to slay the dragon, and finding the dragon too much for you, and running away—but going out again the next day. It's the little chips of tolerance that you finally knock off the granite of your own ego: not saying 'I told you so,' not noticing the dented fender in the family car. It's the gradual acceptance of limitations—your own as well as others. It's discarding some of the ambitions you had for yourself, and planting them in your children. . . ." His voice trailed off into the listening night.

"Are you talking," she asked finally, "about living, or loving?"

"You'll find there's not much of one without the other."

"When . . . when did you learn that?"

"Quite a while ago. Before your mother died." His hands touched her shining hair. "Better go to bed now, Baby. Tomorrow's your big day."

She clung to him suddenly. "Oh, Daddy, I'm going to miss you so!"

"Nonsense," he said. "I'll be seeing you all the time. Run along now."

After she was gone, he sat there for a long time, alone in the moonlight.

Arthur Gordon
Submitted by Linda Ringo

Turning the Page

A friend is the hope of the heart.

Ralph Waldo Emerson

I first met Jeanne on moving day. She appeared sometime after the furniture was unloaded, with brownies in hand, to welcome me to the neighborhood. There was something about her I instantly liked: her attitude, her enthusiasm for life.

Recently single again, I was forced to move from my country dream home to a small duplex in town, and my spirits were about as high as the grass in the front yard. I detested the word "single." It was meant for slices of cheese, or those old records I collected as a teenager. Singleness was a mystery to be solved before the channel changed; not a lifestyle to claim for very long.

But Jeanne was doing it well, and her zest was contagious. She soon had me camping, mountain biking, playing marathon Scrabble on Saturday nights. We liked the same movies, read the same kind of books and chuckled at the same things. Every year I hung out with her, the more I laughed, and the less I thought about the past and how it hurt and robbed me. She became the sister I never had, my sidekick.

Singleness wasn't so bad after all. In fact, I was content. My children stopped rebelling, I had a good job, a ministry to singles in my church and a best friend who inspired me to live each day grateful for the blessings.

Then it happened. I met Carl. I didn't plan to fall in love, but I knew, after ten years of being single, that he was the right man for me. I prayed for a husband for Jeanne, so we could make the transition together, but it didn't happen. She shared my hopes and dreams with me, and helped me plan the wedding, but I could see the hurt as she readied herself to go solo.

The weekend before the wedding, she kidnapped me for a mountain getaway, our last jaunt as single sisters. As we sat in front of the roaring fire, gazing at the snow-capped peaks, we finally shed some tears. I told her how bittersweet it was for me, that I couldn't enter into a new life with Carl without a twinge of sadness at how things will change. Nobody but us could understand that though our friendship would remain as deep and faithful, it would never be quite the same. She wouldn't be popping over in her pajamas anymore, or calling me at five in the morning or planning a last-minute card game and leaving a message to tell me what time to be there.

Ending a chapter in your life is never easy. All the years of romantic yearnings about being married again, I never imagined it might come attached to an ache like this. It was odd that a part of my life I once spurned was now so cherished. But it was time to turn the page.

The night before I walked down the aisle again, I wrote Jeanne a long letter full of memories of all the special things we did together, and how she would always be my best friend and have a place in my heart that no one, not even my husband, could claim. Life has seasons, and we must change with them as best we can.

It's been four years now, and Jeanne hasn't found Mr. Right, but she's not sitting around waiting. She's been on a missionary trip to the Philippines. She makes every day count, and she motivates me to do it, too.

We have to work harder at staying close now, but Jeanne doesn't feel awkward anymore about popping in for a game of Scrabble. Carl always smiles and slips away to his office. I set up the board while Jeanne's feet slide snugly into her slippers. It may be a very long night.

Jan Coleman

Full Circle

Becoming single again was one of the greatest shocks of my life. I had only been married for two years. During that time I had been diagnosed with thyroid cancer. After two operations I was one year away from being able to talk and drive again. I knew that my marriage was having difficulties, but I was too weak and sick to know what to do.

My marriage ended at noon on a Saturday in October. A friend had taken me for a drive to see the leaves, and when I came home there was a note on the kitchen table. My husband had packed his things and gone, and I was single again.

The degree of my helplessness was immediately driven home to me. I couldn't even call my family to let them know what happened. I had no income and no way to get around. Being single was not something I felt ready for. I had forgotten what it was like to be alone, and I needed to learn all over again how to function by myself.

I had met my elderly next-door neighbors, Pete and Floye Hull, and I really liked them, but I had no idea how close we would become. From the minute they heard I was alone, they went out of their way to look after me as if I belonged to them. Floye cooked my favorite foods and called me every day. Pete caught mice in the middle of the night, carried out my trash every Wednesday morning and fixed whatever broke down in my house. The phone would ring and Floye would say, "We just made popcorn, and Pete's bringing some over to you," or "Get your coat on and let's go see the Christmas lights." Pete and Floye not only made it possible for me to live through that year, but they actually made it fun.

Gradually my voice came back, and I was able to drive longer and longer distances. I adjusted to being on my own, and I began to enjoy myself again. It felt good to have no one to answer to and to be able to do just as I liked. Even though I was better, Pete and Floye and I had become like a family, and we did things together frequently. I realized I had felt more alone in my unhappy marriage than I did being single. It was a wonderful impulsive time in my life, and I couldn't imagine giving up this newfound freedom for anyone.

When Pete had his heart attack I drove Floye to the hospital. My heart was pounding as the doctor told us he could not recover. After sixty-four years of marriage, I didn't know how Floye could bear this terrible blow. I asked if I could be alone with Pete for a moment. He was unconscious but very agitated. I felt as though he might hear me, and I desperately wanted to put his mind to rest. I told him out loud over and over that he mustn't worry—that I would look after Floye just as they had looked after me. After I spoke to him, he seemed to quiet down. Pete died the next morning, and I set out to keep my promise.

Floye and I were a team now. We were both single again. I learned about hearing aids, put in eye drops and tried to drive her everywhere she needed to go. It was a very hard time for her after Pete died. I don't know how she made it, but something kept holding her to life. Floye had such an instinctive gift for happiness. Whatever situation she found herself in, she found something to enjoy or laugh about. At eighty-six she took us on drive-bys of her high school boyfriend's old house, we went out to lunch, and we discussed our philosophies about men, marriage and life. But she always missed Pete. I often felt as though he was right there waiting for her, but I never told this to anyone.

A year and a half after Pete's death, I met my future husband. I had no intention of getting married again, but Floye noticed him from the start. She continually asked me how much I liked him and if I thought he liked me. I wasn't ready to admit that I cared about him at all, but from the start, Floye seemed to know something about this relationship that I didn't. She wasn't a bit surprised when months later I told her we were going to get married.

She was radiant the day of our wedding and seemed to love Sam as much as I did. He fixed things for her and carried out her trash. One morning after Sam had gone over to change a light bulb, he said to me, "I never knew Pete, but I felt so strongly just now that he is right there with Floye." That afternoon while we were at work, Floye was rushed to the hospital. We went over as soon as we heard.

Sam and I were both with her by her hospital bed, holding her hands, when she died. It was just one year after she saw us married. We hoped in our hearts that now she and Pete were together again.

When I look back on those precious difficult eight years, I can see that life has room for a little of everything. Sometimes you dance with a partner, and sometimes you dance alone. But the important thing is to keep dancing.

Meredith Hodges

More Chicken Soup?

Many of the stories and poems you have read in this book were submitted by readers like you who had read earlier *Chicken Soup for the Soul* books. We are planning to publish five or six *Chicken Soup for the Soul* books every year. We invite you to contribute a story to one of these future volumes.

Stories may be up to 1,200 words and must uplift or inspire. You may submit an original piece or something you clip out of the local newspaper, a magazine, a church bulletin or a company newsletter. It could also be your favorite quotation you've put on your refrigerator door or a personal experience that has touched you deeply.

To obtain a copy of our submission guidelines and a listing of upcoming *Chicken Soup* books, please write, fax or check one of our Web sites.

Chicken Soup for the *(Specify Which Edition)* Soul
P.O. Box 30880 • Santa Barbara, CA 93130
fax: 805-563-2945
Web site: *www.chickensoup.com*

You can also visit the Chicken Soup for the Soul site on America Online at keyword: chickensoup.

Just send a copy of your stories and other pieces, indicating which edition they are for, to any of the above addresses.

We will be sure that both you and the author are credited for your submission.

For information about speaking engagements, other books, audiotapes, workshops and training programs, please contact any of the authors directly.

Supporting People Around the World

In the spirit of *Chicken Soup for the Soul,* the publisher and coauthors of *Chicken Soup for the Single's Soul* will donate a portion of the proceeds from this book to the following charities:

Big Brothers Big Sisters of America (BBBSA) is the nation's oldest and largest youth mentoring organization. Established in 1904, they are the leaders in one-to-one mentoring relationships between adult volunteers and children at-risk. Volunteer Big Brothers and Big Sisters help youth increase their self-confidence, reach their highest potential and successfully meet the challenges of childhood and adolescence. Today, there are more than 500 Big Brother Big Sister agencies serving more than 130,000 children.

You may contact this organization at:

Big Brothers Big Sisters of America
230 North 13th Street
Philadelphia, PA 19107-1538
Tel: (215) 567-7000
Fax: (215) 567-0394
www.bbsa.org

Single Volunteers is a nonprofit organization whose mission is to provide singles with a fun, creative way to meet one another while working to benefit their local communities through volunteer activities. With chapters throughout the U.S., Canada and Australia, and more chapters being added regularly, Single Volunteers is quickly becoming a premier volunteer organization for singles throughout the world.

For more information, please contact this organization at:

Single Volunteers
9519 49th Place
College Park, MD 20740
Tel: (301) 474-2399
www.singlevolunteers.org

Heifer Project International, a nonprofit organization working to end global hunger while caring for the earth, provides livestock and training to people in need. HPI creates sustainable small-scale farm enterprises that help people lift themselves out of poverty. All recipients agree to "pass on the gift" of offspring to others in need, building stronger communities and, ultimately, a better world.

You may contact this organization at:

Heifer Project International
1015 Louisiana Street
Little Rock, AR 72202
Tel: (800) 422-0474
www.heifer.org

Operation Smile is a private, not-for-profit volunteer medical services organization providing reconstructive surgery and related health care to indigent children and young adults in developing countries and the United States. Operation Smile provides education and training around the world to physicians and other health care professionals to achieve long-term self-sufficiency.

For more information, please contact Operation Smile headquarters at:

Operation Smile
6435 Tidewater Drive
Norfolk, VA 23509
Tel: (757) 321-7645 • Fax: (757) 321-7660
www.operationsmile.org

Who Is Jack Canfield?

Jack Canfield is a bestselling author with over twenty-three books published, including nine *New York Times* bestsellers. In 1998 *USA Today* declared that Jack Canfield and his writing partner, Mark Victor Hansen, sold more books during the previous year than any other author in the United States. Jack and Mark also have a syndicated *Chicken Soup for the Soul* newspaper column through King Features and a weekly column in *Woman's World* magazine.

Jack is the author and narrator of several bestselling audiocassette and videocassette programs, including *Self-Esteem and Peak Performance, How to Build High Self-Esteem* and *The STAR Program.* He is a regularly consulted expert for radio and television broadcasts and has published a total of twenty-seven books—all bestsellers within their categories—including twenty-two *Chicken Soup for the Soul* books, *The Aladdin Factor, Heart at Work, 100 Ways to Build Self-Concept in the Classroom* and *Dare to Win.*

Jack conducts keynote speeches for about seventy-five groups each year. His clients have included schools and school districts in all fifty states, over one hundred education associations including the American School Counselors Association and Californians for a Drug Free Youth, plus corporate clients such as AT&T, Campbell Soup, Clairol, Domino's Pizza, GE, New England Telephone, Re/Max, Sunkist, Supercuts and Virgin Records.

Jack conducts an annual seven-day Training of Trainers program in the areas of building self-esteem and achieving peak performance in all areas of your life. The program attracts educators, counselors, parenting trainers, corporate trainers, professional speakers, ministers, youth workers and interested others.

To contact Jack for further information about his books, tapes and trainings, or to schedule him for a keynote speech, please contact:

The Canfield Training Group
P.O. Box 30880 • Santa Barbara, CA 93130
phone: 805-563-2935 • fax: 805-563-2945
To send e-mail or to visit his Web site: *www.chickensoup.com*

Who Is Mark Victor Hansen?

Mark Victor Hansen is a professional speaker who, in more than two decades, has made over four thousand presentations to more than 2 million people in thirty-two countries. His presentations cover sales excellence and strategies; personal empowerment and development; and how to triple your income and double your time off.

Mark has spent a lifetime dedicated to his mission of making a profound and positive difference in people's lives. Throughout his career, he has inspired hundreds of thousands of people to create a more powerful and purposeful future for themselves while stimulating the sale of billions of dollars worth of goods and services.

Mark is a prolific writer and has authored *Future Diary, How to Achieve Total Prosperity* and *The Miracle of Tithing.* He is coauthor of the *Chicken Soup for the Soul* series, *Dare to Win* and *The Aladdin Factor* (all with Jack Canfield) and *The Master Motivator* (with Joe Batten).

Mark has also produced a complete library of personal empowerment audio- and videocassette programs that have enabled his listeners to recognize and use their innate abilities in their business and personal lives. His message has made him a popular television and radio personality, with appearances on ABC, NBC, CBS, HBO, PBS, CNN, Prime Time Country, Crook & Chase and TNN News. He has also appeared on the cover of numerous magazines, including *Success, Entrepreneur* and *Changes.*

Mark is a big man with a heart and spirit to match—an inspiration to all who seek to better themselves.

For further information about Mark contact:

P.O. Box 7665 • Newport Beach, CA 92658
phone: 949-759-9304 or 800-433-2314
fax: 949-722-6912
To send e-mail or to visit his Web site: *www.chickensoup.com*

Who Is Jennifer Read Hawthorne?

Jennifer Read Hawthorne is coauthor of the #1 *New York Times* bestsellers *Chicken Soup for the Woman's Soul* and *Chicken Soup for the Mother's Soul,* as well as the bestselling *A Second Chicken Soup for the Woman's Soul.* Currently at work on future *Chicken Soup for the Soul* books, she also delivers *Chicken Soup for the Soul* presentations worldwide, sharing inspirational stories of love and hope, courage and dreams.

Jennifer is known as a dynamic and insightful speaker, with a great sense of humor and a gift for telling stories. From an early age she developed a deep appreciation for language, cultivated by her parents. She attributes her love of storytelling to the legacy of her late father, Brooks Read, a renowned Master Storyteller whose original Brer Rabbit stories filled her childhood with magic and a sense of the power of words.

As a Peace Corps volunteer in West Africa teaching English as a foreign language, Jennifer discovered the universality of stories to teach, move, uplift and connect people. Her *Chicken Soup for the Soul* presentations make audiences laugh and cry; many people say their lives are changed for the better as a result of hearing her speak.

Jennifer is cofounder of The Esteem Group, a company specializing in self-esteem and inspirational programs for women. A professional speaker since 1975, she has spoken to thousands of people around the world about personal growth, self-development and professional success. Her clients have included professional associations, Fortune 500 companies, and government and educational organizations such as AT&T, Delta Airlines, National Association of Home Builders, American Society of Travel Agents, Avon, Hallmark Cards, American Business Women's Association and Sales and Marketing Executives of Topeka.

Jennifer is a native of Baton Rouge, Louisiana, where she graduated from Louisiana State University with a degree in journalism. She lives in Fairfield, Iowa, with her husband, Dan, and two stepchildren, Amy and William.

If you would like to schedule Jennifer for a *Chicken Soup for the Soul* keynote address, you may contact her at:

Jennifer Hawthorne Inc.
1105 South D Street
Fairfield, IA 52556
phone: 515-472-7136 • fax: 515-469-6908

Who Is Marci Shimoff?

Marci Shimoff is coauthor of the #1 *New York Times* bestsellers *Chicken Soup for the Woman's Soul* and *Chicken Soup for the Mother's Soul* as well as the bestselling *A Second Chicken Soup for the Woman's Soul.* She is a top-rated professional speaker who, for the last seventeen years, has inspired thousands of people with her message of personal and professional growth. Since 1994, she has specialized in delivering *Chicken Soup for the Soul* keynote addresses to audiences around the world.

Marci is cofounder and president of The Esteem Group, a company that offers self-esteem and inspirational programs for women. She has been a featured speaker for numerous professional organizations, universities, women's associations, health-care organizations and Fortune 500 companies. Her clients have included AT&T, American Airlines, Sears, Junior League, the Pampered Chef, Jazzercise and Bristol-Myers Squibb. She is appreciated by her audiences for her lively humor, her dynamic delivery and her ability to open hearts and uplift spirits.

Marci combines her energetic style with a strong knowledge base. She earned her MBA from UCLA; she also studied for one year in the U.S. and Europe to earn an advanced certificate as a stress-management consultant. Since 1989, Marci has studied self-esteem with Jack Canfield, and has assisted in his annual Training of Trainers program for professionals.

In 1983, Marci coauthored a highly acclaimed study of the fifty top business women in America. Since that time, she has specialized in addressing women's audiences, focusing on helping women discover the extraordinary within themselves.

Of all the projects Marci has worked on in her career, none have been as fulfilling as creating *Chicken Soup for the Soul* books. Currently at work on future editions of *Chicken Soup for the Soul,* she feels blessed to have the opportunity to help touch the hearts and rekindle the spirits of millions of people throughout the world.

If you would like to schedule Marci for a *Chicken Soup for the Soul* keynote address or seminar, you can reach her at:

The Esteem Group
4754 West Blvd.
Naples, FL 34103
phone: 877-472-9394 • fax: 877-472-5065

Contributors

Brenda Nichols Ainley is a medical transcriptionist, editor, a mother and grandmother and a sometimes dabbler in the written word. Her head is bursting with wonderful stories that beg telling. With publication of this short memoir, she will be passionately inspired to commit more of them to paper. You may e-mail Brenda at *Brendaree@aol.com.*

Joan Wester Anderson is a bestselling author and is recognized around the world as an authority on angelic and miraculous intervention in everyday life. Over two million copies of her books have been sold. She can be reached at P.O. Box 127, Prospect Heights, IL 60070.

Bill Asenjo is a Ph.D. candidate in the Rehabilitation Counselor Education Program at the University of Iowa, minoring in Aging Studies. To maintain sanity, he writes stories when not working on his dissertation. Bill can be reached at 714 5th Ave., Iowa City, IA 52245 or by e-mail at *basenjo@avalon.net.* His phone number is 319-358-7474.

Bryan Aubrey is a former English professor of literature who is now a freelance writer and editor. He has contributed stories to other *Chicken Soup* books, including *Chicken Soup for the Dog and Cat Lover's Soul* and is being considered for *Chicken Soup for the Jewish Soul.* Bryan can be reached by e-mail at *wotan@kdsi.net.*

T. J. Banks of Avon, Connecticut, has written fiction, poetry books, book reviews and essays for numerous publications, including *Poets and Writers, Cat Fancy, Just Cats!, Writing for Our Lives, Women and Earth* and *Our Mothers Our Selves: Writers and Poets Celebrate Motherhood.* She is an editorial associate with the Writer's Digest School and has won awards for her fiction and journalism from the Cat Writer's Association and The Writing Self, and she has written a novel for young adults, *Houdini.* T. J. may be reached at 860-678-7978.

Barbara Baumgardner lives in Bend, Oregon, with Molly, a golden retriever who runs everything in the house except the vacuum cleaner. Barbara is a widow and a hospice volunteer which laid the foundation for her first book, *A Passage Through Grief: An Interactive Journal.* A year later, *A Passage Through Divorce* was published. She divides her time between writing, travel, quilting and long walks with Molly. Barbara can be contacted by e-mail at *barbara@empnet.com.*

Maggie Baxter's God has been faithful since her lightning experience: She was hired as a school administrator in Springfield, where she found a wonderful church as "singles" director, and built a home out in the country where she still jogs every day (when it is not storming). Maggie is still single and LIVING life.

Christine E. Belleris is the editorial codirector for Health Communications, Inc., publisher of the *Chicken Soup for the Soul* series. She has happily worked on every book in the series except for the original. While her grandmother couldn't read, Christine's love of the written word has always been her passion. A native of Denver, she lives in Boca Raton, Florida, with her husband, Jeff, and their son, Nicholas. She can be reached at 3201 S.W. 15th St., Deerfield Beach, FL 33442, or call 800-851-9100, ext. 208 or e-mail her at *christineb@hcibooks.com.*

Bits & Pieces. Reprinted by permission. ©1998, *Bits & Pieces* (Rob Gilbert, Ph.D., editor), *The Economics Press,* Inc., 12 Daniel Rd., Fairfield, NJ 07004-2565 U.S. Phone: 800-526-2554 (U.S./Canada) or (+1 973) 227-1224 (worldwide). Fax: 973-227-9742 (U.S./Canada) or (+1 973) 227-9742 (worldwide). E-mail: *info@epinc.com.* Web site: *www.epinc.com.* Contact The Economic Press, Inc. directly for subscription information to the pocket magazine *Bits & Pieces,* or for a free sample issue.

Judith Black is a spirited performer, comedian, writer, mother and recording artist. She holds a degree from Wheelock College in early childhood development and studied acting at The Royal Academy of Dramatic Arts in London, England. She has served on the faculty of Lesley College's Art Institute for over fifteen years. Her original works have been commissioned by National Public Radio, the U.S.S. Constitution Museum, the U.S. Department of the Interior, and performed on stages as far-ranging as the Smithsonian Institution, The Montreal Comedy Festival and Hebrew University in Jerusalem. Visit Judith's Web page at *http://www.storiesalive.com/.*

Kay Bolden is a freelance writer and social worker in Joliet, Illinois. Her stories have appeared in several local newspapers and nationally in *Woman's Day.* She is the single mother of two children, and has been foster mother to dozens more. She can be reached via e-mail at *Ksparky130@aol.com.*

Jean Bronaugh's "Santa Redeemed" story was her mother's favorite. Michelle, Jean's daughter, grew to love the story as her Grandma had, and she asked that Mom put it in writing. This writing was submitted by Michelle in honor of her mom and grandma.

Cindy Jevne Buck is a professional writer and writing instructor who is currently compiling a book of heartwarming stories related to gardening. She warmly encourages all writers, gardeners and flower lovers to send their stories to 51 N. Cromwell St., Fairfield, IA 52556, or by phone/fax at 515-472-6022 or e-mail her at *cbuck@kdsi.net.*

Steve Burt's stories appear in places like *Green Mountain Trading Post, Coastal Journal* and *Down East.* "Unk's Fiddle" comes in his collection, *Unk's Fiddle and Other Stories.* His agent is seeking a publisher for a new collection, *Christmas 1944 and Other Stories.* Mail c/o Hagermans, P.O. Box 1176, Southold, NY 11971.

Linda Butler still keeps her hand very busy raising her five children. Occasionally her hands find time for gardening, needlework and writing. Linda also enjoys bicycling, stargazing and taking walks. Linda writes feature articles for a local weekly newspaper, and she is working on several children's books. Linda and her family make their home in Pleasant Grove, Utah.

Nardi Reeder Campion, a freelance writer in Hanover, New Hampshire, has been published in *The New Yorker, Reader's Digest, Family Circle, Gourmet, Yankee* and has written ten op-ed pieces for *The New York Times.* Her column, "Everyday Matters," appears in the *Valley News* of White River Junction, Vermont. The author of *Mother Ann Lee—Morning Star of the Shakers,* her forthcoming memoir is called *One Woman's Wellesley, the Continuing Education of a Slow Learner.*

Pamela J. Chandler is a sixth grade teacher, writer and mother of two in Redding, California. She is an avid reader constantly seeking new knowledge and ways to share her excitement about learning new things with others, especially her children, her students and her educator colleagues. She can be contacted at 984 Montcrest Dr., Redding, CA, or through e-mail at *pamelacate@aol.com.*

Michael Clay is a true Texas-born author. He grew up in the state of Texas learning the "Old School Ways." He was also educated in Texas. Michael has two books he's currently working. His hope is to enrich the life of every reader with a humble approach to this complex life.

Jan Coleman is a freelance writer with experience in magazine, stage and television. After a painful divorce she devoted her time and talents to singles ministry, helping others go successfully solo. Her seminar, "Dodging Those Dating Landmines," is humorous and enlightening. You may contact Jan at 2050 Canal St., Auburn, California 95603 or by e-mail at *jwriter@foothill.net.*

B. J. Connor and her husband, Michael, have a daughter, Nichole, and a son, Sean. B. J. met Doris Delventhal at Bible Study at their church in Ann Arbor, Michigan. A former newspaper writer, B. J. has been published in six books and numerous magazines including *Guideposts* and *Focus on the Family.*

Christie Craig is a writer, photographer and teacher. With over three hundred magazine credits and one published novel she shares her experience and inspiration through classes and workshops. For more information call 281-376-6474.

Cathy Lee Crosby, one of America's most popular and respected entertainers, has excelled in virtually every aspect of show business, including acting, directing, singing, writing, speaking and producing. The star of ABC's hit television series, *That's Incredible!* for six years, Cathy Lee has starred in more than sixty feature films, television movies and miniseries. She has also given years of service to numerous children's charities, and was the founder of the Get High on Yourself Foundation, one of the most successful, positive alternative to drug abuse foundations in the United States.

Doris Delventhal, a Michigan native, is a retired registered nurse busy with family and volunteer work. After graduating, she and three friends moved to

Denver, Colorado. There she met Leo, a graphic arts professor. Their children, Mari Lee, Fred and Barb, and spouses and six grandchildren, help make Doris's life beautiful.

Tom Durkin is a Phi Beta Kappa graduate of UCLA with degrees in psychology and theater arts (TV/film). During his career, he has worked in virtually every genre and medium of writing. He was a charter member of the Sacramento Single Fathers Support Group, which inspired him to write "What I Did on My Son's Summer Vacation." You may reach Tom at *tdurkin@vfr.net.*

Vivian Eisenecher holds a B.S. in business administration and is gerontology certified. She is the author of *Double Vision* and is currently working on her second book, a collaboration on aging. She may be reached at 17439 Gibraltar Court, San Diego, CA 92128. You may e-mail her at *WAE0335@aol.com.*

Pamela Elessa lives in Seattle, Washington. She is the program director of Elessa Services, a community-based counseling service. Pamela, along with her husband, Dumbe, are certified marriage and family therapists who conduct quarterly marriage seminars throughout the Pacific Northwest. For information regarding seminars and training materials, please contact Pamela by calling 888-870-1088.

Terry Fairchild is a transplanted urbanite who loves the friendliness and slow pace of Southeastern Iowa that he shares with his wife, Paula, and son, Spencer. A college professor of literature, Terry's passions are contemporary film, modern poetry, mystery fiction and professional sports. Terry is a long-suffering Cleveland Indians fan.

Arnold Fine has been the senior editor of *The Jewish Press,* the largest Anglo-Jewish publication in the world for the past forty-nine years. He was coordinator of special education at Samuel J. Tilden High School in Brooklyn, teaching handicapped and brain-injured children. Since retiring from the New York City Public School System, Mr. Fine has become an adjunct instructor in the Behavioral Science Department at Kingsborough College of the City University of New York. He has been honored by the National Committee for the Furtherance of Jewish Education and the Jewish Teachers Association of New York State. His column "I Remember When" has continually been published in *The Jewish Press* for the past forty-nine years. He is married, has three sons and six grandchildren.

Barbara Jeanne Fisher currently works as a writing tutor at Terra State Community College. Ms. Fisher is a prolific writer and has published numerous magazine articles. Although fictional, in her first novel, *Stolen Moments* many of the emotions portrayed by the characters come from her experience in dealing with lupus disease in her own life. Her goal in writing the book was to use the feelings of her heart to touch the hearts of others. *Stolen Moments* may be obtained by contacting Barbara at *mentorsfriend@yahoo.com* or writing to Stolen Moments, P.O. Box 563, Fremont, OH 43420.

Tina French is an educator, writer and inventor of the game "Prouato Beme" which is a game that increases communication and self-esteem in children. She is happily married to Paul French for eleven years and has three wonderful children. Tina's husband and children inspire her to continue writing and to follow her dreams.

Toni Fulco has authored over 150 articles, stories and poems in national magazines and anthologies. Her stories also appear in *Chicken Soup for the Pet Lover's Soul* and *A Second Chicken Soup for the Woman's Soul.* She raises cockatiels and conures at home and is known locally as "the bird lady." You can reach Toni at 89 Penn Estates, E. Stroudsburg, PA 18301.

Judith Gillis is an award-winning poet and writer. Her work has appeared in *Christianity and the Arts, Women of Spirit, Focus on the Family Single Parent* magazine and others. She lives in Christian Community in the Ozark Mountains of Arkansas with her husband Fred. Besides learning to make soap and quilt, her latest effort is founding the Ozark Mountain Christian Writer's Guild. She hopes your faith is boosted by her story, and that you, too, will trust God with the impossible in your life.

Cathy Gohlke is a freelance writer and dramatic reader. She also writes for and directs the Mom Street Players, a theatrical troupe of mothers dedicated to the promotion of literacy through plays, puppet shows and storytelling. Cathy can be reached by writing Laurelea, 162 Deaver Rd., Elkton, Maryland 21921 or by calling 410-392-3099.

Diane Goldberg is a wife, mother, gardener, daydreamer, part-time social worker and freelance writer living in the Southeast. She is lucky enough to be married to "the right one." Her successes are attributable to her sister, Donna, her husband, Ronnie and her son, Jacob. Her failures are entirely her own.

Arthur Gordon attended Yale University. He was a Rhodes Scholar at Oxford in England and served as an Air Force officer in World War II. He then spent several years in New York City, on the staffs of prominent magazines. He has served as editorial director at *Guideposts,* and his articles and stories have appeared in *The Saturday Evening Post, This Week, Colliers, Redbook* and *Reader's Digest.* The author of the bestselling *A Touch of Wonder,* he is currently a freelance writer from his home in Savannah, Georgia.

Yitta Halberstam is the coauthor of the national bestselling series *Small Miracles: Extraordinary Coincidences from Everyday Life* and a lecturer on spirituality. The most recent book in the series *Small Miracles of Love and Friendship* will be published in September 1999. for speaking engagements, please contact her at YMYE@aol.com.

David Haldane is a staff writer for the *Los Angeles Times,* where he has covered virtually everything under the sun. His work has also appeared in numerous magazines including *Penthouse, Forum, Los Angeles Times Magazine, The Progressive, Aqua* and *Salon.* He can be reached c/o LA Times, 1375 Sunflower

Ave., Costa Mesa, California 92626, by e-mail at *david.haldane@latimes.com* or by calling 714-966-5997. "Looking Toward the Light" first appeared in the September, 1998 edition of *Aqua*.

Bonnie Harris is a general assignment reporter for the *Los Angeles Times* in Orange County, California. She has covered earthquakes, mudslides, wildfires, bombings, riots, and, fortunately for her own soul, a few treasured human interest features that make people feel good. Bonnie, twenty-eight, is a native of St. Petersburg, Florida, and a journalism graduate of the University of Maryland. Her e-mail address is: *Bonnie.Harris@LATimes.com*

Jennifer Harris, LPN, CD (DONA) is a wife, nurse, doula (professional childbirth support person) and writer who lives in Bremerton, Washington. She plans to become a midwife and is currently writing her first novel. Her passion in empowering women—helping them to discover their worth. You may e-mail her at *Doula2Care@aol.com.*

Christine Harris-Amos is a multimedia artist who has studied at Colorado State University, Wayne State University, the Students League and Honolulu Academy of Arts. For the last fourteen years, she has enhanced her print making skills in etching and photogravure under Dodie Warren. She lives in Lanikai, Hawaii, with her husband Wally Amos and her daughter, Sarah Amos. When she is not baking cookies with Wally, you can find her at her desk painting watermelons on his shoes and shirts.

C. J. Herrmann lives in the woods outside of Los Angeles with his lovely wife of ten years and their magical two-year-old son. Ever since he can remember he's been fascinated by stories about peak performance and the infinite reach of human potential and has taught various seminars on this subject. He has published numerous articles on a variety of topics ranging from political issues, financial tips, music, poetry, spiritual healing and general culture. He is currently seeking representation for his first suspense novel and can be reached at 1715 Sylvania Lane, Topanga, CA 90290 or by calling 310-455-1843 or by e-mail at *Siege@ix.netcom.com.*

Wilma Hankins Hlawiczka was born in 1922 and raised in Tampa, Florida. She received a B.S. in education in 1945 from the University of Tennessee and her master's from Sam Houston State in 1973. She taught history, competitive swimming and diving, gymnastics and physical education in both Florida and Texas. In 1981 she retired, taking up golf and oil painting. She lives in Missouri City, TX.

Meredith Hodges is a freelance writer who currently lives with her husband in Falls Church, Virginia. Together they run a cashmere business over the Internet from their home. You may reach Meredith at *Smhodges@erols.com* or by writing Royal Cashmere, P.O. Box 4051, Merrifield, VA 22116.

C. L. Howard raised four children and now lives in a small Nebraska town near her two daughters and four grandsons. Her sons live near Puget Sound.

Her job as a classroom teacher and director of high school forensics and drama keep her very busy.

Barb Irwin reared and educated six children in southern Indiana and then moved to Indianapolis and continued her own education. She now works for the state and volunteers for singles projects at St. Luke's UMC, the largest singles group in the state (when she isn't playing with some of her sixteen grandchildren).

J. A. Jance writes two police procedural series. Detective J. P. Beaumont hails from Seattle while Sheriff Joanna Brady calls southeastern Arizona home. As biregional as her characters, J. A. has divided her life between Arizona and Washington State. She has a husband, five children, three grandchildren and three dogs.

James M. Jertson resides in Globe, Arizona, where he is a child/family therapist and Clinical Supervisor with Arizona's Children Association. He has spent twenty-five years working with Native American people in Arizona and New Mexico. His son Marty is an engineering student at Colorado School of Mines, where he plays intercollegiate golf. His son Jimmy is a recent graduate of Benedictine College in Atchison, Kansas.

Cielle Kollander, the proud grandmommy of four-year-old Teddy Eddy May, is an international gold-record recording artist, composer and teacher. At the height of her career, a catastrophic car accident shattered her body and her future. Not expected to live or ever sing again, her recovery is a story of many miracles. Currently she is writing her autobiography *The Heart of a Singer,* producing her WholeBodySinging™ seminar video and recording a CD with Roger Kellaway who the *Wall Street Journal* calls "the most respected unknown in jazz." You may reach her at 413 N. B St., Fairfield, IA 51556, or by calling 515-472-2248, or via e-mail at *ciellewbs@yahoo.com.*

Shirley Byers Lalonde is a writer and mother of two grown children. She is the author of two books, numerous articles and short stories and serves as a contributing editor for *WITH* magazine. She can be reached by voice or by fax at 306-327-4822.

Linda LaRocque has written short stories for *Guideposts* and *Signs of the Times.* Her first book is currently under review by a publisher. This award-winning author of five plays contends all writing to be a form of ministry. She writes from her home in South Haven, Michigan.

Jeanne Marie Laskas is a columnist for the *Washington Post Magazine,* where her essays appear weekly. She is also a contributing writer at *Esquire, Good Housekeeping,* and *Health Magazine.* Her third book, *Fifty Acres and a Poodle,* a memoir about life on her farm in Scenery Hill, Pennsylvania, will be published by Bantam in 2000.

Rosemary Laurey is a writer, novelist and transplanted Brit now living in Ohio. Visit Rosemary's Web site at *http://www.eclectics.com/rosemarylaurey.com.*

Eileen Lawrence is vice president of Chadwyck-Healey, Inc., a publisher of scholarly works in electronic format ("The Home of the Humanities on the Web"), based in Alexandria, Virginia, with offices in England and Spain. A former teacher and educational consultant, she entered publishing-related work in 1980. She also runs a consulting company, Eileen Lawrence Communications, which she started in 1986. Eileen lives in Silver Spring, Maryland.

Judith Leventhal is the coauthor of *Small Miracles, Small Miracles II* and *Small Miracles for Love and Friendship.* She is a psychotherapist in private practice in Brooklyn, New York. Ms. Leventhal is an inspirational public speaker and may be reached at *jlsmiracle@aol.com.*

Patricia Lorenz is an internationally known inspirational, art-of-living writer, speaker, columnist and teacher. She is a frequent contributor to the *Chicken Soup for the Soul* books. She is the author of *Stuff That Matters for Single Parents* and *A Hug A Day for Single Parents* and the writer of over 400 articles published in many national magazines. Patricia is a speaker who entertains her audiences from the get-go and packs a wallop with her take-away messages. You may e-mail her at *patricialorenz@juno.com.*

Rob Loughran is remarried, with three more children—eight in all. He lives in Rohnert Park, California, and works as a freelance writer. "Eight-year-old Rachel" is twenty-one and will graduate from the University of California Santa Barbara in 1999. Rob hasn't received any field trip permission slips from UCSB.

Anne Marion lives in Madison, Wisconsin, where she continues a lifelong involvement in the creative arts. She paints, sculpts, writes and performs songs, creates videos which tie together the visual and musical realms, and teaches her crafts to others. Originally from New York, she is a self-taught musician and artist. As a young woman, she performed in the "borscht belt" hotels in the Catskills, singing, writing skits, directing plays, playing in bands and performing as an on-stage hypnotist. She is the mother of two adult sons and a grandmother of five.

Cliff Marsh left the Big Apple thirty years ago for the idyllic life of Hawaii. He has been freelance writing for over twenty years for ads, commercials, marketing videos and children's stories. Christine Amos has wonderful stories to tell, and Cliff loves to write them. Cliff says all he is today is due to his wife's incredible Italian cooking!

Megan Martin is a successful wife, mother and teacher who considers herself quite lucky to have fascinating friends and family to write about. She can be reached at 1908 Chapel Hill Rd., Columbia, MO 65203 or by calling 573-446-4899. You may e-mail her at *martinme@missouri.edu.*

Katie Mauro, twenty-four, has been writing since she was little. At the age of five, her first short story "Mrs. Comfort and Her Cat" won the rave reviews of family and neighbors. Since then, she has turned her sights to children's books and novels. After graduating from Stanford University (B.A. '95, M.A. '96), she spent a summer at Oxford University as a student in the Programme in English Literature, before venturing to Washington, D.C., as a publicist. A California native, Katie looks forward to returning home with the love of her life to be near her family—and of course, continue dancing with everyone.

Dawn McKenna lives in Southern California. Still single, her children are now grown; her youngest lives nearby and her oldest in Texas. Watch for her forthcoming frontier novel *Sorry Creek.* For more about Dawn's writing, visit her Web site at *http://www.dawnmckenna.com.*

Maggy Rose McLarty lives in the Pacific Northwest with her son, daughter and cocker spaniel, Winnie. Maggy loves to write, read, cross-stitch and garden. One day soon she expects to have her first romantic suspense novel published. At present, she is a receptionist/secretary.

Cynthia Mercati is a playwright, with over thirty published plays. She is also a professional actress, currently touring with a children's theater company that does many of her scripts. She often writes about growing up in Chicago and baseball. As a White Sox fan, she's learned to hang her hat on hope—and wait for next year! She can be reached at P.O. Box 20, Waukee, IA 50263 or by calling 515-987-2587.

Barbara Feder Mindel still feels the magic in combining words, imagination and self-expression since childhood. Her sons are her gourmet meal in life; however, writing is her dessert to gorge on. She is a staff writer at work and edits for organizations, friends and writer penpals. She conducts creative writing classes and workshops; writes stories, articles and poems for publication. She beams when her sons get published, too! You may contact Barbara at 12 Meadow Rd., Poughkeepsie, NY 12603 or by e-mail at *bmindel@usa.net.*

John Morris and his wife, Linda are independent Nikken Distributors, a leading health care provider from Japan. Diamond Communications in South Bend, Indiana, has recently published John's first book *Bullet Bob Come to Louisville.* These twenty-two stories from John's professional baseball career cover a variety of themes from everyday life. You may contact John at 800-480-3717 to order.

Jan Nations is a managing producer of a national daily radio broadcast and producer of an international tape series. Jan's previous publishers include Multnomah, Starburst and *Teachers in Focus* magazine. She had three children (twin boys and one daughter) and five young grandchildren.

Oriah Mountain Dreamer is a Canadian retreat leader and writer. She has studied with Native American elders who gave her the medicine name, Mountain Dreamer. *The Invitation,* a book expanding on this smaller piece by the same title, is published by HarperSanFrancisco, a division of HarperCollins (May 1999—ISBN 0-06-251584-5).

Laurie Oswald is assistant editor of *Mennonite Weekly Review,* a weekly national newspaper based in Newton, Kansas, covering Mennonite and Anabaptist concerns around the globe. She is also a contributing editor for *WITH,* an Anabaptist Christian magazine for teens. Laurie enjoys deepening her relationship to Jesus Christ, writing poetry and music and serving in lay ministry. She grew up in Manson, Iowa, and graduated from Goshen, Indiana College with a bachelor's degree in communications. Laurie may be reached at 609 Highland Ave., Newton, KS 67114 or by calling 316-284-0223 or by e-mail at *heartil@juno.com.*

Janice Lane Palko is a freelance writer who pens a bimonthly column for the *Pittsburgh Tribune Review New Record.* She is married and the mother of three children. Her address is 118 Brookmeade Dr., Pittsburgh, PA 15237.

Shirley Pease is a freelance writer and speaker, chairperson of two writer's clubs and coauthor of one book and working on another for widows. Her articles have been published in several secular and Christian magazines. You may e-mail her at *mocrane@aol.com* or write 1818 Skyline Dr. #31, Wenatchee, WA 98801.

Carol A. Price-Lopata is a first-grade teacher and has been a public speaker for twenty years. She has been a criminal investigator for Crimes Compensation, a coordinator for juvenile court program, a medical practice developer, emergency shelter founder and behavioral management counselor.

Dick Purnell is an internationally recognized speaker/author on single adult relationships. He speaks at seminars, conventions and special events for singles. Dick is the director of Single Life Resources, a division of Campus Crusade for Christ. His Web site *www.slr.org* features books for singles. For a catalog, call 888-758-6329 or contact him at P.O. Box 1166, Cary, NC 27512.

Bobbie Reed, Ph.D., D. Min., author of thirty-six books on education, parenting, relationships, and successful living, is a nationally known inspirational speaker and consultant on leadership and single-adult ministry. Her career included serving as training director, hospital administrator and chief deputy warden for a maximum security men's prison. She and her husband, Ed, live in San Diego, California.

Judith Robinson is a wife, mother, writer and office manager. She is vice president of Inspirational Writers Alive! in East Texas, she is published regularly in a local Christian newspaper, self-publishes a monthly newsletter and is involved in the church prison ministry. Her favorite time is spent with God, her family and friends. You may write to Judith at 13582 Indian Dr., Tyler, TX 75709.

Carol Fannin Rohwedder is a third-generation Arizonan, who has two grown daughters and is married to a physician. Inspired by her restoration of a century-old Arizona territorial adobe home, she recently published her first novel, a suspense/romance *CONCHE* under the pen name Sedona Davis. Her e-mail is *abanico20@aol.com.*

Nancy Rue is a former high school English and theater teacher. She is now a full-time freelance writer, having written more than fifty books, most of them for young people (or middle-aged readers like herself, who still steal away with the occasional Nancy Drew mystery). She lives in Lebanon, Tennessee, with her husband, Jim, and daughter, Marijean, when she isn't off at college. Nancy's philosophy is "If you aren't enjoying it, think about whether you really need to be doing it. God wants us to have joy!"

Jackie Shelton is a marketing professional based in northern Nevada. Jackie started a home-based business upon the birth of her son, Noah. In addition to playing with Noah, she now has more time to write and plant flowers. She also volunteers time to a number of nonprofit organizations, including Tengo Un Sueno, a language preschool.

Lizanne Southgate is the author of *Mother Musing, An Unlikely Princess* and *The Boy Who Swallowed a Dream.* She is a ghostwriter and the mother of five. To contact her regarding her books or ghostwriting services, write to: P.O. Box 878, Brownsville, Oregon 97327 or e-mail *lizannes@proaxis.com.*

Linda Stafford is painting pictures of old whaling ships when she isn't sailing on the ocean. She has just written a novel set in Hawaii. She is still happily single and enjoys walking on the beach and watching Kilauea Volcano eruptions turn the sky a fiery red. You may reach Linda at P.O. Box 6161, Hilo, HI 96720.

Carren Strock is a writer, photographer and painter. Her work has appeared in numerous publications in the United States and abroad. She is the author of *Married Women Who Love Women* (Doubleday) and is also a workshop leader, teacher and regional representative for the International Women's Writers Guild. Reach her at: *http://www.erols.com/carrens.*

Linda Ross Swanson recently left an active job as a church administrator, and went to work part time for her husband, David, who is the CEO of a credit union. This move created time for two of her passions—writing and hospice work. Linda recently completed a memoir entitled *Beheading the Hydrangea* which awaits publication and is planning a book about her spiritual experiences with the dying. Her articles and stories may be seen in various periodicals and newspapers throughout the country. You may contact Linda at 503-292-4755 or by e-mail at *forestparkfcu@msn.com.*

LeAnn Thieman is an author and nationally acclaimed speaker. A member of the National Speakers Association, LeAnn inspires audiences to truly live their priorities and balance their lives physically, mentally and spiritually while making a difference in the world. She coauthored *This Must Be My Brother,* a book recounting her role in the daring rescue of 300 babies during the Vietnam Orphan Airlift. To inquire about her book, tapes and presentations, contact LeAnn at 112 North College, Fort Collins, CO 80524 or call 877-THIEMAN. You may visit LeAnn's Web site at *www.LeAnnThieman.com.*

Deb Gatlin Towney was born in Richardson, Texas. A graduate of the University of North Texas and KD Studio of Dallas, she has varying degrees in child development, English and fine arts. She is a writer of poetry, fiction and children's books. Currently she lives in San Jose, California, with her husband and two children, where she enjoys writing and acting in a local theatre. She is a lifelong advocate for children, the elderly and the homeless. Please write to her at *lifewrites@aol.com.*

Louise Lenahan Wallace received her B.A. in human services from Western Washington University in 1992. She likes to bowl and square dance and do the publicity for her county unit of the American Cancer Society. She has been published in *Grit* magazine. Ogden Publications will publish her novel *The Longing of the Dove* in summer of 1999.

Melanie M. Watkins is a graduate of the University of Nevada, Reno. She enjoys playing with her five-year-old Jonathan and volunteering with teenage mothers. Melanie is a second-year medical student at Stanford University. She hopes to become a motivational speaker and an obstetrician/gynecologist. You may reach her at 650-497-4373 or at *melmarie@leland.stanford.edu.*

Kari West is a freelance writer and speaker and coauthored *When He Leaves* (Victor Books). Her words have appeared in national and international magazines, including *Single-Parent Family* and are on audiotapes for the blind. Today she lives on a sun-splashed hilltop with her second husband, Richard, four dogs and a goat named Sigmund. You can write her at P.O. Box 11692, Pleasanton, CA 94588 or at *kariwest@juno.com.*

Cara Wilson is an inspirational speaker, marketing communications writer and the author of the internationally acclaimed *Love, Otto—The Legacy of Anne Frank.* Her writing has appeared in *Reader's Digest* and in *A Second Chicken Soup for the Woman's Soul.* She is presently working on many writing projects. Cara may be reached at Creative Impact Marketing, 1838 Westcliff Dr., Ste. #4, Newport Beach, CA 92660 or by calling 949-650-0300. Her fax number is 949-650-0337 and e-mail creativeimpact@msn.com.

Michelle Wolins resides in Durban, South Africa, with her husband, Barry, and his son, Lee. She has started her own motivational training company and is currently teaching high school senior boys about life skills. The Wolinses love South Africa and have been blessed to be able to visit the States regularly. If you were encouraged by their story, they would love to hear from you. E-mail them at mwolins@iafrica.com.

Permissions *(continued from page iv)*

Have Freedom, Will Travel. Reprinted by permission of Dawn McKenna. ©1999 Dawn McKenna.

The Visit. Reprinted by permission of C. J. Herrmann. ©1999 C. J. Herrmann.

Fascination with Dree. Reprinted by permission of Megan Martin. ©1998 Megan Martin.

I Don't Even Know Your Name. Reprinted by permission of Jean Fulton. ©1999 Jean Fulton.

Surviving the Shipwreck. Reprinted by permission of Cara Wilson. ©1999 Cara Wilson.

A-Head of the Game. Reprinted by permission of Katie Mauro. ©1998 Katie Mauro.

Bowled Over. Reprinted by permission of Jan Coleman. ©1998 Jan Coleman.

Reply to Box 222B. Reprinted by permission of Barbara Baumgardner. ©1985 Barbara Baumgardner.

New Year's Eve Dilemma. Reprinted by permission of Judith Robinson. ©1998 Judith Robinson.

Dave Barry's Guide to Finding a Mate. Reprinted from *Dave Barry's Guide to Marriage and/or Sex.* ©1987 by Dave Barry. Permission granted by Rodale Press, Inc. Emmaus, PA 18098.

On the Rocks. Reprinted by permission of Dick Purnell. ©1999 Dick Purnell.

A Good Catch. Reprinted by permission of Jeanne Marie Laskas. ©1999 Jeanne Marie Laskas.

The Surprise Date. Reprinted by permission of Rosemary Laurey. ©1998 Rosemary Laurey.

A Cure for Cold Feet. Reprinted by permission of Pamela Elessa. ©1998 Pamela Elessa.

Dating Again. Specified Excerpts (pp.18-19, 208-210) from *Bouncing Back* by Joan Rivers. Copyright ©1997 by Joan Rivers. Reprinted by permission of HarperCollins Publishers, Inc.

Loving Henry. Reprinted by permission of Terry Fairchild. ©1999 Terry Fairchild.

The Last Date. Reprinted by permission of Cindy Jevne Buck. ©1999 Cindy Jevne Buck.

The Invitation. © 1999 by Oriah Mountain Dreamer. Reprinted by permission of HarperCollins Publishers, Inc.

How David and Lily Got Together. Reprinted by permission of Arnold Fine. ©1998 Arnold Fine.

The Moment It Happens. Reprinted by permission of Carol Price-Lopata. ©1994 Carol Price-Lopata.

The High School English Teacher. Reprinted by permission of Arnold Fine. ©1998 Arnold Fine.

Perennials. Reprinted by permission of Jacqueline Shelton. ©1996 Jacqueline Shelton.

Hope Is Where the Heart Is. Excerpted from *Angels We Have Heard on High* by Joan Wester Anderson. ©1997 by Joan Wester Anderson. Reprinted by Ballantine Books, a division of Random House Inc.

The Letter. Reprinted by permission of Shirley Byers Lalonde. ©1998 Shirley Byers Lalonde.

What's Your Sign? Reprinted by permission of Janice Lane Palko. ©1998 Janice Lane Palko.

An Educated Woman. Reprinted by permission of Christine Belleris. ©1998 Christine Belleris.

Love at First Bite. Reprinted by permission of Christine Harris-Amos. ©1998 Christine Harris-Amos.

A Chance of a Lifetime. Reprinted by permission of LeAnn Thieman. ©1998 LeAnn Thieman.

The Right One. Reprinted by permission of Diane Goldberg. ©1998 Diane Goldberg.

Mrs. Grodefsky. Reprinted by permission of Arnold Fine. ©1999 Arnold Fine.

One Day at a Time. Reprinted by permission of Cathy Gohlke. ©1999 Cathy Gohlke.

Can You Love Me? Reprinted by permission of Pamela Chandler. ©1999 Pamela Chandler.

Christmas Is Coming! Reprinted by permission of Deb Gatlin Towney. ©1997 Deb Gatlin Towney.

Mama's Heart. Reprinted by permission of Toni Fulco. ©1998 Toni Fulco.

The Angel at the Bank. Reprinted by permission of Arnold Fine. ©1998 Arnold Fine.

Hands to Go 'Round. Reprinted by permission of Linda S. Butler. ©1999 Linda S. Butler.

Take Heart, Mom. Reprinted by permission of Cielle Kollander. ©1999 Cielle Kollander.

A True Christmas. Reprinted by permission of Nancy Rue. ©1997 Nancy Rue.

Sidelined. Reprinted by permission of Judith Black. ©1998 Judith Black.

One Man and a Baby. Written by Paul Breon. Excerpted from *Seventeen* magazine. Used by permission of the Los Angeles Times Syndicate, Inc.

Marty's Friends. Reprinted by permission of James M. Jertson. ©1999 James M. Jertson.

Outside the Circle of Possibility. Reprinted by permission of Patricia Lorenz. ©1987 Patricia Lorenz.

For Forever. Reprinted by permission of The Economics Press. Excerpted from *Bits & Pieces* by Rob Gilbert and Karen Wydra. ©1998, The Economics Press, Inc.

Where the Heart Is. Reprinted by permission of Brenda Nichols Ainley. ©1999 Brenda Nichols Ainley.

For the Record. Reprinted by permission of Rob Loughran. ©1999 Rob Loughran.

A Wish Seed. Reprinted by permission of Lizanne Southgate. ©1997 Lizanne Southgate.

Message in a Mug. Reprinted by permission of Tina French. ©1999 Tina French.

Dr. Mom. Reprinted by permission of Melanie Watkins. ©1999 Melanie Watkins.

A Real Family Christmas. Reprinted by permission of Kay Bolden. ©1998 Kay Bolden.

No Time for Dreams. Reprinted by permission of Barbara Feder Mindel. ©1999 Barbara Feder Mindel.

A Faded Card. Reprinted by permission of Louise Lenahan Wallace. ©1998 Louise Lenahan Wallace.

What I Did on My Son's Summer Vacation. Reprinted by permission of Tom Durkin. ©1984, 1998 Tom Durkin.

Making the Grade. Reprinted by permission of C. L. Howard. ©1998 C. L. Howard.

Love Is Just Like a Broken Arm. Reprinted by permission of Christie Craig. ©1998 Christie Craig.

LET the MAGIC BEGIN. Reprinted by permission of Cathy Lee Crosby. ©1998 Cathy Lee Crosby.

The Drawer Wouldn't Close. Reprinted by permission of Jan Nations. ©1997 Jan Nations.

The Ten-Dollar Bill. Reprinted by permission of J. A. Jance. ©1999 J. A. Jance.

Looking Toward the Light. Reprinted by permission of David Haldane. ©1998 David Haldane.

Lightning's Gift. Reprinted by permission of Maggie Baxter. ©1997 Maggie Baxter.

Starting Over. Reprinted by permission of Jennifer Harris. ©1998 Jennifer Harris.

My Sailor Man. Reprinted by permission of Linda Ross Swanson. ©1997 Linda Ross Swanson.

Paid in Full. Reprinted by permission of Bobbie Reed. ©1996 Bobbie Reed.

Rudy's Angel. Reprinted by permission of Wilma Hankins Hlawiczka. ©1999 Wilma Hankins Hlawiczka.

He Has Not Left Me. Reprinted by permission of Simon & Schuster, Inc. from *WIDOWED* by Dr. Joyce Brothers. Copyright ©1990 by Joyce B. Enterprises.

Love, Leo. Reprinted by permission of B. J. Connor. ©1999 B. J. Connor.

Cultivating My Garden. Reprinted by permission of T. J. Banks. ©1998 T. J. Banks.

A Widow's Workshop. Reprinted by permission of Shirley Pease. ©1999 Shirley Pease.

The Journey. Reprinted by permission of Christie Craig. ©1999 Christie Craig.

The Voyage. Reprinted by permission of Eileen Lawrence and Anne Marion. ©1999 Eileen Lawrence and Anne Marion.

Unk's Fiddle. Reprinted by permission of Steven E. Burt. ©1994 Steve E. Burt.

A Single Long-Stemmed Rose. Excerpted from *Jack Benny* by Mary Livingstone Benny and Hilliard Marks as told to Marcia Borie. Reprinted by permission of Albert T. Brod and Ruth Hagy Brod Literary Agency. ©1975 Albert T. Brod.

Angels, Once in a While. Reprinted by permission of Barb Irwin. ©1999 Barb Irwin.

A Small Miracle in Nashville. Excerpted from *Small Miracles II: Heartwarming Gifts of Extraordinary Coincidences* by Yitta Halberstam and Judith Leventhal. ©1998 Adams Media Corporation. Published by Adams Media Corporation.

The Best Seat in the House. Reprinted by permission of John Morris. ©1999 John Morris.

Santa Redeemed. Reprinted by permission of Jean Bronaugh. ©1997 Jean Bronaugh.

A Bunch of Violets. Reprinted by permission of Carol Fannin Rohwedder. ©1999 Carol Fannin Rohwedder.

Everything He Had. Reprinted by permission of Judith Gillis. ©1999 Judith Gillis.

Nine Years and Nine Days. Written by Bonnie Harris. *Seventeen* magazine. Reprinted by permission.

Rescued by a Drowning Dog. Reprinted by permission of Carren Strock. ©1998 Carren Strock.

The Face of Compassion. Reprinted by permission of Michael Clay. ©1998 Michael Clay.

A Lasagna Kind of Christmas. Reprinted by permission of Linda LaRocque. ©1996 Linda LaRocque.

Between Two Worlds. Reprinted by permission of Kari West. ©1999 Kari West.

Dad Is There For Me Again—and Always. Reprinted by permission of Cynthia Mercati. ©1999 Cynthia Mercati.

Life's Final Pieces. Reprinted by permission of Barbara Jeanne Fisher. ©1998 Barbara Jeanne Fisher.

The Makeover. Reprinted by permission of Maggy Rose McLarty. ©1998 Maggy Rose McLarty.

Unbroken Circle. Reprinted by permission of Laurie Oswald. ©1998 Laurie Oswald.

A Shining Thing. Reprinted by permission of Arthur Gordon. ©1983 Arthur Gordon.

Turning the Page. Reprinted by permission of Jan Coleman. ©1998 Jan Coleman.

Full Circle. Reprinted by permission of Meredith Hodges. ©1999 Meredith Hodges.

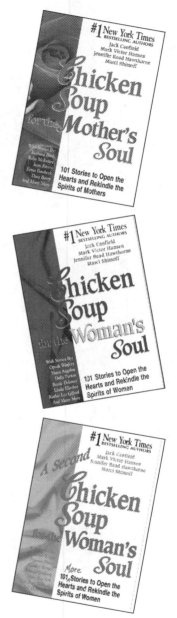

#1 New York Times BESTSELLER
Jack Canfield
Mark Victor Hansen
Mark & Chrissy Donnelly
and
Barbara De Angelis, Ph.D.
Chicken Soup for the Couple's Soul
With Stories By:
Paul Reiser
Marianne Williamson
Deepak Chopra
George Burns
Joan Wester Anderson
Charlton Heston
And Many More
Inspirational Stories About
Love and Relationships

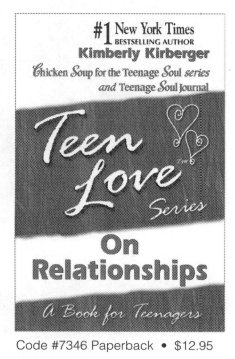

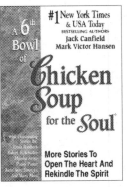

The Schwarzbein Principle

The Latest Evolution in Health and Fitness

It's not just a diet. It's a lifestyle revolution.

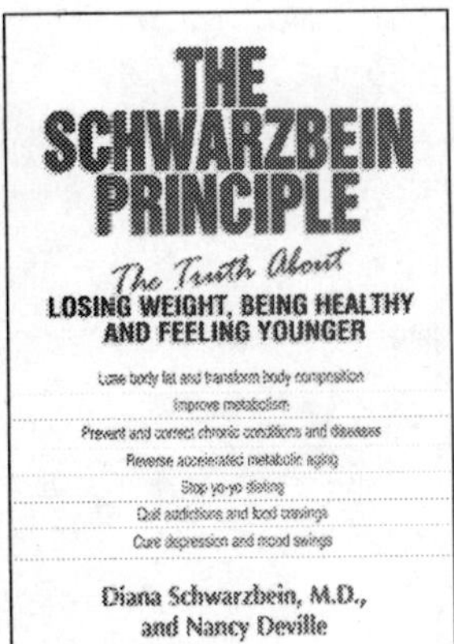

Maximize your metabolism and achieve lasting weight loss with *The Schwarzbein Principle*. Through real-life stories, this book reveals how excess weight, "accelerated aging" and degenerative disease can be controlled and reversed.

Code #6803 Paperback • $12.95

Don't forget the cookbooks—filled with delicious, healing recipes to accompany your new choice in lifestyle and nutrition.

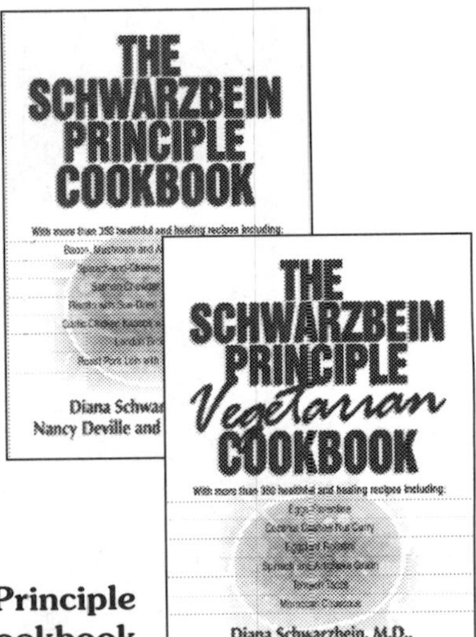

The Schwarzbein Principle Cookbook
Code #6811 Paperback • $12.95

The Schwarzbein Principle Vegetarian Cookbook
Code #682X Paperback • $12.95

Available in bookstores everywhere or call **1.800.441.5569** for Visa or MasterCard orders.
Prices do not including shipping. Your response code is **CCS**.
Order online at ***www.hci-online.com***

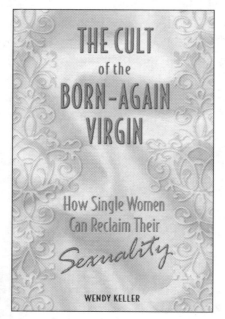